Alabama
ROAD TRIPS

SECOND EDITION

Foreword by
Lee Sentell

AdvanceLocal / AL.com
in cooperation with
The Alabama Tourism Department

Birmingham, Alabama

ACKNOWLEDGEMENTS

More than a dozen of Alabama's most prominent writers and authorities on Alabama travel contributed pieces to this book:

They are:
Lee Sentell, Alabama Tourism Department
Erin Bass, *Deep South Magazine*
Grey Brennan, Alabama Tourism Department
Colette Boehm, Gulf Shores
Verna Gates, Birmingham, AL

Rick Harmon, Alabama Tourism Department
Brian S. Jones, Alabama Tourism Department
Jennifer Kornegay, Montgomery, AL
J.P. Parsons, Scottsboro, AL
Carolanne Roberts, Birmingham, AL
Marilyn Jones Stamps, Montgomery, AL
Annette Thompson, Birmingham, AL

Also Special Recognition to:
Tommy Cauthen, Alabama Tourism Department
Pam Smith, Alabama Tourism Department

COVER PHOTO: Meg McKinney/Leisa Cole/Rich Albright

Photography: Art Meripol, Chris Granger, Tom Starkey PhD , Raphael Tenshert, Meg McKinney

Graphic design by Sandra Slate

Library of Congress Number applied for

ISBN: 978-1-57571-036-5

To order copies of this book, please contact
    Advance Local
    Carl Bates
    1731 1st Ave. North
    Birmingham, AL 35203
    cbates@advancelocal.com
    (205) 325-2237

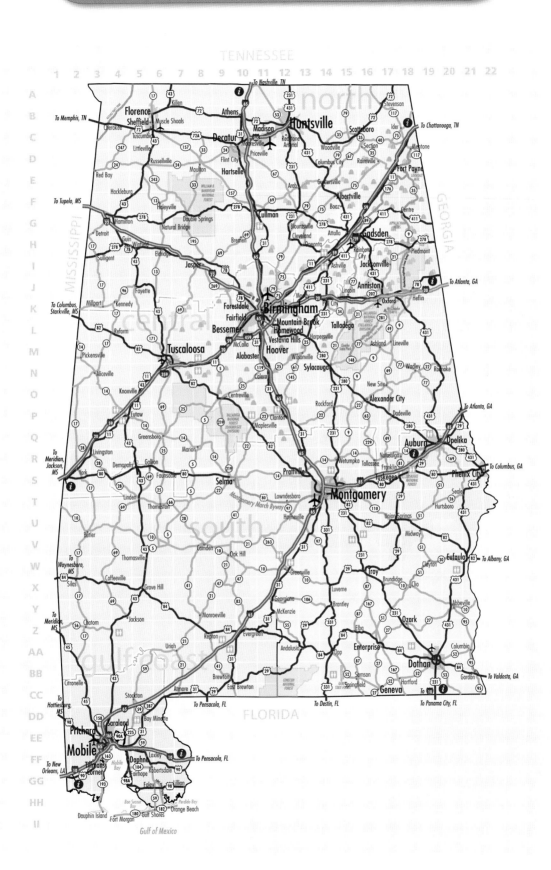

CONTENTS

Music Hall of Fame

Vulcan Park

Point Mallard Wave Pool

CONTENTS

Alabama State Capitol Building

Dauphin Island

Gulf State Park

Whether you've been in the state for 40 years or 40 hours, most people agree: "Alabama is such a beautiful place."

Waterfalls cascade among the foothills of the Appalachian Mountains. Down along the Gulf Coast, five rivers flow into Mobile Bay, the place that a famous naturalist refers to as "America's Amazon." Wherever you roam, the diverse scenery is breathtaking.

Are you on a quest to learn more about a Southern subject? Trails direct visitors to a range of topics spotlighting botanical gardens, civil rights landmarks, some of the best golf courses in the world, music that shaped America, some of North America's best birding, top foodie spots from barbecue to fine dining, scenic rivers and craft beer.

In North Alabama, the lakes of the Tennessee River offer world-class bass fishing. Make cabin or room reservations at Joe Wheeler State Park and Lake Guntersville State Park at the river's edge or overlooking Huntsville at Monte Sano State Park. Take relaxing walks in the park or slow drives into and around Florence, Athens, Decatur, Scottsboro and Guntersville.

Two centuries ago Alabama pioneers wrote the first state constitution in Huntsville. Visit the recreated neighborhood where it happened. The nation's space program began in Huntsville in 1950 and developed rockets that put Neil Armstrong and Buzz Aldrin on the Moon. Today Alabama scientists and engineers are planning missions to Mars.

Plan most of a day to explore the U.S. Space and Rocket Center. Walk among actual space hardware. Gasp with fellow "astronauts" on a simulator while being thrust skyward. Register your kids to explore at the U.S. Space Camp.

Absorb the history of Muscle Shoals music studios near Florence. It's where Aretha Franklin laid down the track "I Never Loved A Man (The Way I Love You)" and Percy Sledge recorded "When A Man Loves A Woman." See the piano where Paul Simon performed "Ko-dachrome." And where the Rolling Stones recorded "Brown Sugar" and "Wild Horses." Cut your own record at the Alabama Music Hall of Fame. Back home, stream the "Muscle Shoals" documentary about legendary producer Rick Hall and the Shoals music.

Head south of the Tennessee River in Decatur and marvel at the live honey bees and other critters inside the Cook Museum of Natural Science. When it's warm, take your bathing suits to Point Mallard and ride the waves.

Visit a pair of Catholic destinations in Cullman, settled by German immigrants a decade after the Civil War. Denied from being a priest at St. Bernard Abbey because of a physical deformity, Benedictine monk Brother Joseph Zoettel crafted scores of miniature reproductions of famous churches, shrines and landmarks between 1918 and 1958. Catholics globally who watch EWTN (Eternal Word Television Network) broadcast from Irondale often make the pilgrimage to the studios and later travel to Hanceville to worship at the Shrine of the Most Blessed Sacrament.

Birmingham is one of the nation's top foodie towns, with multiple restaurants honored with James Beard awards. Frank Stitt began the South's farm-to-table movement more than 30 years before his Highlands Bar and Grill was named the nation's best restaurant. Chris Hastings's Hot and Hot Fish Club has received numerous honors as well. The Bright Star, open in nearby Bessemer since 1917, is another Beard winner.

Birmingham is also known for its role in the civil rights movement. In 1963, the Rev. Martin Luther King Jr. called Birmingham the most segregated city in America. After weeks of demonstrations to end Jim Crow laws, the Ku Klux Klan dynamited the 16th Street Baptist Church and killed four little girls. Tour the church and then visit the Birmingham Civil Rights Institute.

Hear the hum of motorcycles on the track past the Barber Vintage

Colorful leaves brighten a scenic drive through Noccalula State Park.

Motorsports Museum outside Birmingham. George Barber collected bikes since his youth and opened the world's largest motorcycle collection in 2003. Harleys date from 1902. It's is also the busiest Porsche driving school in the world. A short drive east, NASCAR fans are discovering the Talladega Superspeedway's Garage Experience and Celebration Plaza in the track's massive infield.

On the way to Tuscaloosa, stop at Vance and tour the Mercedes Benz plant. You might see the most expensive vehicle made in America, the Mercedes Maybach GLS, rolling down the assembly line. You can drive one home for north of $200,000.

Get tickets in advance for a daily tour of Bryant-Denny Stadium that includes about one mile of walking. The tours give you access to locker rooms, but, sadly, no sighting of national championship trophies. Next, visit the Paul Bryant Museum near the Coleman Coliseum.

Many serious golfers put the Robert Trent Jones Golf Trail on their bucket list and head for the Grand National courses outside Opelika. Golf course architect Robert Trent Jones declared the land around the 600-acre lake near Opelika to be the single greatest site for a golf complex.

The 1851 Alabama State Capitol hosted delegates from seven states who seceded from the U.S. and gathered in the Senate chamber to form the Confederate States of America hoping to preserve slavery. Jefferson Davis of Mississippi was sworn in on the front steps as president of the ill-fated effort. Walk south of the Capitol to tour the Museum of Alabama inside the Alabama Department of Archives and History.

Just below the statue of Jeff Davis, the historic 1965 Selma to Montgomery Voting Rights March ended a few feet from the Capitol grounds. Dr. Martin Luther King Jr. delivered his "How Long? Not Long" speech in the street when Gov. George Wallace refused him permission to speak from the Capitol steps.

Read 16 bronze panels in Bicentennial Park that were dedicated on in late 2019. Walk a few steps to Dexter Avenue King Memorial Baptist Church. Tours begin in the basement where King and dozens of other black pastors organized the 1955 Montgomery Bus Boycott. Nearby is the Civil Rights Memorial that sculptor Maya Linn created for the Southern Poverty Law Center. It honors 41 victims who died fighting for racial equality from 1954 to 1968.

Tour the Rosa Parks Museum, then head to the Equal Justice Initiative's powerful National Memorial for Peace and Justice and nearby Legacy Museum. White terrorists lynched thousands of blacks across the South in hopes of preserving white supremacy. The lynching memorial features 800 steel columns with names of 4,000 victims.

Enjoy an evening of comedy or drama inside one of the two professional theaters at the renowned Alabama Shakespeare Festival. Winton "Red" Blount, a wealthy Montgomery businessman who privatized the post service under President Richard Nixon, built it.

In 1965 in Selma, State Troopers brutally ended a peaceful march for voting rights by 600 blacks. The attack on the Edmund Pettus Bridge is remembered as Bloody Sunday. Since the Oscar-winning movie "Selma," even more tourists make the trip to walk across the bridge.

Drive south to Monroeville, which hometown novelist Nelle Harper Lee renamed Maycomb in her classic "To Kill a Mockingbird." Enter the restored 1903 courthouse. Sit in the balcony of the courtroom and recall Atticus Finch's passionate defense of a black man wrongly accused. Come see local actors perform the "Mockingbird" play in April and May.

Travel south to a section of Alabama that feels different, older, like part of a European country, and for good reason. Two French brothers founded Mobile in 1702 as France's first capital of the Louisiana territory.

Downtown Mobile is packed with attractions that showcase its rich traditions. Housed in an 1857 landmark, the History Museum of Mobile showcases portraits, sterling silver sets, maps, swords and a full-scale model of a Confederate submarine. The Mobile Carnival Museum displays handmade gowns that have been worn by Mardi Gras royalty since the 1860s. Walk in to admire the elegant lobby of the Battle House Hotel, which dates from 1852.

The USS Alabama battleship, along with the USS Drum submarine, guards the Mobile causeway. Many state residents remember donating dimes during their childhood to bring the ship from Seattle.

Visit Bellingrath Gardens and Home to see some of the state's most spectacular gardens. Traffic backed up for miles in April 1932 when Coca-Cola bottler Walter Bellingrath and wife Bessie opened their gardens framed by live oaks that sheltered countless azaleas and camellias.

Soak up the sunshine along Alabama's crystal white beaches. Choose from 20,000 rooms, cabins and houses in Gulf Shores and Orange Beach. Delicious seafood served here is the freshest anywhere in Sweet Home Alabama.

— *Lee Sentell*

Geography shapes the history and traditions of a region, and nowhere is this better experienced than in North Alabama at the end of the Appalachian Mountains.

Drop in on Fort Payne, the hometown of the country band Alabama, for some of the South's most beautiful mountain scenery. For more than a century, Mentone has been a secluded escape for travelers seeking the cool tranquility of plunging waterfalls.

At Guntersville, you can step off a ski boat on the smooth lakes of the Tennessee River and in only a few minutes be on top of a mountain where eagles fly.

Make the pilgrimage to a rural church at Henagar to hear the ancient tradition of Shaped Note singing.

Learn the sad legend of the Indian princess whose name graces a waterfall in Gadsden. Drive around mountainous Blount County and discover that covered bridges were built out of necessity, not simply for charm.

There's more fun on the river in Decatur where the first wave pool in America still rocks the waves each summer.

In Florence, visit the birthplace of W.C. Handy, "father of the blues," and then go to the studio where the Muscle Shoals Sound was born.

There's a reason why the Cullman phone book is laced with lots of German surnames.

A visit to Huntsville shows you how astronauts in the U.S. trained for space travel.

Scottsboro, once tainted by the legacy of tragic racial trials, is best known today for shopping bargains made famous by Oprah Winfrey.

Waterfalls are scattered through the northeastern corner of the state.

HUNTSVILLE:
TO THE MOON & BACK BY DINNER
by Brian S. Jones

The U.S. Space & Rocket Center (One Tranquility Base; 1-800-63-SPACE) in Huntsville is the largest and most comprehensive American space flight museum in the world. Located just off I-565, the center is

There is a great photo opportunity when you enter the Davidson Center and climb the stairs to the main exhibit hall. The Quick monoplane that was invented by William Lafayette Quick and flown in 1908 in Hazel Green, Ala. is suspended from the ceiling. A photo taken of the Quick plane from the top of the staircase will also show the 38-story replica of the Saturn V rocket visible outside the window. It is awe-inspiring to think of the progression that led man from the Quick plane to the Space Shuttle in less than 80 years.

easy to spot from miles away by the 38-story replica of the Saturn V rocket standing in front of it. The space center's side parking lot is located alongside the futuristic dormitories used for Space Camp and an 89-ton mockup of the Pathfinder space shuttle.

Walking up the sidewalk to the center, you will see both the grave of Miss Baker, a squirrel monkey launched into space and successfully recovered, and an SR-71 Blackbird spy plane on display. The SR-71 Blackbird planes were used by the U.S. Air Force from 1964

to 1998 as strategic reconnaissance aircraft. They cruised at Mach 3 (three times the speed of sound) and set a jet speed record by traveling from New York to London in one hour and 54 minutes.

Once inside the space center, you can purchase a ticket and visit a gift shop full of NASA and science souvenirs, including flights suits, space craft models, and Apollo and shuttle program collectibles. The six-story IMAX SpaceDome Theater is being converted into a state-of-the-art digital theater, with new seating and lighting and state-of-the-art screens, and a planetarium, which will be a new addition to the center in early 2019. The theater will show STEM-focused productions and planetarium shows. Tickets for the theater and planetarium can be purchased individually as well as part of combination admission.

EXPLORE EXHIBITS AND COLLECTIONS

The U.S. Space & Rocket Center, created by the state of Alabama in 1970, has an extensive collection of original space exploration hardware, including Mercury and Gemini capsule trainers, the Apollo 16 capsule and one of the few V-2 rockets in the nation. You can also see the actual desk where Dr. Wernher von Braun worked as director of the Marshall Space Flight Center and his 1969 calendar where written by his hand in pencil on July 20 are the words: "lunar surface achieved."

DISCOVER WONDERS OF THE SATURN V CENTER

A short walk through Rocket Park will lead you to the Davidson Center for Space Exploration, which was specially designed to house the original engineering model, the first Saturn V rocket. It was never launched into space. The rocket is suspended 10 feet above the floor, allowing visitors to walk underneath it. The Saturn V is a National Register of Historic Landmark and was named one of the Seven Wonders of America by "Good Morning America."

Once in the main area of the Davidson Center, you will be overwhelmed by the awesome size of the Saturn V rocket as you walk directly underneath this engineering marvel. The Saturn V on display is one of only three remaining in the world. The rest of the 68,000 square-foot Davidson Center is filled with artifacts from the Apollo era, including an actual moon rock from the Apollo 12 mission, a lunar excursion module, lunar rover vehicle, a mobile quarantine facility, the Apollo 16 capsule and actual spacesuits worn by the astronauts. You can walk across the same metal access arm walkway that the astronauts used to enter their space capsules.

A special program offered at the rocket center is Space Camp. The idea for Space Camp came from Dr. von Braun in 1977 when he was touring the rocket center and noticed a group of children studying the exhibits and taking notes. Dr. von Braun said, "We have band camp, football, cheerleading; why don't we have a science camp?" Space Camp was founded in 1982 to provide residential and day camp educational programs for children and adults. Space Camp and Space Academy programs include the original simulated astronaut training camps conceived by Dr. von Braun and its sister program, Aviation Challenge, which offers simulated jet pilot training.

Space Camp was also featured in the Hallmark Hall of Fame movie *A Smile as Big as the Moon* on ABC television.

Guests enjoy a tour of the U.S. Space and Rocket Center in Huntsville led by a former astronaut.

The movie is based on a true story about a special education teacher's dream of helping his students attend Space Camp.

OTHER SPACE FUN IN HUNTSVILLE

Drive to the top of Huntsville's Monte Sano to see the Von Braun Astronomical Society's Planetarium and Observatory (5105 Nolen Ave.; 256-539-0316) located inside Monte Sano State Park, just past the park office. Dr. Wernher von Braun and his colleagues used the observatory's telescope to search for possible landing sites for the Apollo program. The planetarium offers programs to the public every Saturday night.

Watch a presentation projected onto the domed theater ceiling, such as a depiction of that night's visible constellations, and, when the weather permits, view wonders of the sky through the planetarium's telescopes. Knowledgeable presenters ready to answer your questions lead each show. All programs are family-friendly, but some are more suited for younger audiences than others. Admission is $5 for adults, $3 for students, and free for children under 6, as well as VBAS members.

ABOUT HUNTSVILLE

Huntsville is nicknamed "The Rocket City" because it is the birthplace of the U.S. space program and it was here that the Saturn V rockets were developed that put man on the moon. Huntsville was a sleepy North Alabama cotton-farming town when the U.S. Army chose a site just southwest of the city for the building of three munitions facilities in early 1941.

The three facilities were combined to form one large site called Redstone Arsenal at the end of World War II. The Redstone Arsenal site was selected for the Army's rocket and missile development program, and 1,000 personnel were transferred there in 1950. Central to this group was Dr. Wernher von Braun and his team of German rocket scientists who had been brought to the U.S. from Germany after the war. They were given the mission to develop what became known as the Redstone Rocket based on their wartime V-2 rocket technology. The Redstone Rocket was used to launch America's first satellite, Explorer I, in 1958 and America's first man, Alan Shepard, in 1961. The massive Saturn V rocket that took man to the moon during the Apollo program was developed in Huntsville by the von Braun team during the mid-1960s.

Don't Miss This

MOON SHOT AND OTHER SPACE TRAVEL SIMULATORS

Be sure to experience Moon Shot, where you can rocket 140 feet straight up in 2.5 seconds with 4 G's of force and experience 2-3 seconds of weightlessness followed by a 1 G free fall, and other space travel simulations while at the U.S. Space & Rocket Center.

OTHERS INCLUDE:

G-Force Accelerator, where you can spin at approximately 24 revolutions per minute and experience three times the force of gravity — what astronauts felt during a shuttle launch.

Hyper Ship motion-based simulator, a five-minute, multi-sensory experience that combines a movie-like audiovisual presentation using a high-definition projection screen and surround sound, with the motion of the ride compartment. There are different rides available, including "Red Baron" and "Black Hole."

Mars Climbing Wall, where you can learn about the red planet and scale part of the tallest volcano in the solar system.

WHERE TO STAY

Whether you're looking for a luxurious hotel, a RV camping spot with hookups or a cozy and quiet bed and breakfast, Huntsville offers nearly 6,200 rooms to choose from. You can share a view of the Saturn V rocket or be close to the hottest shopping and dining spots. For a list of lodging and dining options in the area, visit www.huntsville.org.

FORT PAYNE:
THE VIEW FROM LOOKOUT MOUNTAIN
by Brian S. Jones

The largest city along the Alabama portion of Lookout Mountain Parkway is Fort Payne (256-845-1524). It is located on what was originally an important village in the Cherokee Nation and was home to Sequoyah who created the Cherokee alphabet that made reading and writing in that language possible. History tells us that Sequoyah is the only person ever to conceive an alphabet in its entirety.

A canvas of scenic beauty year-round is the best way to describe the Lookout Mountain area of northeastern Alabama, especially in DeKalb County, near Fort Payne. Native poplars, dogwoods, maples and hickories explode throughout the area in the fall and provide a panoramic showcase of vibrant yellow, gold and orange. Chock-full of natural splendor, the area is also known for its protected forestlands, which are rich with greenery in the spring. Little River Canyon, considered a marvel of nature and a recreational wonder, boasts a river that begins and ends entirely on top of a mountain and attracts visitors throughout the year.

Many come here simply to view the beautiful waterfalls; others come to enjoy some of the country's best whitewater kayaking.

HISTORY OF FORT PAYNE

Fort Payne derived its name from the fort commanded by Maj. John Payne that was built here in the 1830s by the U.S. Army and used to corral American Indians, whose Cherokee ancestors had lived in the area for thousands of years before removal to the West. As a stop on the railroad line between Birmingham and Chattanooga, Fort Payne flourished and became a boomtown during the late 1880s. Unlike the gold rush out West, this area experienced a coal and iron rush when an influx of workers came here from New England with the lure of instant riches. Many of the town's historic buildings date from this period, including the Fort Payne Opera House, the W.B. Davis Mill Building and the Fort Payne Depot Museum.

Sadly, the boom that brought attention to the town in the latter 1800s was soon a bust. The area fell into decline before coming back in the early 1900s as the center of hosiery manufacturing – an industry that earned Fort Payne the nickname of "Sock Capital of the World." Fort Payne is credited with developing athletic socks. As textile industries began moving overseas in the 1990s, the area around Fort Payne began to diversify again. This time, city leaders used tourism as the means of attracting people to the Lookout Mountain area to enjoy its scenic beauty and nature-based activities. Today, in addition to being a scenic mountain town, Fort Payne is home to members of the country music group Alabama.

FORT PAYNE DEPOT MUSEUM

When visiting the area, there are a number of attractions you'll want to be sure to see. Among them is the Fort Payne Depot (105 Fifth St. N.E.; 256-845-5714). Constructed in 1891 out of pink sandstone in the Richardson Romanesque style of architecture, the depot was a main stop on the railroad line with two express mail trains and six passenger trains passing through daily. With its central location, the depot also became the town's unofficial community center. Locals used it as a gathering place to catch up with friends and family who would come into town from their farms.

Politics and "just a little friendly gossip" was usually the talk of the day at the depot,

ABOUT FORT PAYNE

Fort Payne, the largest town along the Alabama portion of the Lookout Mountain Parkway, boasts an intriguing history – from the famed Sequoyah, who developed an entire alphabet for the Cherokee Nation, and the tragic Trail of Tears Indian removal to a great industrial boom era, subsequent bust and thriving hosiery industry.

In 1780, the area now known as Fort Payne was named after the Cherokee Chief "Red-Haired" Will Weber. The name of this locale was known as Willisi and then Will's Town. What is now officially DeKalb County was known as Will's County until 1836.

The first general use of the name "Fort Payne" came several years after the Indian removal stockades had been abandoned in 1838. Fort Payne became an official name in 1869 and on May 5, 1878, it became the county seat of DeKalb County. Among its famous people are Jeff Cook, Teddy Gentry and Randy Owens, founders of the country music group Alabama; former Agricultural Commissioner and 2010 Democratic gubernatorial nominee Ron Sparks; and Katherine Stinson, who was the fourth woman in Alabama to become a licensed pilot.

especially on Sunday afternoons when many stopped to visit after church before heading back to their rural areas. The depot remained in service as a train station until 1970 and was placed on the National Register of Historic Places the following year.

Fort Payne Depot Museum

Today, the depot serves as a museum of local history with separate collections for railroad history, Native American heritage, war memorabilia and DeKalb County history.

FORT PAYNE OPERA HOUSE

The Fort Payne Opera House (510 Gault Ave. N.; 256–845–6888) was built in 1889 and is still in use today. It began life as a venue for live performances and was used for public forums before being converted to use as a theater during the silent movie era. The Fort Payne Opera House has been completely restored and is today used as a cultural center for the community. It is on the National Register of Historic Places and the National Register of 19th Century Theaters in America.

MOUNTAIN MUSIC – THE BAND ALABAMA

"My home's in Alabama," so sing the members of the legendary music group who grew up in Fort Payne and took the state's name for their band. When visiting their hometown, you'll find life-sized bronze statues of group members on display on the corner of Union Park facing the intersection of Gault Avenue and Fourth Street North downtown. The band was formed in 1969 by Randy Owen and his cousin Teddy Gentry. Their musician friend and Fort Payne native Jeff Cook soon joined them. Alabama released 21 gold, platinum and multiplatinum albums, had 42 No. 1 singles and sold more than 73 million records. They have a star on the Hollywood Walk of Fame and were named the Country Group of the Century in 1999 by the Recording Industry Association of America.

A must-see for any fan or country music lover is the Alabama Fan Club and Museum (101 Glenn Blvd. S.W.; 256-845-1646) located at the intersection of AL Highway 35 and U.S. Highway 11 less than a mile off I–59 at Exit 218. This museum houses the group's many awards, collections from their touring days and a great gift shop.

Fall colors reflect on the water.

At Little River, there is a 23-mile drive along the canyon's rim that offers spectacular views into the 700-foot-deep gorge. The drive features several stop-off points where you can pull over and get photographs. The 15,000-acre site encompassing Little River Canyon was made a part of a national preserve by an act of Congress in 1992 to ensure that its beauty can be enjoyed for generations to come.

LITTLE RIVER CANYON NATIONAL PRESERVE

Little River Canyon was carved out by the river after thousands of years and is one of the deepest canyons in this part of the United States. To get there via AL Highway 35, take the I–59 exit and go east about 10 miles.

There are three major waterfalls in Little River Canyon. Little River Falls marks the beginning of the canyon and is located off Highway 35 next to the bridge separating the town of Gaylesville from Fort Payne. This is your first stop on a scenic tour entering from the north. An expanded boardwalk project completed in 2012 leads you directly to the 45-foot waterfall.

Next is DeSoto Falls, which is located on the West Fork of the river and is 104 feet high. Grace's High Falls is the last of the major three and is Alabama's highest waterfall at 133 feet. The waterfalls are seasonal. The best time to view them is in the fall, winter or spring. Lack of rain often diminishes the power of the falls in the summer.

Besides the beautiful falls, visitors will discover that Little River Canyon is a hiker's delight with beautiful natural forests and sandstone cliffs towering 600 feet above the canyon floor. There are several hiking trails you can take along the edges of the canyon. These trails allow you to get some great views of the entire canyon area. Eberhart Point is the best point for hiking down to Pine Tree Hole at the bottom of the canyon.

The more adventurous can even put in there for some whitewater rafting fun. As visitors will discover, the Little River Canyon area is also a land of beauty and legends. One of the most interesting legends is the local one about Littlefoot.

Several years ago, a small petting zoo was in operation near Little River Canyon. The family running the zoo ran into financial difficulties and ended up closing. The remaining animals were being moved to another facility when an escape occurred. A small family of monkeys took advantage of an open transport cage and ran off into the woods. Then the reports started.

As the legend goes, a group of rafters noticed something moving in the trees and that it appeared to be following them down the river. A Cub Scout troop had pine cones playfully thrown at them from the treetops. A group of hikers left their backpacks along the riverbank and returned to find their snacks missing and several small footprints in the surrounding mud.

A retired engineer from Huntsville took a blurry photo of a small hairy figure walking upright and dragging what appeared to be an Igloo cooler. These occurrences soon became known as Littlefoot sightings. So when hiking Little River Canyon, just remember to keep one eye on the tree branches and the other on your snacks.

THE BEAUTY OF DESOTO STATE PARK

DeSoto State Park (7104 DeSoto Parkway N.E.; 256-845-0051) is located eight miles northeast of Fort Payne. One visit and it's easy to see why DeSoto was voted as one of America's Top 10 State Parks by Camping Life magazine. The park spreads over 3,500 acres along the outer ridge of Lookout Mountain and embraces some of the state's most dazzling natural wonders. The best way to enjoy this wonderful state park is to get out and experience it.

DeSoto State Park has 25 miles of hiking

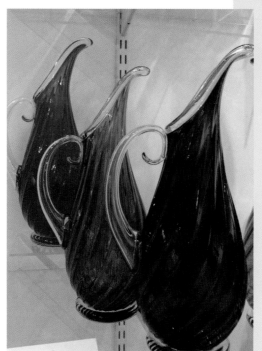
Original works of glass

and biking trails. Talmadge Butler Boardwalk Trail offers a 360-yard walk designed for hikers of all experience levels. There is a 20-foot octagon deck at the end of the trail that overlooks a natural pool created by the Azalea Cascade.

The area was named for the beautiful wild azaleas that bloom here in mid-April. During the summer and fall seasons, weekend interpretive programs and guided hikes are offered.

The Lodge at DeSoto State Park (1299 Blalock Drive N.E.; 256-845-5380) was built during the 1930s. At the time, it was used as a group lodge and a dance hall. During the late 1970s, additions were made around the main part of the lodge and a motel constructed next to it. Inside the lobby you can still see the front center stone with the word "Lodge" carved into it.

The original part of the structure was turned into the Mountain Inn Restaurant, which is in operation today. Right outside the restaurant is a large deck that's great for

Don't Miss This

THE "COOL" EXPERIENCE AT ORBIX HOT GLASS

An unexpected find in Fort Payne is Orbix Hot Glass (3869 County Road 275; 256-523-3188).

Located on 26 acres atop Lookout Mountain bordering the Little River Canyon National Preserve, this glass-blowing studio and gallery offers fine handcrafted decorative and functional glass, as well as glass-blowing classes. Orbix was started in the late 1990s by Cal and Christy Breed. Cal leads a team of glass blowers who handcraft each piece with great attention to form, balance and color. These master artisans are a wonder to watch. They use a blowpipe to inflate molten glass into a bubble. During the blowing process, the partially blown glass is then turned around and around and bits of glass are often added with the use of a smaller metal rod. Various colorants are also added in the process to make dazzling translucent colors. The form of glass blowing practiced at Orbix was first invented by the Phoenicians around 50 B.C.

relaxing and enjoying the mountainous view. Lodging options available at the state park include chalets, log cabins, motel rooms and plenty of campsites. There is also a picnic area with a playground, an Olympic-size swimming pool and a nature center.

WHERE TO EAT

Make sure you try the JoJo potatoes at the Bar-B-Q Place (1502 Gault Ave. S.; 256–845–6155). This is one of those hole-in-the-wall places that serve up good authentic Southern barbecue and plenty of it.

MENTONE:
A MOUNTAINTOP TREASURE

by Brian S. Jones

Mentone is best described as a mountain resort town with Southern manners and a unique artistic flair. The small town is located on Lookout Mountain in the northeastern corner of the state, just a few miles from the Georgia border. The Lookout Mountain Parkway is known for its beautiful waterfalls and great white-water kayaking. An especially popular time to visit is in autumn when native poplars, dogwoods, maples and hickories provide a dazzling blanket of vibrant red, yellow and orange across the mountain.

Mentone sits on the western rim of Lookout Mountain, 1,000 feet from the valley floor. Lookout Mountain is 83 miles long and is part of the Cumberland Plateau of the Appalachian chain that begins in Maine and ends in Alabama. For more information on the Lookout Mountain area, contact the DeKalb County Tourist Association at 888-805-4740 or online at Lookout-MountainAlabama.com.

DISCOVER MENTONE

Nestled among the woodlands atop the western brow of Lookout Mountain, the historic and scenic village of Mentone hosts antique stores, arts and crafts shops, galleries and restaurants. Also tucked away in the mountaintop town is the notable bed and breakfast lodge, Mentone Inn, which opened in 1921. Just a short drive south on the tree-covered parkway, you will find DeSoto State Park and its gorgeous waterfall. This beautiful state park offers a lodge and restaurant, rental cabins and a renovated campground.

"If you want to rent a cabin, Mentone has them. If beautiful scenery, waterfalls, pretty hikes, neat shops and restaurants sound good, then Mentone with its cool, clear mountain air is for you. And don't forget to look for three annual arts and crafts festivals in May, July and October," says John Dersham, photographer and DeKalb County Tourist Association's executive director.

TAKE IN THE HISTORY OF MENTONE

Mentone is every bit as picturesque as Dersham describes it with the lands surrounding the town providing an element of romance and mystique. It is believed that the ancestors of the Creek and Cherokee tribes inhabited the area dating back as far as 8000 B.C. Settlers arrived shortly after the Cherokee removal of 1838-1839. The first house, built by Robert Vernon, now forms the central structure of St. Joseph's-on-the-Mountain Episcopal Church.

The natural spring water from the mountain is said to have health-restoring properties because of its purity and iron content. The development and promotion of the area as a health resort dates from 1872 with the arrival of the John Mason family from Iowa and Dr. Frank Caldwell from Pennsylvania. Dr. Caldwell became convinced of the healing properties of the area's mineral water after drinking it while visiting the Mason family and having his own health restored. He returned to Pennsylvania and sold all his possessions so he could move back and build a hotel. Dr. Caldwell lived with the Mason family while building the hotel. One night, he was telling the family of his dilemma with coming up with a name for his hotel when Alice, one of the youngest daughters, spoke up. She had just read of Queen Victoria's visit to the French town of Mentone and noted that the name meant "a musical mountain spring." Dr. Caldwell loved her suggestion and decided on the name Mentone Springs Hotel. The beloved hotel that Dr. Caldwell built in 1884 remained the state's oldest

The Old Union Crossing Covered Bridge, originally built in 1863, is located off Contry Road 614. The bridge was rebuilt in 1980.

operational hotel, and a true Alabama gem, until an electrical fire burned it to the ground in 2014. Though the Mentone Springs Hotel is gone, its legacy endures in the city named after it.

VISIT THE WILDFLOWER CAFÉ

Laura Catherine Moon, a self-proclaimed hippie chick who grew up in Birmingham, left her home behind to see the world. Upon arriving on the West Coast, she became fascinated with the heathy-eating culture for which California is known. Moon, as she is appropriately known, began to learn about edible and medicinal plants and decided to come home to Alabama to hone her craft. She landed in Mentone, where she grew

Don't Miss This

The Tomato Pie is The Wildflower Café's most popular dish and is highly applauded by locals and the flocks of tourists who come to the mountain town of Mentone each year. It is found on the Alabama Tourism Department's list of "100 Dishes to Eat in Alabama Before You Die."

Mentone Inn

herbs and vegetables to study and sell to local businesses.

One of her customers was Margaret Baker, the original owner of Wildflower Café. Moon eventually became a partner in the café, and it is now known for her organic recipes and gourmet café fare. The menu offers specials ranging from sushi to Mexican, with vegan, vegetarian and gluten-free options available. The Wildflower Café has won numerous awards and was named Best Café in Alabama in an Alabama magazine readers' poll.

WANDER THROUGH MENTONE

The Mentone Inn (6139 AL Hwy. 117; 256-634-4836) is a 12-room bed and breakfast that was built in 1921 and features a large front porch and an outdoor meeting pavilion with a fireplace. The Mentone Inn hosts a year-round farmers market every Wednesday from 3-6 p.m. and on Saturdays from 10 a.m.-1 p.m. Area farmers set up their booths in the town square to the left of the Mentone Inn. The market features vegetables, fruits, flowers, plants, cage-free eggs, honey and other locally produced goods.

Directly behind the farmers market is St. Joseph's-on-the-Mountain Episcopal Church (21145 Scenic Hwy.; 256-634-4476). The current building grew around an original log cabin worship site that dates to around 1870. Over the years, additions were built using wood reclaimed from old buildings of

the same vintage as the original cabin. Near the altar in the main worship hall are several long dark pews donated by the Advent Episcopal Church in Tuskegee. They were hand-finished by George Washington Carver, with a stain he made especially for them. St. Joseph's also has several tranquil garden areas for meditation and reflection underneath a canopy of trees. The church and its beautiful grounds have hosted numerous weddings and other events over the past generations.

A walking tour through downtown Mentone will lead you to the Hitching Post (6081 AL Hwy. 117). is now Magnolia Rose and Co. Housed within the Hitching Post are several businesses: The Gourdie Shop (256-634-4776), a gift and clothing boutique; Mountain Properties (256-635-8760), a real estate office; Magnolia Rose and Co. (256-634-2077), an antique and gift shop; and Tip Top Bake Shop (205-410-8965), a shop selling desserts, breads, and home-décor gifts, as well as gifts for wine- and tea-lovers. Built in 1896, the Hitching Post was originally a general merchandise store. By the 1940s, the site housed a cafe, gas pumps, a post office and a dance hall. The building began to be known as the Hitching Post because a group of fox hunters would hitch their horses to the building and eat an early breakfast in the cafe before their hunts. Weekend dances were held regularly in the second-floor dance hall during the 1940s and 1950s until the behavior of some of the participants began to get a little rowdy. Some of their post-dance

behavior was also cited as perhaps a little "inappropriate" to be taking place so close to St. Joseph's Episcopal Church.

Across from the Hitching Post are the Log Cabin Village Shops (6086 AL Hwy. 117; 828-508-0576). These eight unique stores are housed in log cabins clustered on top of a small hill. You will find a large selection of native jewelry, handmade soaps, weavings, quilts, antiques, and food in these locally owned venues. The village is constructed from several log cabins from Piedmont, Ala., that were taken down and reassembled board by board. Make sure and stop in for an old-fashioned ice cream at the Cones of Mentone in the village.

Down the hill from the Log Cabin Village Shops is Kaw-Liga's Wood Carving. You may notice the sound of a chain saw running when you approach Kaw-Liga's. Don't be alarmed – that's just how they carve wood up here in the mountains. The wood sculptures range from busts to life-size bear carvings. About a three-minute walk down the street from Kaw-Liga's is the wonderful Wildflower Café and Country Store.

Lookout Mountain Parkway was named "One of America's Most Scenic Drives" by Reader's Digest.

WHERE TO EAT

Just down the street from the Hitching Post, you'll find the Green Leaf Grill (6080 AL-117; 256-634-2110), which offers local, farm-fresh meats and seafood. In 2018, the Alabama Farmers Federation named Green Leaf Grill Best Catfish Restaurant in the state. Across the street, you'll see the acclaimed Wildflower Café. Past Green Leaf Grill, visit Helena's Gas & Deli (6081 AL-117; 256-634-2111), a long-established local favorite to grab a breakfast sandwich or burger—and a refill on gas, if you need it! Following highway 117 a few more yards will lead you to Plowshares Bistro (5951 AL-117; 256-634-3001), which offers breakfast, sandwiches, and dinner entrées, such as Appalachian Pork Chop and Lobster Ravioli. On the walls, you may see art from the Kamama Art Gallery that formerly occupied the building. Construction of the Mentone Arts and Culture Center is underway, which will create a new home for the gallery and other art in the area. Further still down the road, walk to the Mentone Market (5872 AL-117; 256-634-4686). This working gas station also offers delicious lunch offerings in a quaint, vintage setting.

EXPLORE NEARBY

Miracle Pottery (7871 AL Hwy. 117; 256-635-6863) is about halfway up the mountain between Valley Head and Mentone. Miracle Pottery has a large selection of functional and decorative pottery and art.

All of the pottery is made on-site by Valinda Miracle with stoneware or porcelain clay. Valinda used her art as therapy while recovering from health problems and now uses it as an inspiration to others. All of the pottery is oven and microwave safe and dishwasher friendly.

A ski resort in Alabama? Sure there is. The Cloudmont Ski Resort (721 County Road 614; 256-634-4344) is located in Mentone just off Lookout Mountain Parkway. Since 1970, a collection of advanced snow-making equipment has produced a ski resort right here in the mountains of Alabama. Snow comes to Cloudmont as soon as overnight temperatures drop to 28 degrees or colder, allowing the manufacture of a deep-base snow. Cloudmont offers personalized instruction to skiers of all ages and abilities in both group and private lessons. Skis, boots, poles and snowboards are available for rent.

The resort offers a variety of chalets and cabin rentals year-round. If you are visiting during the summer, you can enjoy the adjoining golf course and the Shady Grove Dude Ranch. The dude ranch offers horseback riding, wagon rides, square dancing and a real cowboy experience. The ranch includes 800 acres of beautiful wooded wilderness laced with miles of picturesque trails that are used by these part-time cowboys and nature enthusiasts for hiking or trail ride.

Don't Miss This

A PLACE FOR ROMANCE

The Lodge at Gorham's Bluff near Pisgah is among the state's most romantic destinations. Choose from a suite in the main lodge or bring friends and share a cottage. Create memories and enjoy the peace and quiet while overlooking the Tennessee River. Visitors say it is hard to find, impossible to forget. 256-451-8439. www.gorhamsbluff.com.

GUNTERSVILLE:
WHERE EAGLES FLY
by Brian S. Jones

Bald Eagle perched high above Guntersville Lake

It's the name of a famous song, but Guntersville is truly a place "where eagles fly." This area in North Alabama attracts so many migrating bald eagles during the winter that Lake Guntersville State Park specifically created an event for folks to come, watch and enjoy the graceful symbol of our American heritage each year.

Eagle Awareness is a must-attend event for bird watchers and outdoor lovers. Covering six weekends from early January through early February, the event has been a tradition at Lake Guntersville for more than 30 years. The program was started as an activity for people of all ages to experience the joy of watching eagles and other birds in their natural habitat and as a way of educating the public about the importance of protecting the area's wildlife.

ENJOY A STAY AT LAKE GUNTERSVILLE STATE PARK LODGE

The event kicks off at Lake Guntersville State Park Lodge (1155 Lodge Dr., Guntersville; 256-571-5540), the centerpiece of the 6,000-acre park. Here, you can relax in comfort, enjoying wonderful overnight accommodations as well as exceptional meals at the park's Pinecrest Dining Room. Be sure to inquire about lodging packages and other deals prior to your arrival for an Eagle Awareness weekend. After settling into the lodge following check-in, you'll want to attend the orientation that will let you know what's on tap for the weekend. The warm apple cider and music the lodge provides will certainly put you in the mood for your exciting outdoor adventure to eagle nesting sites and beyond.

TAKE A FEW FIELD TRIPS

Prepare to get up early and meet in the lobby of the lodge for breakfast and come back later, following your guided day tour, for informative talks, special exhibits and great food. The guided trips begin around 5:30 a.m. and include an easy-to-follow schedule of activities.

During your trip to this area, you will discover a series of small grassy islands, each home to an abundance of waterfowl and other birds. Here, you might encounter Canada geese, blue and gray herons, various varieties of ducks and river otters.

Eagle Awareness weekends feature guided field trips, knowledgeable guest speakers and talks from the park naturalist, making the programs both enjoyable and educational. Programs are free and include noted speakers with live birds, magnificent scenery and guided trips to High Falls Park in Geraldine, Cathedral Caverns in nearby Grant, and waterfowl areas at Guntersville Lake and Dam.

Eagle Awareness programs include noted speakers with live birds, magnificent scenery and guided field trips to High Falls Park in Geraldine, Cathedral Caverns in nearby Grant, and waterfowl areas at Guntersville Lake and Dam.

The tours are open to the public, so be prepared to have others just show up and be a part of the eagle-watching experience.

High Falls Park (969 County Road 144, Grove Oak; 256-659-4683), located in nearby DeKalb County, is a gorgeous area that has been called a "surprise of nature." The centerpiece of the 38-acre park is the 35-foot

ABOUT GUNTERSVILLE

Guntersville is named for John Gunter, one of the area's famous personalities. His famous great-grandson, Will Rogers, is an honorary son of the city. Rogers rose to prominence as an American cowboy, vaudeville performer, humorist, social commentator and motion picture actor.

Another notable figure is "Mississippi Bill" Harris. Bill is said to have tamed the Big Muddy (and many other rivers as well) from the stern of his 12-foot fishing boat named Miss Guntersville. Bill took a total of 23 trips over a 30-year span. The combined distance of his trips was 55,000 miles, more than twice the circumference of the earth.

Harris' first significant trip started at Guntersville Lake and ended in the New Orleans French Quarter and spanned more than five days, during which he called local radio shows to update them on his progress. He slept on boat docks at night and narrowly escaped being killed by several angry dock owners over the course of his journey. In the 1980s, Guntersville celebrated "Bill Harris" day, when the legendary boater would give every kid in attendance a quarter to buy bubblegum. Harris died in 2004.

Don't Miss This

GUNTERSVILLE MUSEUM AND CULTURAL CENTER

Sunday afternoon, after your Eagle Awareness weekend has ended, you'll want to come indoors for a visit to the Guntersville Museum & Cultural Center (1215 Rayburn Ave.; 256-571-7597). Located at the historic rock armory, the museum features a little bit of everything, from Native American artifacts to information about famous local figures.

Of particular interest for bird lovers is a special exhibit that, as attendants will tell you, is "for the birds." A display of almost exclusively native mounted birds that once resided at Guntersville's City Elementary "Rock School" now calls the museum home. Created by Bessie Rayburn Samuel, a self-taught taxidermist, in the 1920s, the display is considered a local treasure and was used as a reference for the state's first ornithology book.

You can also learn about the Tennessee Valley Authority and its role in the making of Guntersville Lake and Dam as well as about steamboats, gunboats and race boats that play a big role in Guntersville's past and present. Exhibits feature photos and replicas that depict life on the river before and after the formation of Lake Guntersville.

Guntersville Museum and Cultural Center

waterfall that spans 300 feet across in some points. At the base of the falls is a 25-foot, arched natural bridge that has been eroded by water over the course of the years. Hikers can get perfect upstream and downstream views of the falls from a pedestrian bridge on the far side of Town Creek. In addition, the park features six hiking trails where you can truly enjoy a get-back-to-nature moment. A day-use park, High Falls is a perfect location for viewing migratory waterfowl, a variety of songbirds, woodpeckers and bald eagles.

The trip to Cathedral Caverns (637 Cave Rd., Woodville; 256-728-8193) is not a bird-watching adventure but a cave tour that's well worth the trip. The first thing you will notice is the large entrance, which measures 126 feet wide and 25 feet high. Inside, you'll find Big Rock Canyon, Mystery River and other natural rock formations such as Stalagmite Mountain, The Frozen Waterfall and Goliath, a stalagmite column that reaches 45 feet to the ceiling of the cave. You can visit anytime – in winter and even in hot summer months – because the cave maintains a comfortable 60-degree temperature. Cathedral Caverns Park is open daily at 9 a.m. and closes after the last tour comes out of the cave.

One of the most popular spots for eagle watching is the area around Guntersville Lake and Dam. Guntersville Lake, Alabama's largest, contains 69,100 acres and stretches for 75 miles from Nickajack Dam to Guntersville Dam. The 30-mile-long body of water on the mighty Tennessee River sets the stage for all kinds of outdoor recreational activities, including fishing, boating and camping, and provides a picturesque setting for photographing bald eagles as they fly gracefully through the skies across the scenic landscape of Guntersville or swoop down into the water to catch a fish. While the vast majority of the eagles gather around the dam during the winter months, it's not unusual for many to stay here all year. Perhaps that's because they have learned what human visitors have known for quite some time – that Lake Guntersville is a beautiful place to hang out. Okay, maybe it's the other way around – humans have taken their cue from the birds.

Be sure and dress for the weather and remember to bring your camera, as there will be plenty of picture-taking opportunities in the great outdoors of North Alabama, particularly around Town Creek. This spot is not only perfect for watching the American bald eagle but enjoying other migratory birds as well.

Jones Cove Pinnacle at Guntersville Lake

FLORENCE:
ALABAMA'S RENAISSANCE CITY
by Brian S. Jones

Trowbridge's has served Florence residents and visitors since 1918.

Florence, the county seat of Lauderdale County, was surveyed in 1818 by Ferdinand Sannoner, an Italian native who named the city after Florence, Italy. The history of the area dates to 8000 B.C. and includes the influences of archaic hunter-gatherers as well as the Woodland and Mississippian cultures that established the great Indian mounds found here.

OVER THE BRIDGE AND ACROSS THE RIVER

Coming into Florence (about an hour and half from Huntsville via U.S. Highway 72), you will cross over the Tennessee River on the O'Neal Bridge. If you look to your left, you will see McFarland Park (200 James Spain Drive; 256-760-6416). This area has been a local favorite for about the past 10,000 years, dating back to when the river drew archaic hunter-gatherers. Mound builders, who later inhabited the area, also enjoyed the site.

Present-day McFarland Park has 60 campsites, a driving range, fishing piers, a playground and picnic area, walking trails, a floating restaurant, a lighthouse, beach area and soccer fields. This is a perfect place to enjoy some time on the river as well as special events such as the Trail of Tears Motorcycle Ride and the Bassmaster Fishing Tournament.

DOWNTOWN

Court Street is the main street of Florence. It takes you right into the downtown area. You'll know you are heading in the right direction when you start seeing purple paw prints on the street. They represent the lion mascot of the University of North Alabama, which is the center of academic and sports excellence in this part of the state. Be sure to take notice of the historic architecture along Court Street.

If you catch the aroma of freshly ground coffee, it is from Rivertown Coffee House (117 N Seminary St., 256-765-7128). This cozy café offers breakfast, lunch, and dinner in addition to coffee, tea, smoothies and craft beer. Make sure you try their Poblano Pimento Cheese Sandwich, their dinner burrito and any of their brewed beverages made with Muletown Roasted Coffee. If you feel like having a cool libation, check next door at On the Rocks (110 N. Court St.; 256-760-2212). Located in a two-story historic building, this pub features great afternoon specials and live music later at night.

Across the street you can experience a true slice of Italy at Ricatoni's (107 N. Court St.; 256-718-1002). Opened in 1996, Ricatoni's has become a local favorite with several signature items, including pizzas cooked in a wood-burning oven, freshly baked bread with herbs and olive oil and "old country"-style entrees. The man behind it all is owner Rick Elliott, better known as Ricatoni Valentino from his numerous TV commercials. Next to Ricatoni's is City Hardware (105 N. Court St.; 256-275-3666). Don't come looking for nails and light bulbs at City Hardware though. This restaurant/cafe features seafood, roasted chicken, burgers and sizzling steaks with outside seating on an upstairs deck to catch the evening breezes.

HIGH FASHION WITH A SOUTHERN FLAIR

No trip to downtown Florence is complete without visiting award-winning designer Billy Reid's store (114 N. Court St.; 256-767-4692). Reid was named best new menswear designer in America by *GQ* magazine and won the 2012 Menswear Designer of the Year award from the Council of Fashion Designers of America.

Reid's designs for both men and women capture classic Southern elements of fashion in lively fabrics that he showcases in his flagship shop and studio. The store itself is interesting to walk through and experience. It is a converted turn-of-the-20th-century bookstore furnished with Reid family heirlooms.

Florence boasts an old-fashioned downtown area with businesses lining a wide street leading to the University of North Alabama. The best way to experience this lovely downtown area is to park your car on one side of Court Street and start exploring.

Among his selections of shirts, suits, dresses, shoes and jeans, you'll also find designer T-shirts he created to help promote organizations like the Alabama Seafood Marketing Commission that sports logos like "Make Cornbread Not War" and "Eat Oysters, Love Longer."

FOLLOWING THE BRICK ROAD TO SEMINARY

After your fashion tour, head back down Court Street until you reach Mobile Street. It's a wonderful old brick road that will take you past the Chicago Cafe (106 E. Mobile St.; 256-710-3607), offering flavors of the "Windy City," and the House of Heroes (110 E. Mobile St.; 256-810-0604), a comic book store where you can get your geek on.

Continue down Mobile Street to the stylish art deco Shoals Theatre (123 N. Seminary St.; 256-764-1700) on the corner of Mobile and Seminary. Across from the theatre is a waterfall sculpture in the shape of nearby Wilson Dam, the only neoclassical-style dam in the TVA system, integrating themes of ancient Roman and Greek architecture into the modern structure. It spans the Tennessee River between Lauderdale and Colbert counties. The quad-cities of the area are represented on the dam sculpture: Tuscumbia (founded in 1820), Florence (founded in1826), Sheffield (founded in 1885) and Muscle Shoals (founded in 1923). Right behind the sculpture is Legends Steakhouse (201 N. Seminary St, 256-766-5072).

Walking down Seminary Street you will come to Ye Ole General Store (219 N. Seminary St.; 256-764-0601), which has been in operation since the 1940s. Named one of the 25 Best Vintage Stores in America by GQ magazine, the store has a little bit of everything including long johns, work gloves, socks, overalls, boots and even skillets. Don't be surprised if proprietor Gordon O. Glasscock comes out to talk with you. When Mr. Glasscock comes out to greet you, he actually wants to talk with you and not just sell you something.

"THE FATHER OF THE BLUES"

Across the street from Ye Olde General Store, you will see a statue of "Father of the Blues" W.C. Handy, who was born in Florence in 1873. Handy's most famous recording was "Beale Street Blues." The W.C. Handy Home, Museum & Library (620 W. College St.; 256-760-6434) is less than a mile away and houses a collection of memorabilia, including musical instruments, personal papers and original sheet music.

EXPERIENCE WILSON PARK

Just past the W.C. Handy statue downtown is Wilson Park (North Woods Avenue at East Tuscaloosa Street), a one-block park between Seminary Street and Wood Avenue named for President Woodrow Wilson. The park is the site of several annual events including the Alabama Renaissance Faire that draws 40,000 people to the area each October to enjoy some medieval entertainment.

A short walk will take you past a large European-style fountain in the center of the park to a great view of the replica of the historic Forks of Cypress plantation (321 N. Seminary St.). The original Forks of Cypress, completed in 1822 on a knoll five miles from Florence, was the only Greek Revival house in Alabama to feature a two-story colonnade, composed of 24 ionic columns around the entire structure. It was struck by lightning and burned in 1966. The replica was built in 1983 and is now the city headquarters for Regions Bank.

As you walk past the Forks of Cypress, you will be headed back to Court Street where you'll see Rosie's

W.C. HANDY FESTIVAL

The Florence area celebrates Handy with the annual W.C. Handy Festival (256-766-7642), featuring blues, jazz and gospel music, educational events, coordinated art shows, athletic events, street parties, great food and more over a 10-day period each summer. During the tribute to the "Father of the Blues," great jazz and blues music can be heard throughout The Shoals at restaurants, theaters, malls, parks and other locations.

Altogether, the festival features more than 100 events, including the popular Street Strut, Handy Nights and the Handy Run, which makes it a great all-around family-oriented celebration. Some of these events require admission, but most are free.

The event is held around the last full week in July and draws about 150,000 people. In addition to the Handy Festival, downtown Florence comes alive with art, music, shopping and family entertainment during First Friday celebrations from March through December.

Scores turn out for the Handy Festival.

University Of North Alabama Bibb Graves Hall

Mexican Cantina (302 N. Court St.; 256-767-5599) on your left. Known for its fresh, authentic Mexican food and wide variety of margaritas, Rosie's is only about a five-minute walk from the University of North Alabama.

UNIVERSITY OF NORTH ALABAMA: WHERE THE LIONS ROAR

The University of North Alabama (UNA) (One Harrison Plaza; 800-TALK-UNA) is the state's oldest four-year public university. It opened its doors in 1830 and was the first state-chartered institution to begin operation in Alabama. UNA was re-established in 1872 as the first state-supported teachers college south of the Ohio River and a year

later became one of the nation's first coeducational colleges. Throughout the year, UNA offers a variety of cultural events, such as the George Lindsey UNA Film Festival, named for alumnus George Lindsey of The Andy Griffith Show fame. It is also home to cultural organizations such as the Entertainment Industry Center, where many students have taken their first steps toward careers in music and entertainment.

Rogers Hall, a Greek Revival mansion built in 1855, is the first building you'll see as you are walking toward UNA on Court Street. Turning right and following the sidewalk, you will soon be at the main entrance (a visitors' parking lot is off to the right if you decide to drive). Just past the entrance is the president's house on your right and in front of you will be a large Italian limestone fountain at Laura Harrison Plaza in front of Bibb Graves Hall.

Mascots Leo III and Una reside on the campus in the 12,764-square-foot climate-controlled George H. Carroll Lion Habitat that is to the right of Bibb Graves Hall. UNA's live lion mascot tradition began in 1973, when then-President Dr. Robert Guillot personally acquired a 12-pound lion cub, now known as Leo I, from a Knoxville zoo. Since then, the cub's birth date, April 14, has been celebrated as the official lion mascot birthday – an annual event that attracts kindergarten and elementary school children from throughout the region.

After making friends with the king of the jungle, you'll want to continue to explore the historic campus that spreads out over 130 acres and includes Wesleyan Hall where infamous Civil War General William Tecumseh Sherman coined the phrase "War is hell."

AFTERNOON DELIGHT

After strolling through the UNA campus, wander back down Court Street for a tasty end to your exploration. Trowbridge's Ice Cream and Sandwich Bar (316 N. Court St.; 256-764-1503) has been a Florence institution since 1918. The old-fashioned diner still has a lunch counter and serves up malteds. Taste Trowbridge's signature orange-pineapple ice cream and you'll quickly discover why Travel Leisure magazine listed it among its "50 Reasons to Love the USA."

WHERE TO STAY

Inspired by Southern hospitality, the Marriott Shoals Hotel & Spa (10 Hightower Place; 800-593-6450) is a AAA four-diamond hotel with a relaxing European spa, great dining in its rotating restaurant, and live music in Swampers lounge. Set in the Tennessee River Valley, the resort also offers great views from each room's private balcony and features two championship Robert Trent Jones Golf Trail courses. For a list of other lodging and dining options in the area, visit Florence Lauderdale Tourism (200 Spain Drive; 888-356-8687). The GunRunner Hotel is in the heart of downtown Florence (310 E Tennessee Street; 855-269-4724). It includes 10 luxury suites, seven with private balconies.

ABOUT FLORENCE

Florence, the county seat of Lauderdale County, was surveyed in 1818 by Ferdinand Sannoner, an Italian native who named the city after Florence, Italy. The history of the area dates to 8000 B.C. and includes the influences of archaic hunter-gatherers as well as the Woodland and Mississippian cultures that established the great Indian mounds found here.

GADSDEN, ATTALLA AND BEYOND:
WONDER FALLS AND MORE

by Jennifer Kornegay

Take two days to explore the stunning scenic splendor of northeastern Alabama with visits to waterfalls in Gadsden and Fort Payne and the federally protected magnificence of Little River Canyon. There are also opportunities for antiques shopping, taking a walk on the wild side and enjoying a taste (or two) of Alabama wine before you leave.

TRAGIC BEAUTY

Start in Gadsden with a visit to one of the area's prettiest gems, Noccalula Falls (Noccalula Falls Road; 256-549-4663). Torrents of shimmering water take a dramatic plunge into Black Creek Ravine to form this 90-foot-high waterfall. According to local legend, so did a Cherokee princess with the same name. In a tragic end to a Romeo and Juliet-style love story, Noccalula threw herself over the falls rather than forsake her true love by a forced

Noccalula Falls statue

marriage to another. A statue at the edge of the falls illustrates and honors her sacrifice.

The city of Gadsden has long recognized the allure of the waterfall, and has protected it and built a 250-acre park around it, complete with a pioneer village, a botanical garden, a mini-zoo, a train that traverses the property and a fabulous playground with pavilions. You can take in great views of the waterfall simply by walking into the park, but taking the steep trail down to and under the falls is well worth some heavy breathing.

During summer's swelter, it is at least 10 degrees cooler in the shade of the woodland path than in the sun, and when you get up to the waterfall, the soft mist dancing in the air is a soothing refresher.

DOWNTOWN DELIGHTS

In the heart of Gadsden's revitalized downtown, the Mary G. Hardin Center for Cultural Arts (501 Broad St.; 256-543-2787) is worth a stop when you leave Noccalula Falls. It hosts a variety of visual, musical and theatrical presentations each year, including performances by the nationally renowned Etowah Youth Symphony Orchestra, and houses the Café 5 (256-547-1066), which serves daily meat-and-veggie-plate specials with amazing cornbread muffins.

Right next door, the Gadsden Museum of Art (515 Broad St., 256-546-7365) showcases local talent and rotating exhibits of other Southern art. Downtown also hosts First Fridays on (yep, you guessed it) the first Friday of each month. These events include local live entertainment, food and drink specials from area restaurants, classic car shows and more, and they're free.

LIONS, TIGERS & BEARS, OH YES!

From Noccalula Falls, take AL Hwy. 211 for 15 miles to Attalla to visit Untamed Mountain and Tigers for Tomorrow. (708 County Road 345; 256-524-4150). This exotic animal preserve and environmental learning center is a sanctuary for more than 160 tigers, cougars, bears, lions, wolves and other creatures that have been rescued from roadside circuses, owners who tried to keep them as pets and other situations that put these majestic animals at risk. Owner Susan Steffens worked for years in some of the country's best zoos and believes that wild animals should never be kept as pets or be subjected to terrible living conditions for the sake of our entertainment. She believes letting the public get up close to the big cats and other animals is a means of education, teaching visitors about the animals' beauty and power and their habitat needs. Tigers for Tomorrow is also a sanctuary for injured raptors and birds of prey that are native to Alabama as well.

ATTALLA ANTIQUING AND FLEA MARKET TREASURES

Downtown Attalla has a bevy of antiques shops with wares ranging from fine furnishings, china and glass to old books, bottles, collectibles, lamps and even some "junk." Somewhere in Time (402 Fourth St.; 256-538-4056) is a great place to step back into yesterday. Olde Walker Drug Store Antique Mall (328 Fifth Ave. NW, 256-538-6678) has items, from 15 vendors, including some great vintage signs, all housed in the historic main street drugstore. Owners Melton "Cowboy" and Janie Terrell have been operating the Mountain Top Flea Market ((11301 U.S. Hwy 278; 1-800-535-2286) since 1973. The market features everything from homemade ice cream, hot dogs, hamburgers, red-hot chili peppers, fruits and vegetables to toys, games, CDs, DVDs, tools, birds, fishing poles, hats, purses, clothes, shoes

Little River Canyon boasting beautiful fall colors.

and a bargain special that includes 18 pairs of socks for $5.

The Terrells can always be found mingling with the crowd on Sundays. Visitors have come from all 50 states and experienced a "true" Southern flea market at Mountain Top.

WINE DOWN

After enjoying the area's flora, fauna and shopping, relax with a glass of all-natural wine for a perfect ending to an exciting day. At Wills Creek Vineyards (10522 Duck Springs Road; 256-538-5452) in Attalla, just four miles from Untamed Mountain, you can indulge in the sweet juices of Alabama's native grape, the muscadine.

Nestled in a picturesque valley, this vineyard is family owned and operated and welcomes visitors with free wine tastings, tours of the vineyard and, of course, its wine and gift shop where you can purchase the wines you just sampled.

PLAY AT THE PARK

Travel north of Gadsden on I-59 and get off at exit 231 toward Valley Head to discover an abundance of natural wonder awaiting you at and around DeSoto Falls located right outside of Mentone and marked by signage on County Road 89. The Little River hurls itself over a craggy rock ledge, creating a 104-foot cataract and a thunderous roar.

A short stroll from the DeSoto Falls parking area takes you to an observation point. Just down the road, you'll find several smaller waterfalls in DeSoto State Park (7104 DeSoto Parkway NE; 256-845-5380). This 3,205-acre outdoor paradise has cabins, primitive camping sites and 25 miles of hiking and biking trails. Each season is a new revelation; you'll find the forest ablaze with color in fall and filled with the blooms of native wildflowers like Catesby's trillium, mountain laurel and sweet shrub in spring and summer.

But the park's true treasures are the waterfalls tucked among the rocks and trees. Traverse the trails in the park to find them. Indian Falls is the easiest to reach and drops 20 feet into a glassy pool. Laurel Falls is a pretty little drop and Lost Falls deep in the park, is aptly named because when there's not enough water flowing, there is no waterfall. The 360-yard Boardwalk Trail is an easy trek that takes you to a round deck overlooking the lovely Azalea Cascade. A detailed trail map with the location of each waterfall can be found on the park's website or at the park's lodge.

INTO THE DEEP

Thirteen miles from DeSoto Falls is Little River Falls. It plummets 45 feet and is the glittering showpiece of Little River Canyon.

Little River is one of the country's longest rivers to form and flow on top of a mountain. Over eons, its clear waters have cut through sandstone and carved an extensive canyon and gorge system as they descend.

Drive on 89 South to Highway 35 to visit the Little River Canyon Center (4322 Little River Trail NE ; 256-845-3548) and watch the 15-minute video to learn more before going to view Little River Falls. Continue to Highway 176, also known as Canyon Rim Parkway, and drive 11 miles along the edge of the canyon through the 15,000-acre Little River Canyon National Preserve. Multiple scenic overlooks offer majestic views of the falls as well as sheer rock faces, soaring hawks and the Little River. Grace's High Falls are also visible on this drive, but they are a bit fickle, only appearing when there's been enough rain. Tall and slim with a gentler flow, the falls are a treat for those who catch them at the right time. Further into the preserve, Canyon Mouth Park has picnic tables and access to trails that weave through the lower canyon's boulders and creeks.

Don't Miss This

Smoke on the Falls Barbecue Festival

The annual Smoke on the Falls Barbecue Festival is held each April at Noccalula Falls and attracts thousands of visitors for two days of family fun. The event features live music and plenty of kids activities along with the barbecue cook-off featuring both backyard cooks and professionals competing for thousands of dollars in prize money and bragging rights. And around the holidays, Christmas at the Falls showcases brilliantly colored lights that set the park aglow. Several lighted scenes are synchronized to popular holiday tunes. You can take it all in on foot or aboard the train. Kids of all ages enjoy hot cocoa, kettle corn and activities like decorating their own Christmas cookies.

PORK, BLUES AND INNER TUBES:
AN ALABAMA BARBECUE TOUR

In Alabama, barbecue is a culture all in itself. The state serves some of the nation's best, with iconic and award-winning restaurants just about everywhere. Take a tour of some of North and Central Alabama's best – from the fruits of lifelong professional pitmasters to new kids on the barbecue block – and pick up a side of fun along the way.

THE HOME OF BAMA WHITE SAUCE

Over the past 85 years, Big Bob Gibson Bar-B-Q (1715 6th Ave., SE, Decatur; 256-350-6969) has grown from a table in Gibson's backyard to a regional barbecue staple – garnering attention from news outlets and cooking competitions all over the country.

In the 1920s, vinegar-and-mustard-based Carolina-style sauce was the predominant barbecue sauce choice. Big Bob Gibson didn't think it complemented his chicken very well, so he came up with his own mayonnaise-based condiment.

Big Bob Gibson's split, seasoned chickens are laid open on the pit for several hours and then dipped in white sauce.

The flavor of the sauce, combined with meat smoked in hickory-fired brick pits, established white barbecue sauce as a North Alabama regional specialty. Four generations of the Gibson family have continued the restaurant's tasty traditions.

While in Decatur, visit Point Mallard Park (2901 Point Mallard Dr., 256-341-4900). This more than 500-acre park features a host of actvities, including camping, hiking and biking trails, a golf course and year-round ice skating, as well as the popular Point Mallard Water Park at the J. Gilmer Blackburn Aquatic Center.

PORK WITH A SIDE OF SOUL

In Florence you'll find the W.C. Handy Home, Museum and Library (620 W. College St.; 256-760-6434) which houses a collection of musical instruments, personal papers and original sheet music belonging to W.C. Handy, "Father of the Blues."

Each July, a festival celebrates the Florence

Champion of the Pit Chris Lilly with award-winning meats

Big Bob Gibson's sauces have become so popular that they are now available at more than 2,000 grocery stores in eight states and online. Locals use the white sauce as a marinade, basting and table sauce.

native's musical talents and those of other blues musicians.

Bunyan's BBQ (901 W. College St.; 256-766-3522) is less than a half-mile from the W.C. Handy Home, Museum and Library. Bunyan's is known for its pork and hot slaw. Grab a spot at one of the small tables inside or dine al fresco at one of several outdoor tables.

Need a place to stay for the night? Check into the Marriott Shoals Hotel & Spa (10 Hightower Place; 800-593-6450). The AAA four-diamond hotel boasts a European spa, rotating restaurant and two championship Robert Trent Jones Golf Trail courses.

Don't Miss This

THE ORIGINAL DREAMLAND BAR-B-QUE

No trip to Tuscaloosa is complete without a meal at the original Dreamland Bar-B-Que (5535 15th Ave. E., off Jug Factory Rd.; 205-758-8135). Opened by John "Big Daddy" Bishop in 1958, the idea to build the restaurant on the land next to his home came to Bishop in a dream. Once known for serving only ribs, white bread and sauce, today the restaurant's ten locations all serve pulled pork, chicken, traditional side items and desserts. The sauce recipe is a tightly kept secret, but what we do know is that its vinegar-based with hints of garlic and brown sugar. Dreamland encourages its customers to use the slices of white bread served with the ribs to soak up their extra sauce.

Ribs from the original Dreamland Bar-B-Que

GET YOUR FILL IN BIRMINGHAM

Birmingham is a barbecue lover's mecca. From pulled pork at Jim 'N Nick's to Full Moon's famous chow-chow, there's plenty to keep your tastebuds entertained.

Jim 'N Nick's Bar-B-Q (1908 11th Ave. S.; 205-320-1060) has served Birmingham for over 30 years. Known for pulled pork, cheese biscuits and homemade slaw, the restaurant consistently receives accolades from local and national publications. It boasts more than 25 locations throughout the South and in Colorado. Jim 'N Nick's was crowned the winner in the Alabama Tourism Department's inaugural Alabama BBQ Bracket.

Also on Birmingham's Southside is Full Moon Bar-B-Que (525 25th St. S.; 205-324-1007). Once owned by Pat James, the restaurant famous for its half-moon cookies and chow-chow – a spicy, sweet Southern relish – was bought in 1996 by brothers David and Joe Maluff. Full Moon now has fourteen locations, including the original.

Some of the Magic City's most popular attractions are minutes from both restaurants. Visit Vulcan, the world's largest cast-iron statue, at Vulcan Park and Museum (1701 Valley View Dr.; 205-933-1409); walk on the wild side at the Birmingham Zoo (2630 Cahaba Rd.; 205-879-0409); or head downtown to explore McWane Science Center (200 19th St. N.; 205-714-8300).

Another must-try barbecue joint is Saw's BBQ (1008 Oxmoor Rd.; 205-879-1937) in Homewood. It's young compared to longstanding porkhouses like Full Moon, Jim 'N Nick's and Dreamland, but it hasn't taken long for it to become a local favorite.

Saw's barbecue is North Carolina-style and served in a signature vinegar-based sauce. There are three locations in Birmingham serving pulled pork, ribs, chicken with white sauce, stuffed potatoes and home-style sides. Saw's Sauce is available online, in Alabama stores and at retailers throughout the country.

Want some authentic Alabama barbecue sauce to take home? Stop by Alabama Goods (2933 18th St. S.; 205-803-3900) in downtown Homewood. You'll also discover a bevy of Alabama-made products.

You'll need a relaxing place to stay during your time in Birmingham. Renaissance Ross Bridge Golf Resort & Spa (4000 Grand Ave.; 205-916-7677) fits the bill. Also check out the Sheraton Birmingham Hotel (2101 Richard Arrington Jr. Blvd. N.; 205-324-5000), the historic Tutwiler Hotel Hampton Inn and Suites (2021 Park Pl.; 205-322-2100) or Aloft (1903 29th Ave. S.; 205-874-8055).

Birmingham's Saw's BBQ

RIB IT UP IN TUSCALOOSA

Head down to Tuscaloosa and prepare to get your hands a little dirty. Your first stop? Lunch at Archibald's (1211 Martin Luther King Blvd.; 205-345-6861) in Northport.

George Archibald Jr. was 12 when he started working in the family barbecue business his father started in 1962. Today, George and his sister, Paulette, keep this diamond in the rough going, serving the ribs and sauce that have garnered local admiration and national attention. After lunch, stop by the Kentuck Gallery Shop and Courtyard (503 Main Ave., Northport; 205-758-1257). Kentuck also hosts the acclaimed Kentuck Festival of Arts each October.

From Northport, head to the University of Alabama campus to explore Bryant-Denny Stadium (920 Paul W. Bryant Dr.; 205-348-3680) and the Paul W. Bryant Museum (300 Paul W. Bryant Dr.; 205-348-4668), where you can take in more than 100 years of Crimson Tide football history. There's plenty to see and do on campus, and you're sure to work up a championship-sized appetite.

Full Moon barbecue chicken, cooked low and slow over a hickory wood-fired pit and spiced with a mouthwatering, award-winning sauce

The observation tower at Vulcan Park and Museum is open until 10 p.m. It's the perfect place to watch a sunset or get a spectacular nighttime view of Birmingham's skyline.

JUDGE HORTON AND THE SCOTTSBORO BOYS

by Lee Sentell

Take a 110-mile journey through scenic northeastern Alabama to visit train depots and courthouses in Stevenson, Scottsboro, Decatur and Athens, where the saga of the Scottsboro Boys case played out over seven years. It began the modern Civil Rights era. The chief hero was Judge James Edwin Horton Jr., who might have inspired Harper Lee's Atticus Finch, the courageous attorney she immortalized in *To Kill a Mockingbird*.

HOW THE SAGA BEGAN

During the Depression, African-Americans and whites looking for work commonly traveled by hopping on freight trains. On March 25, 1931, two poor, white female cotton mill workers climbed aboard a Southern Railway freight train pulling out of Chattanooga and met some white boys sitting on a load of gravel in an open boxcar.

Five black Chattanooga teens, Clarence Norris, Haywood Patterson, Eugene Williams and brothers Andy and Roy Wright, had also climbed aboard. When the Memphis-bound train dipped into Georgia, Charlie Weems, Olen Montgomery, Willie Roberson and Ozie Powell, among others, hopped aboard.

A fistfight broke out in the boxcar while passing through Jackson County, Ala. Six white boys that the African-American boys forced off the train ran back to the Stevenson depot to press charges. The stationmaster contacted Sheriff Matt Wann, who authorized an armed posse to stop the train 38 miles down the line at Paint Rock Depot, 20 miles past Scottsboro.

When 75 armed men stopped the train, Victoria Price (age 26) and Ruby Bates (19) climbed down from the boxcar and chatted with locals for 20 minutes while the posse rounded up the African-American boys and shackled them for starting the fight.

Ruby told Paint Rock station agent W.H. Hill and Deputy Sheriff Charlie Latham that the black boys had raped them on the train. It was a lie that would resonate for years and transform the lives of all involved. When the group was transferred to the Scottsboro jail, Ruby and Victoria identified nine of those arrested, aged 12 to 20, as their attackers.

THE SCOTTSBORO BOYS TRIALS

Amidst a racially charged atmosphere, Judge Alfred E. Hawkins began the trials April 6 in the Jackson County Courthouse. Four all-white juries reached multiple guilty verdicts in four days. Eight of the nine defendants, who had scant interaction with a lawyer, were sentenced to die in the electric chair.

Lawyers appealed to the U.S. Supreme Court. On Nov. 7, 1932, the court ruled in Patterson v. Alabama that the defendants had been denied the right to adequate counsel, a violation of the 14th Amendment, and ordered new trials. The Alabama Supreme Court granted a change of venue to Decatur and selected James Edwin Horton Jr., a highly respected circuit judge, to preside.

A communist-connected legal defense group recruited Samuel Leibowitz, a legendary Jewish lawyer from New York, to defend the men.

When Patterson's retrial began at the Morgan County Courthouse on March 27, 1933, reporters came from all over the nation. In a stunning turn of events, Ruby Bates testified she had not been raped. Victoria Price, on the other hand, remained steadfast that she (Victoria) had indeed been attacked.

When Scottsboro physician Dr. Marvin Lynch had examined the girls, he found no bruises or physical evidence to back up their accusations. He declined to testify for fear of losing business, but told the judge privately he didn't believe rape had occurred.

Based primarily on Victoria's testimony, the all-white jury ignored Ruby's testimony and returned with a guilty verdict on May 9, and asked for the death penalty.

On June 22, Judge Horton held a hearing in the Limestone County Courthouse in his hometown of Athens to discuss defense motions. He read a lengthy review of the evidence and said it did not corroborate the accuser's testimony. He shocked the courtroom by setting aside Patterson's conviction and ordered another trial. Northern

Morgan County Archives

Attorney Leibowitz with Patterson and other defendants

Stevenson Railroad Depot Museum

newspaper editorials cheered the decision, but most Southerners strongly disagreed.

The unhappy justices of the Alabama Supreme Court replaced Horton. He lost re-election the following year, although his home county supported him.

Meanwhile, the ambitious prosecutor Attorney General Thomas Knight Jr. was elected lieutenant governor. The men languished in prison amidst a series of more convictions and death sentences in Decatur. Trials continued into 1937. The last Scottsboro Boy left prison in 1950. The last of the nine died in 1989.

Judge Horton died in 1973 at age 95. Accuser Victoria Price, who never wavered from her story during a dozen trials, surfaced after a 1977 television movie about the case and died in 1982 at a Huntsville hospital at age 77.

The 82-year saga came to a legal conclusion on April 19, 2013, when Alabama Gov. Robert Bentley signed two pieces of legislation unanimously approved by the Alabama Legislature that exonerated the defendants.

Fittingly, the ceremony took place in Scottsboro at the former African-American church where attorney Leibowitz supposedly first met with the young defendants. The governor handed a signing pen to Clarence Norris Jr., a son of the defendant whose ap-

peal triggered the landmark Supreme Court decision Norris v. Alabama.

FOLLOW THE DRAMA

Begin your journey at the restored 1872 Stevenson Railroad Depot Museum (207 W. Main St.; 256-437-3012). It is packed with local history exhibits, although none on the Scottsboro Boys case.

Drive 18 miles through the lush countryside to the Scottsboro town square and read the historic marker in front of the remodeled Jackson County Courthouse (102 E. Laurel St.). At the Circuit Clerk's office, ask to see the folder of the original case documents. On weekdays when court isn't in session, visit the second floor courtroom to see the original bench from which Judge Hawkins officiated during the first round of speedy convictions.

STOP IN PAINT ROCK AND CONTINUE TO HUNTSVILLE

From Scottsboro, drive west on U.S. Hwy. 72 for 20 miles and stop at Paint Rock (population 210) where the train was stopped in 1931 because of the racial fight and the Scottsboro Boys were arrested. A concrete pad marks the rail station where the

WHERE TO EAT IN SCOTTSBORO

Chances are that some of the crowds in town for the 1931 trials ate at Payne's (101 E. Laurel St.; 256-574-2140) on the west corner of the square. It opened in 1869 and is famous for its hot dog with red slaw.

girls first lied that they had been gang raped. A historic marker unveiled in 2013 explains the importance of the location.

Arrive in Huntsville, the hometown of the two young women. A day before accusing the Scottsboro Boys, Victoria and Ruby left the freight depot, which is a block from the historic 1860 Huntsville Depot & Museum (320 Church St. NW; 256-564-8100). The Huntsville Visitor Information Center (500 Church St.; 256-551-2370) is a block west of the depot museum, across the train tracks. Huntsville, best known for Army and NASA programs, offers a range of great places to eat.

WHERE TO EAT IN HUNTSVILLE

For award-winning dining, visit James Boyce's Cotton Row downtown (100 South Side Square; 256-382-9500).

HEAD TO DECATUR

A half-hour's drive west of Huntsville is Decatur. The site of the old Morgan County Courthouse is now a park to the north of the current courthouse at 302 Lee St. NE.

By the time Haywood Patterson was retried in Decatur, the case was drawing international media coverage. Local portrait photographer Fred Hiroshige captured iconic images. See an exhibition at the Morgan County Archives (624 Bank St. NE; 256-351-4726). Open weekdays until 4.

Late in life, Judge Horton was asked about his decision to overturn Patterson's conviction in 1933. He replied in Latin his grandfather's motto that translates, "Let justice be done, though the heavens may fall." Timothy Hutton starred in a 2006 motion picture about the trial titled *Heavens Fall.* In 2010, a Broadway musical about the case (by the creators of *Cabaret* and *Chicago*) captured 12 Tony nominations.

END YOUR TOUR IN ATHENS

From Decatur, cross the Tennessee River and drive 12 miles north to Athens to see the handsome 1919 Limestone County Courthouse (200 West Washington St.; 256-233-6400). Visit the large third-floor courtroom where Judge Horton stunned onlookers as he set aside Patterson's conviction for lack of corroborating evidence, dooming his own political future. After Horton died, local officials installed a bronze plaque on the south wall of the courtroom that quotes his charge to the Decatur jury 40 years earlier: "So far as the law is concerned, it knows neither native nor alien, Jew nor Gentile, black nor white. This case is no different from any other. We have only to do our duty without fear or favor." The statue of Judge Horton is located on the west side of the courthouse.

These days, the top tourist attraction in Scottsboro is Unclaimed Baggage Center (509 W. Willow; 256-259-1525), a block west of the museum. The Jackson County tourist information office is located at 407 E. Willow St. (256-259-5500).

WHERE TO EAT AND STAY IN DECATUR

After visiting the Morgan County Archives, walk a block to Simp McGhee's (725 Bank St. NW; 256-353-6284). Order fish served Pontchartrain style. Stay overnight down the road at the Double Tree Hilton Hotel, only two blocks from the Tennessee River waterfront (101 6th Ave NE; 855-605-0318).

Don't Miss This

THE SCOTTSBORO BOYS MUSEUM

The former Joyce Chapel United Methodist Church where Leibowitz possibly first met with the defendants is now the Scottsboro Boys Museum (428 W. Willow St.; 256-912-0471). Community activist Shelia Washington opened the museum in 2010 and accelerated efforts to exonerate the men, who by that time were all long deceased. The rail tracks that carried the Scottsboro Boys to Paint Rock in 1931 are a block behind the museum. Open hours are limited, so check in advance.

Limestone County Courthouse

DECATUR:
THE RIVER CITY
by Brian S. Jones

Located on the banks of the Tennessee River in North Alabama, Decatur is called "The River City" and is known for its great outdoor recreation. A few minutes off I-65 is Point Mallard Park (2901 Point Mallard Dr., 256-341-4900). This 500-acre family park lets you stay in tune with nature 365 days a year. The park borders the Wheeler National Wildlife Refuge (2700 Refuge Headquarters Rd.; 256-353-7243) and is home to an 18-hole golf course, a 25-acre wooded campground, an indoor ice skating rink, a tennis center, an athletic complex, soccer fields and one of the state's most popular water-themed attractions.

MAKING WAVES AT POINT MALLARD

Point Mallard is home to America's first wave pool. It was developed in the early 1970s after the mayor of Decatur saw enclosed "wave-making" swimming pools in Germany and thought one could be a tourist attraction in the United States. The Point Mallard Aquatic Center features the original Wave Pool, Pro Bowl Slide, Towering Sky Pond and Speed Slide, Lazy River, three Flume Tube Rides, Olympic Pool, Sandy Beach, a scenic lagoon and a children's area featuring the Squirt Factory & Duck Pond.

A sloping entrance allows you to walk directly into the shallow end of the pool. This is the perfect place for small children to play and waders to enjoy the cool water on their toes. Those who want to really ride the waves can head for the deeper end. Swimming with the waves is great fun, but a float or inner tube lets you ride the waves without tiring out. The waves run on a cycle so you can easily get in and out of the pool.

After some wave-pool fun, head to Sandy Beach located right along Flint Creek – a

major tributary to the Tennessee River. There are plenty of complimentary beach lounge chairs, so bring your sunscreen and relax by the water. The Squirt Factory & Duck Pond area is nearby and offers plenty of playground slides and swings to keep the younger ones happy.

Point Mallard Floaters

Next on your summer fun tour is the Towering Sky Pond, which takes you on an inner tube plunge off a 40-foot tower into an Olympic-sized pool. You can ride the inner tube by yourself or with a friend. There are also championship diving boards and plenty of room for swimming. A short walk through a wooded picnic area will lead you to the Lazy River where you can enjoy a relaxing inner tube ride through a winding water-filled quarter mile long track. Right next to the Lazy River is the Speed Slide, which features three flumes of waterslide fun on top of a small hill.

DRY LAND ADVENTURE

Of course, the Aquatic Center is only part of the fun at Point Mallard. There are plenty of other activities to keep the family entertained for a weekend or a week. The Strike Zone features softball and baseball pitching machines that are available for hourly rental. Next to the batting cages is the golf driving range, which features target greens and putting areas with rental clubs available.

The Jimmy Johns Tennis Center has 12 championship hard courts, four championship clay courts, and two indoor hard courts. The tennis center is located alongside the

Don't Miss This

POINT MALLARD'S SPECIAL EVENTS

Whether you choose to visit Decatur and Point Mallard Park in the spring, summer, fall or winter, you'll discover a myriad of other exciting activities to keep the family entertained.

The Alabama Jubilee Hot-Air Balloon Classic is a free family event held annually at Point Mallard on Memorial Day weekend. The Jubilee hosts more than 60 local and national hot-air balloons and features a balloon glow at night, an antique car and tractor show, an assortment of arts and crafts, live stage acts and food. Balloons launch early in the morning and late in the afternoon.

The Spirit of America Festival, North Alabama's largest free patriotic event, features children's activities, live music, Miss Point Mallard Pageant and a large fireworks display held July 3-4 each year. The festival provides a unique opportunity for friends and family to gather and honor the nation's true heroes and celebrate hometown spirit and traditions.

Ronald Reagan Spirit of America fields. The 10-acre facility boasts laser-graded and lighted soccer fields with a permanent outdoor stage at the east end. The Spirit of America

Stage is the home of the Spirit of America Festival that takes place at Point Mallard each July 3-4.

Right next to the Spirit of America fields are campgrounds offering 239 campsites on 25 wooded acres complete with an enclosed meeting facility, kids' playground, and grills. A small trail running through the campground connects the three-mile hiking/biking trails that run alongside the Tennessee River and the side of the golf course. The Point Mallard Golf Course is an 18-hole championship course that lies on 200 acres of wooded flatlands surrounding Point Mallard Park. The course is open year-round with bargain-priced weekly green fees.

After swimming, playing tennis, golfing, enjoying batting cage practices or any of the other assorted Point Mallard activities, you may be ready to cool off for a bit. The perfect place to do that is at the indoor ice skating rink. Point Mallard Ice Complex offers a regulation-size indoor ice rink that is also open year-round.

Decatur's Old State Bank Building

War-related items. The historical reenactment is held in honor of Gen. Joe Wheeler and Confederate Gen. John Hunt Morgan, who both resided in North Alabama at some point during their military careers.

BATTLE FOR DECATUR CIVIL WAR REENACTMENT

History buffs in the family can return to the grit and glory days of the Civil War and relive the struggle between advancing Confederates and garrisoned Unions during the September Skirmish. Held every Labor Day weekend, the Civil War reenactment event marks the beginning of the Battle for Decatur, which was a small part of the 1864 Franklin-Nashville Campaign. The event includes open Confederate and Union war camps, troop drills and weapon demonstrations, dinner and a dance in period dress, as well as arts, crafts and live battles.

Over the course of the weekend, Union troops will win the day during one battle reenactment while the Confederates will capture the contested ground during the next day's skirmish. Spectators are encouraged to visit with soldiers, see demonstrations and purchase Civil

COOK MUSEUM OF NATURAL SCIENCE

The Cook Museum (133 4thAve. N.E. Decatur, AL 35601; 256-351-4505) has a shiny new building in downtown Decatur and many more exhibits for the entire family to enjoy.

The original Cook Museum was housed in a humbler facility – but still had much to offer in fun and learning. It was founded in 1968 by John Cook, Sr. and housed his professional collection of insects. Back then, he used the collection to train employees and gave public tours by appointment. In 1980, collections of rocks, minerals, fossils and more were acquired, and it was officially named the Cook's Natural Science Museum.

The Cook family had a vision to expand the museum to offer even more educational opportunities for the community through displays of "God's creation."

The museum boasts a 15,000-gallon saltwater aquarium that's home to fish, live coral, moon jellyfish. Other exhibitions with live animals include terrariums with Gopher snakes, bullfrogs, alligators and more. And, of course, it offers a large insect display.

The Cook Museum also includes three classrooms for field trip groups and a new venue for the community – Monarch Hall. With seating available for up to 480, the hall provides access to a 1,600 square foot patio and a 25-foot screen.

When the family gets hungry, stop at Nature's Table Café within the complex for wraps, sand-

The new Cook's Science Museum

wiches, protein bowls, coffee and smoothies. The restaurant is open to the public without an admission ticket. And before you leave, be sure to stop by the museum store to make a purchase that will help you remember your day and will support the museum's efforts.

DELANO PARK AND ALBANY HISTORIC DISTRICT

Following an exciting morning at the science museum, you and the family can enjoy a picnic at Delano Park (825 Gordon Dr., SE; 256-341-4930), where you can experience the magnificence of a cathedral of more than 400 legacy trees or be dazzled by a gorgeous WPA Rose Garden and the magical Riverwild Garden of native plants and contemporary sculpture.

The park, named after President Franklin Delano Roosevelt, was dedicated in the 1930s by Roosevelt himself.

Kids can explore the park and climb on the back of "Mr. Turtle," stand under the arch of the "Riverwild Heron Gateway," or stare in amazement at a 15-foot-high dragonfly. The middle portion of the park contains a children's playground, a Splash Pad, and a ditch with a concrete bridge donated to the park. The Splash Pad features numerous jets and sprayers that issue water from both the walls and floor of the pad. The floor is a large-scale map of the State of Alabama featuring the main rivers and largest cities in the state.

After the picnic with the kids, mom and dad will enjoy exploring the neighborhood surrounding Delano Park. Decatur's Albany Historic District is home to a wonderful collection of late 19th- and early 20th-century homes, ranging from Queen Anne Victorians to Craftsman Bungalows. The Albany neighborhood is included on the National Register of Historic Places. The district offers a beautiful tour of neighborhood gardens in the spring, and you can see it decorated in its holiday finery during the Christmas tour of homes each December.

Inflating hot-air balloons is a Memorial Day tradition in Decatur.

About Decatur

Nestled in the Tennessee River Valley, Decatur was originally a river crossing for settlers west of the Appalachian Mountains. It was incorporated in 1826. Settlers were drawn to the community by its fertile river valley soil and relatively easy access to other cities. Decatur has several Civil War sites and is well known for its historic homes, commercial buildings and parks.

Big Bob Gibson's

BIG BOB GIBSON'S BAR-B-Q

No trip to Decatur would be complete without a visit to Big Bob Gibson's Bar-B-Q (1715 6th Ave., SE; 256-350-6969). The classic restaurant dates from 1925, when railroad worker Big Bob (6' 4", 300 pounds) Gibson developed a special vinegar-based sauce and began cooking out of a backyard pit. Gibson opened his restaurant on 6th Avenue and soon attracted a loyal following. Third-generation owner Don McLemore and his son-in-law Chris Lilly now operate the restaurant. As the executive chef and head of the Big Bob Gibson Competition Cooking Team, Lilly is also the corporate spokesperson for Kingsford charcoal and author of Big Bob Gibson's BBQ Book. Under Lilly's leadership, the competition team has won multiple state championship cook-offs, more than 10 world championships and has taken the Best Sauce title at the American Royal International

Barbecue Sauce Contest. In 2011, Lilly's team was crowned World Champion at the annual Memphis in May competition.

GEOCACHING

After experiencing the flavor of historic Decatur and enjoying a night of lodging and dining, rouse the family early the next morning for a fun-filled and educational treasure hunt. The search for buried treasures with the Geocaching Passport available from the Decatur/Morgan County Convention and Visitors Bureau will lead you to some of the city's other favorite attractions including the Civil War Trail, the historic Princess Theatre for the Performing Arts, and the Carnegie Visual Arts Center.

To participate, download a copy of the Decatur Geocaching Passport or pick one up at the Decatur-Morgan County Convention and Visitors Bureau (719 6th Ave., SE; 800-232-5449). Once you have found all of the caches and received a stamp for each location, you can take your completed passport to the Visitors Bureau to receive a prize.

CULLMAN:
ALABAMA'S GERMAN VILLAGE
by Brian S. Jones

From its Native American and Civil War past to proud heritage as the site of an authentic 1870s German village, Cullman offers travelers plenty to see and do. You can visit a museum dedicated to the town's German founder, explore a local treasure filled with Civil War memorabilia or stroll the grounds of a Benedictine Abbey where miniatures of some of the world's most famous religious shrines can be found. The town is home to three Alabama governors: Jim Folsom, Guy Hunt and Jim Folsom Jr. Cullman is also the site of the Cullman Oktoberfest each fall. Whatever you choose to do on this road trip, you'll quickly discover why Cullman was selected by bestselling authors Gerald Sweitzer and Kathy Fields as one of "The 50 Best Small Southern Towns."

COL. CULLMANN AND HIS GERMAN INFLUENCE

Your starting point for a tour of Cullman is downtown at the Cullman County Museum (211 Second Avenue NE; 800-533-1258). The museum is a replica of the home of Col. Johann G. Cullmann, who founded the town. It houses thousands of historical items dating to the early 1800s. Displays include the Archeological Room with Native

CULLMAN OKTOBERFEST

Oktoberfest began as a one-day festival in 1977 to celebrate Cullman's German heritage. It has grown to a weeklong festival that features authentic German food, costumes and music. The festival is held the first Saturday in October in Depot Park.

Picturesque Cullman Depot is near the museum and farmer's market.

American artifacts, a clothing store with outfits from the 1800s, a Main Street exhibit with 19th-century storefronts and a photo gallery. Located just outside the museum is a brass statue of Col. Cullmann, who is credited with recruiting more than 10,000 German immigrants to come to this country.

Born in the Bavarian region of Germany, Cullmann traveled to America in the late 1860s to escape the revolutions sweeping across Europe. He first settled in the Philadelphia area and then moved to Cincinnati with the goal of one day setting up his own German colony in America, which he eventually did in Cullman. On his travels, he met former Alabama Gov.

Robert Patton who suggested that he settle in North Alabama. Cullmann was convinced the location was right for his colony, finding that the geography of the Tennessee Valley reminded him of his native Rhine Valley.

In April of 1872, Cullmann and five German families, 10 people in all, left Cincinnati to make the trip to Alabama. By the next year he had recruited 125 families to join the fledgling colony. Land sold for $1.25 an acre, so each family could afford a small farm of their own. Homes and businesses soon sprang up in the new town center. Cullmann built his own house on a half-block lot at the corner of First Avenue and Third Street Southeast. A hotel was built next to his house

About Cullman

The area that would one day become Cullman was originally inhabited by the Cherokee tribe of Native Americans. It contains portions of both the High Town Path and the Black Warrior's Path, two major thoroughfares used by Native Americans for thousands of years. The Black Warrior's Path, which led from the Tennessee River near Florence to a point on the Black Warrior River south of Cullman, figured prominently in the American Indian Wars. Gen. Andrew Jackson dispatched troops down the Black Warrior's Path during the Creek Indian War in 1813. Among the troops sent into Alabama was famous frontiersman Davy Crockett.

Cullman County was created by an act of the Alabama State Legislature Jan. 24, 1877, from portions of land in Blount, Walker, Morgan and Winston counties. The area was named for its founder Johann G. Cullmann (the Americanized version of the name). Cullmann immigrated to America in the 1860s and eventually founded a German colony in North Alabama. For its wealth of history, recreation and cultural opportunities, Cullman is touted by bestselling book authors Gerald Sweitzer and Kathy Fields as one of "The 50 Best Small Southern Towns."

at First Avenue and Fourth Street Southeast. Together the two structures made for an impressive first view of the town when visitors arrived at the nearby train depot.

The city blocks were laid out in perfect squares with wide streets according to Col. Cullmann's specifications. He also had land donated for parks and Protestant and Catholic churches. Cullmann developed a set of zoning laws written to allow shopkeepers to have their businesses on their property and to live there as well.

This made for a downtown very similar to a European village. German was the predominant language spoken in the city for decades. The impact that Col. Cullmann had on North Alabama and the German influence he brought to the area is celebrated annually during Cullman's Oktoberfest.

OTHER THINGS TO SEE AND DO IN CULLMAN

Across the street from the Cullman County Museum is the Cullman Railroad Depot (309 First Ave. NE; 256-739-2948). This pueblo-style stucco building was once used for passenger and freight service. It was restored in 1997 and named a Historic Landmark on the National Register of Historic Places. The lobby of the railroad depot has several displays of vintage railroad-related items. A restored red caboose is on display on the east side of the depot, facing Depot Park. This wonderful downtown park has plenty of walkways and a beautiful fountain in the middle.

Downtown Cullman has three historic districts. The downtown business district features unique specialty shops such as A Touch of German (218 First Ave. SE; 256-739-4592), which offers traditional German clothing, handcrafted nutcrackers, Bavarian steins, old-fashioned metal wind-up toys, Austrian crystal, tapestries, Christmas ornaments, candies and authentic German cuckoo clocks. The residential district of Die Deutsche Kolonie Von Nord Alabama means

"the German Colony of North Alabama." It consists of mostly Victorian-type architecture. The nearby Betz Addition Historic District is composed of 72 residential structures dating from the 1800s.

THE BATTLE OF DAY'S GAP AND MORE

For Civil War buffs, Cullman County offers visitors an opportunity to walk the grounds of an old battle site and tour a museum filled with war memorabilia. During the Civil War, the Cullman area was the site of the Battle of Day's Gap.

This battle was part of a set of skirmishes known collectively as Streight's Raid that

St. Peter's in miniature at Cullman's Ave Maria Grotto.

were fought between the Union forces of Col. Abel Streight and Confederate Gen. Nathan Bedford Forrest. The battle site where Forrest and Streight clashed offers visitors a historic frame of reference for visually recreating the skirmish that left 65 Confederates and 23 Union soldiers wounded. The building known as Penn Cabin was used as a makeshift field hospital for soldiers wounded during the battle.

The Battle of Day's Gap was fought just a few miles from present-day I-65 in a community named Battleground. To get there, from I-65 take exit 310, go north on Highway 157 for eight miles and turn west on County Road 1101 to 1082.

CROOKED CREEK CIVIL WAR MUSEUM IN NEARBY VINEMONT

Travelers wishing to enhance their Civil War experience are encouraged to visit the Crooked Creek Civil War Museum (516 County Road 1127; 256-739-2741) in nearby Vinemont.

The museum features displays of numerous authentic Civil War memorabilia, including uniforms and currency. It is housed in an old log cabin on the site of one of the battles between Forrest and Streight. Following a trail that leads from the hilltop museum to the banks of the creek, you can see areas where Union soldiers entrenched themselves for protection from enemy fire. Some of the trenches still have rocks piled around them that were stacked by the Union soldiers. There are picnic tables and covered pavilions near the site.

Don't Miss This

RELIGIOUS SCULPTURES IN MINIATURE

About 15 or 20 minutes from downtown is the Ave Maria Grotto (1600 Saint Bernard Drive SE; 256-734-4110), a four-acre, landscaped park on the grounds of St. Bernard Abbey. The Grotto provides a garden setting for 125 miniature reproductions of some of the most famous religious shrines in the world created by Brother Joseph Zoettl, a Benedictine monk.

ATHENS:
SOUTHERN SPENDOR
by Brian S. Jones and Jeanette Jones

Athens is a small city in North Alabama with a charming downtown square full of history. Those who enjoy the Southern tradition of "exaggerated remembrances" will feel right at home at the Athens Storytelling Festival. The Delmore Days festival and the Tennessee Valley Old Time Fiddlers Convention have become annual pilgrimages for music lovers. Foodies make their own pilgrimages to the area to enjoy the nationally award-winning goat cheese produced at the nearby Belle Chèvre creamery.

WHERE TO BEGIN: ATHENS STATE UNIVERSITY

Begin your tour of the area at Athens State University (300 N. Beaty St.; 256-233-8100). Founded in 1822, it is located four blocks from the home of George S. Houston, who served as governor of Alabama from 1874 to 1878.

Athens State began as the Athens Female Academy and later became an institution of the Methodist Church before going coeducational. The state of Alabama took control of the college in 1974, changing its name to Athens State College and then Athens State University.

It is the only two-year upper level university in the state. It serves as a complement to the state's junior colleges by offering only junior and senior level classes. Athens State offers more than 30 undergraduate majors through three colleges: Business, Arts and Sciences, and Education. It has an enrollment of about 3,500 students. Calhoun Community College, one of the state's largest, is in the southern part of the county.

The main building on the Athens State campus, Founders Hall, was built in 1842. Local legend says the building was saved from burning by Union troops during the Civil War when college President Jane Hamilton Childs produced a letter from President Abraham Lincoln asking that it be spared. Listed on the National Register of Historic Places, it also houses the majestic Altar of the New Testament woodcarvings. The nearly life-size carvings took 12 years to complete and depict Christ and New Testament figures and verses carved in tulip poplar. Tours are available by appointment.

Northwest corner of the historic Athens town square

This is one of the buildings featured on the annual October Haunts Walks. The Tennessee Valley Old Time Fiddlers Convention is noted for its role in reviving the tradition of competition in old-time music.

TAKE THE SELF-GUIDED DRIVING TOUR ALONG THE CIVIL WAR TRAIL

The self-guided driving tour of the Athens-Limestone County Civil War Trail travels through sites of the battles of Athens and Sulphur Creek Trestle. The Decatur and Nashville railroads in Limestone County played a vital role in the Civil War, and the Athens to Decatur portion of this route still operates today. In southern Limestone County, visitors will see the Memphis & Charleston, which was the longest railroad line in the Confederacy.

This strategic railroad transported soldiers and supplies from the western Confederacy to the eastern Confederacy.

Visitors can follow the trail starting at the Athens Depot, which now serves as the Limestone County Archives (102 W. Washington St.; 256-233-6404). Company F, 9th Alabama Infantry, consisted of 163 men who left from the Athens Depot on June 6, 1861, to fight with Joseph E. Johnston and the Army of the Shenandoah.

Founders Hall at Athens State University

More than 15,000 people, representing more than 30 states, attend the convention each year. In addition to the music fans, the convention brings together some 200 contestants who compete for top prizes. The two days of competition feature 20 categories, including fiddle and guitar, harmonica, mandolin, bluegrass banjo, dulcimer, old-time singing, banjo and buck dancing. The competitions all lead to a "fiddle-off" between the top two fiddlers with the champion taking home a trophy and a cash prize. There are also more than 150 booths packed with vendors, artists and craftsmen.

EXPLORE HISTORIC DOWNTOWN ATHENS

Historic downtown Athens is 1.5 miles from exit 351 on Interstate 65. The 1916 Limestone County Courthouse, crowned by a dome in the French Second Empire style, dominates the business district. The courthouse square offers an eclectic mix of shops featuring a wide variety of antiques, gifts, gourmet foods, clothing and hardware. The courthouse square is also home to the annual Athens Storytelling Festival.

One block off the square on Houston Street is the Houston Memorial Library and Museum (101 N. Houston St.; 256-233-8770), which was the home of George S. Houston, U.S. senator and governor of Alabama (1874-1878). The facility: one of the cornerstones of the historic Athens community and is both a public library and a period museum. The home, said to have "spirits," is another featured stop on the Oc-

WHERE TO STAY

Located about 10 miles west of Athens in the Ripley Community is The Drop Farm (11185 Snake Road; 256-777-0964). There you will find The Drop Inn, a bed and breakfast. The Drop Farm also offers horseback riding lessons and trail rides.

WORTH THE VISIT: BELLE CHÈVRE CREAMERY

The Belle Chèvre creamery (18849 Upper Fort Hampton Rd, Elkmont 256-732-3577), located in nearby Elkmont, has been featured on the "Today Show" and in *Southern Living, Cooking Light* and *Country Living* magazines. Belle Chèvre has been handcrafting fine French-style goat's milk cheeses since 1989 and has earned more than 50 national awards from the American Cheese Society and other institutions. The company is now operated by Tasia Malakasis, who returned to Alabama to learn the art of cheese-making after trying Belle Chèvre's delicious product. Shop around the cheese shop and tasting room or discover more at a special event celebrating these artisan cheeses.

tober Haunts Walks. It is open to the public Monday through Friday, 10 a.m.-5 p.m., and on Saturdays from 9 a.m.-noon.

The U.G. White Mercantile Store (101 N. Jefferson St.; 256-232-4540) has been an anchor of the Athens downtown square for nearly a century. The business was started by Ulysses Grant White in 1917. White moved to the area from Tennessee and decided to open the store after being injured in a farming accident. He sold everything from horse-drawn plows and tractors to radios, heating stoves and cast-iron skillets. The store passed through four generations of White's descendants to the Aycocks, Derrick Young and Johnny Furline. Today, visitors walk along the hardwood floors and roam the historic store looking at the vintage signs and shopping an eclectic blend of old and new offerings.

Tasia Malakasis of Belle Chevre Creamery, Elkmont

THE TENNESSEE VALLEY OLD TIME FIDDLERS CONVENTION

The Tennessee Valley Old Time Fiddlers Convention takes place each year on the campus of Athens State on the first Friday and Saturday in October. Though officially founded in 1966, its roots date back much further.

The Athens area was largely populated by migrant farmers from the southern Appalachian Mountains region. These migrant farmers were descended from immigrants from the British Isles who had a strong heritage and culture of folk fiddle music.

The Tennessee Valley Old Time Fiddlers Convention is known to enthusiasts as the "Granddaddy of Midsouth Fiddlers Conventions."

Located directly across the street from the U.G. White building, Village Pizza (222 West Market St.; 256-233-7627) is an ideal spot for grabbing a bite to eat after a full day of touring and shopping. Offering 8-, 12-, and 16-inch signature and build-you-own pizzas, including gluten-free options, as well as salads and subs, this cozy, brick-walled eatery offers something for everyone. It's open for lunch and dinner every day of the week.

SCOTTSBORO: CLAIM THE TREASURES

by Brian S. Jones and J.P. Parsons

Ask any visitor to Scottsboro about the reason for their trip and they're likely to respond that it's for the shopping experience at Unclaimed Baggage Center. And rightly so. This nationally acclaimed center draws visitors from around the world and has been featured on the Today show, CNN, Oprah, Fox News, Sunday Morning on CBS, the Late Show with David Letterman and in *The New York Times*. But shopping is only part of the allure of this beautiful mountain town.

Located in the foothills of the Appalachian Mountains on 69,000-acre Lake Guntersville, Scottsboro is a treasure-trove of adventure. Here you can tour a quaint museum that chronicles the early history of the Civil Rights Movement in America, see the courthouse where the Scottsboro Boys Trials took place in the 1930s, and enjoy premier outdoor recreation, such as bird watching, boating, camping, fishing and golfing. From nearby canyons and mountains, you'll uncover trails perfect for hiking and biking, and venture along rocky bluffs and into caves located in the very same area that Davy Crockett explored in the late 1700s. To soak in the beauty of the area, be sure to plan visits to coincide with wildflower displays in the spring and the bold and brilliant colors of the leaves in the fall.

WHERE TO BEGIN

The history of Scottsboro and Jackson County is housed in a splendid Greek Revival mansion known as the Scottsboro-Jackson Heritage Center (208 S. Houston St.; 256-259-2122). As both a historical and a cultural museum, the center is dedicated to representing the rich history, customs, traditions and art of Jackson County. The center features three exhibit areas: the antebellum Brown-Proctor House, the pioneer village named "Sagetown" and the Little Courthouse. The center also offers a genealogical research library and hosts various art expositions and traveling exhibits throughout the year.

THE SCOTTSBORO BOYS MUSEUM & CULTURAL CENTER

Three blocks from the Heritage Center is the Scottsboro Boys Museum (428 W. Willow Street; 256-244-1310). It was established in 2010 by founder Shelia Washington and the Scottsboro/Jackson Multi-Cultural Heritage Foundation to tell the compelling story of the Scottsboro Boys.

History records the Scottsboro Boys trials as the beginning of the modern Civil Rights Movement in America. The Supreme Court decision requiring a "jury of one's peers" is considered one of the 10 most important jurisprudence decisions in American history. The trials and their aftermath served as inspirations for Harper Lee's 1960 Pulitzer Prize-winning novel *To Kill a Mockingbird*.

LOST TREASURES AT UNCLAIMED BAGGAGE CENTER

One block from the little chapel that houses the Scottsboro Boys Museum is one of the nation's premier shopping experiences. The Unclaimed Baggage Center (509 W. Willow St.; 256-259-1525), which has received recognition from across the country on television and in newspapers, offers to the public for purchase truckloads of lost luggage and cargo goods that can't be traced to the owners.

Under contract to the airlines and cargo carriers, Unclaimed Baggage receives tons of lost and unclaimed passenger bags and cargo goods each week.

They sort through them then display the merchandise for sale to the public at hugely discounted prices. More than 1 million items pass through the store annually. About 60 percent of the merchandise is clothing with the balance of the store dedicated to cameras, electronics, sporting goods, jewelry, designer glasses, books and, of course, luggage. The vast majority of items are from unclaimed baggage – goods that remain unclaimed after at least 90 days of intensive tracking by the airlines. Cargo and freight shipments that are also unclaimed have been added to the inventory and are available in designated areas of the store.

Some items the Unclaimed Baggage Center receives are just too valuable or intriguing to sell. So store operators opened a small museum to display these "lost treasures." The museum features rotating displays that have included Egyptian artifacts estimated to date from 1567-304 B.C. and a violin from 1770, as well as other rare and unusual items. "Hoggle," the gnome-like gatekeeper from the Jim Henson movie Labyrinth, has a permanent place in the display.

DOWNTOWN SQUARE AND NEARBY ATTRACTIONS

Five blocks from Unclaimed Baggage is Courthouse Square (102 E. Laurel St.) in downtown Scottsboro. Scottsboro is the county seat of Jackson County, and the square is one of the best landscaped in the state. In front of the Neoclassical brick courthouse, constructed in 1911-1912, is a historic marker denoting where the first Scottsboro Boys trials took place.

The front two-story portion is supported by four stone columns of the Doric order. A cupola on the top there contains a Seth Thomas clock.

ART SUNDAY IN THE PARK

If you're visiting Scottsboro in late summer, King Caldwell Park (1004 S. Broad St.) is a must-stop. The park is home to Art Sunday, an arts and crafts festival held the Sunday before Labor Day each year in conjunction with Scottsboro's First Monday Trade Days (among the nation's oldest). Many exhibitors and thousands of people attend the festival annually. Situated near downtown, next to the library and across the street from the police department, the park is largely wooded with several nature trails running through it. It offers picnic tables, a pavilion with restrooms and a playground.

RECREATION ON BEAUTIFUL LAKE GUNTERSVILLE

For outdoor enthusiasts, recreation reigns supreme on beautiful Lake Guntersville. This 69,100-acre lake is Alabama's largest. It was created in 1938 when the Tennessee Valley Authority dammed portions of the Tennessee River to control flooding and provide low-cost hydroelectric power. Today, Lake Guntersville is nationally known for its largemouth bass and has been the site of the National Bassmaster Tournament. Skiing, boating and enjoying personal watercraft are great ways to spend a day on the water.

Located on the banks of Lake Guntersville is Goose Pond Colony (417 Ed Hembree Dr.; 800-268-2884). This public resort features two beautiful 18-hole championship golf courses, lakeside cottages, a main lodge, a waterfront campground and a full-service marina, along with a swimming pool, beach area and The Docks Restaurant.

WHERE TO EAT

The on-site Cups Cafe (256-259-1525) inside Unclaimed Baggage Center is a great place to take a short break from shopping. The menu features Starbucks coffee, salads, sandwiches, barbecue and gourmet desserts. Make sure to try the famous homemade chicken salad. Directions: To get to Unclaimed Baggage Center from U.S. Highway. 72 in Scottsboro, exit on Veterans Drive (AL 35) and continue to Willow Street. Turn left. The store is approximately 1.2 miles from the traffic light, on the left side of the road.

Dining at The Docks is an experience as it is the only fine dining restaurant in the area with lake access for any size boat.

EXPLORE NEARBY ATTRACTIONS

Visitors to Scottsboro will also find a number of attractions within easy driving distance. Cathedral Caverns State Park (637 Cave Rd., Woodville; 256-728-8193) is only a 15-minute drive from Scottsboro. The first thing you notice when you get to Cathedral Caverns is the massive cave entrance. The huge opening measures 126 feet wide and 25

feet high. Inside the cavern, you will find Big Rock Canyon, Mystery River and beautiful rock formations, including a huge stalagmite column that reaches the ceiling of the cave some 45 feet above. You can visit anytime, as the cave maintains a comfortable 60-degree year-round temperature.

The Walls of Jericho, which has been called the "Grand Canyon of the South," is about 25 miles northwest of Scottsboro off Highway 79. The area consists of 12,510 acres of mountainous and wooded terrain with springs, caves, rocky bluffs and portions of the headwaters of the Paint Rock River. The spot gets its name from a traveling minister in the late 1800s who was enthralled with the cathedral-like beauty of the place and decided it needed a biblical name. Visitors can travel to the bottom of the limestone gorge and look up at the 200-foot walls.

About 30 minutes northeast of Scottsboro is the Russell Cave National Monument (256-495-2672) in Bridgeport. This archaeological site was home to prehistoric man for more than 10,000 years and is the only national monument in Alabama. The clues gathered from Russell Cave give a glimpse into the lives of ancient North American inhabitants dating from 10,000 B.C. to A.D. 1650.

FOR MORE INFORMATION

For more information on Scottsboro and the Jackson County area, contact the
Greater Jackson County Chamber of Commerce
407 E. Willow St.; 800-259-5508

Cathedral Caverns is noted for its massive entrance.

HENAGAR:
THE SOUND OF (SACRED HARP) MUSIC

by Grey Brennan

People have been coming to the hills of northeastern Alabama for more than a century to hear and sing the powerful a cappella four-part-harmony music called Sacred Harp. Alabama has been and continues to be in the forefront of making sure this traditional style of music does not fade away. On this road trip, you will hear the sound so associated with the South of the Civil War period and see the town where Sacred Harp songs were recorded for the movie *Cold Mountain*. You can also stay in a *Gone With the Wind*-style antebellum bed and breakfast and visit nearby towns to experience the depths of a cave, hear moving stories of a pottery maker, enjoy views from atop Lookout Mountain and more.

MUSIC HISTORY

Sacred Harp is an early American a cappella singing style based on the fa-sol-la shapes of ovals, diamonds, squares and triangles. This old-fashioned music, sung in a compact formation called a hollow square with singers facing each other, was widely popular during the time of the Civil War. While Sacred Harp singing has faded in other parts of America, the tradition continues to echo in churches on Sand Mountain in Alabama.

There are two Sacred Harp songbooks that are widely used today, and both spring from the efforts of people from Alabama. Singing school instructor Tom Denson and his brother, Seaborn, used the fa-sol-la shape note method to teach folks across North Alabama to sing this music from the late-1800s to the mid-1930s. Later, they founded the Sacred Harp Publishing Company and produced a songbook so widely associated with them that the songbooks are referred to as Denson books, even though several edi-

tions have been published since their deaths. The 1991 Denson Sacred Harp songbook has more than 573 pages and is the book of choice around the world for this type of music. A second well-known Sacred Harp songbook is The Cooper Book, first authored in 1902 by W.M. Cooper of Dothan.

EPICENTER OF SACRED HARP SINGINGS

While many churches and conventions hold Sacred Harp singings, one of the most traditional settings is Sand Mountain in the northeastern corner of Alabama.

This is where you should start your road trip. Grammy winning music director "T Bone" Burnett, who also produced the soundtrack to *O Brother, Where Art Thou?*, recorded nearly 40 Sacred Harp tunes at the small rural Henagar Liberty Baptist Church (1500 Liberty Road; 256-657-1826) for the

Sacred Harp singers

PHOTO TIP

If you want to take pictures inside of Liberty Baptist Church during the convention, use available light. A flash is distracting to the singers. Daylight from the windows is usually bright enough for a good photograph. You can stand at the back of the church or go to one of the side doors that are parallel to the hollow square for a different angle. If you are photographing an individual singer, use one of the breaks and position them so they are angled and looking toward one of the church's windows. This kind of ambient light is very flattering.

If you are using manual settings on your camera, you should set the ISO from 800 to 1600 to allow for a low-light interior. This is critical for low light without a flash. Check your shutter speed to make sure your speed is at least 1/60. If you are shooting at 1/30 or slower you will need to use a tripod or increase your ISO to allow a faster speed.

Sacred Harp songbook

movie *Cold Mountain*. He chose two of the songs for use in pivotal points in the movie. The song "I'm Going Home," is sung when the Civil War is announced, and "Idumea," is used during the horrific battle scene set in Petersburg, Va. In addition, this area of Alabama is where much of *Awake, My Soul*, a documentary about the history and traditions of Sacred Harp singings, was filmed.

Don't Miss This

WINSTON PLACE BED AND BREAKFAST

Looking as if it came from the set of Gone With the Wind, *the Winston Place Bed and Breakfast (353 Railroad Ave., Valley Head; 256-635-6381) is one of Alabama's most beautiful historical mansions and one of the few where you can stay overnight. Enjoy the large verandas and elegant rooms in this 1831 home located just two miles from Mentone.*

BE A LISTENER

The singings at Liberty start in the morning and last to mid-afternoon with a different person called up to lead each song. This is a most sought-out honor, as the leader stands in the middle of the group and enjoys the full force of all the voices directed at that one point.

As a visitor, you can go inside and have a seat in one of the church pews where there is no escaping the music. Those who have attended are quoted as saying the singing feels like a solid force so strong you could stand up and walk on it. Others recall the church vibrating and the singing invading their entire body. "Uplifting," "joyful" and "spiritual" are other words used to describe the experience of hearing the gathering of voices in this small Alabama church.

There are short breaks each hour making it easy to come and go as you please, but you will probably want to stay the entire day, as there is a community lunch at noon each day. Bring some food and join this social event. This social gathering is so popular that some come to the church just for the food. Make friends with the singers and you may be invited to the Saturday night party held in the home of a Henagar Sacred Harp singer, another social event where you may hear traditional mountain music complete with banjoes, fiddles and guitars.

THE SAND MOUNTAIN POTATO FESTIVAL

The singing at Liberty Baptist Church is held close to Independence Day when the people of Sand Mountain celebrate the mountain's farming heritage at Henagar Town Park. The annual Sand Mountain Potato Festival is held each Fourth of July and includes live music, arts and crafts, and an evening of fireworks.

LEARN TO SING

Also during the summer months, the Sacred Harp Musical Heritage Association conducts summer camps to teach people how to sing Sacred Harp. One camp is held in June at Camp McDowell, a retreat in northwest Alabama near Jasper, while another is held in July at Camp Lee near Anniston. The five-day events are called Camp Fasola, named after the singing notes fa-sol-la. Either of these camps combined with the singing at Liberty Church in Henagar make for a complete Sacred Harp experience.

ABOUT THE SAND MOUNTAIN AREA

Henagar is one of the last places in the country with churches that still use Sacred Harp singing in their Sunday morning church services and the town is home to many of the largest and oldest continuous Sacred Harp singings in the country. Henagar is located on Sand Mountain with an average elevation of about 1,500 feet, resulting in the area having one of the coolest climates in the state of Alabama. Look eastward and you will see Lookout Mountain. These two mountains make up a large portion of the southern end of the Cumberland Plateau, a part of the Appalachian mountain chain.

OTHER TIMES TO VISIT

For those who want to visit in cooler times of the year, Liberty Baptist Church in Henagar and the nearby Antioch Church (County Road 783; 256-632-3830) in Ider hold smaller Sacred Harp singings during the fall and winter. Liberty's is on the first Sunday night of the month at 5:30 p.m. from October to April while the singing at Ider's Antioch Church is on the second Sunday night at 5:30 p.m. from October to March.

SUNDAY SERVICE WITH SACRED HARP

There are two Sand Mountain Churches that use Sacred Harp exclusively in their services. They are Liberty Baptist Church and Antioch Baptist Church. A third church in the area called Shady Grove Baptist Church (County Road 408; 256-657-4073) near Dutton uses mostly Sacred Harp music but does not exclusively use it. All of their music is a cappella, however. While Shady Grove meets every Sunday, Liberty meets only on the second and third Sundays of the month, and Antioch meets every Sunday except the second Sunday of the month. Visitors are welcome at all three churches.

TWO POPULAR VINTGAGE STYLE STOPS

While experiencing Henagar, your trip will take you by another type of entertainment from the past – a drive-in theater. These theaters were popular in the early 1960s.

You can still watch a movie projected on a large outdoor screen while seated in your car at the Henagar Drive-In Theatre (168 Gourge Road; 256-657-1340).

After all that singing, you might work up an appetite. Visit Vintage 1889 (151 Eight St. NE; 256-845-3380) in nearby Fort Payne for lunch or dinner. The restaurant is located in the historic old brick Big Mill building, which was the Davis Hosiery Mill 125 years ago. Dine indoors or in the open-air courtyard beneath the old water tower and catch live music Thursday through Saturday. With a large selection of beers and American fare, such as steaks, burgers, and fried green tomatoes, you're sure to leave satisfied. When you're done eating, shop at the art and clothing retail stores also located in the Big Mill building.

VALLEY HEAD

Travel to Valley Head to watch Valinda Miracle make her brilliant colored pottery. Miracle, who is also a painter and author of the book *The Dead Don't Bleed, Those Who Are Alive Do*, operates Miracle Pottery (7871 State Route 117; 256-635-6863) in the foothills of Lookout Mountain near Mentone.

NATURAL WONDERS AND MOUNTAINTOP VILLAGE

Nearby, you'll find Fort Payne, DeSoto State Park, Little River Canyon National Preserve and the mountaintop village of Mentone. All are worth a visit. Learn more about these areas in the Road Trip book on page 12: Fort Payne: The View From Lookout Mountain.

GETTING THERE

It is easy to get to Henagar but a little harder to find Liberty Baptist Church in Henagar or Antioch Baptist Church in Ider. Both are located off the main roads. Combine that with the number of churches in the area and you will quickly find that locating a small country church is no problem, but finding the correct church is a real challenge.

From I-59, take exit 231 and turn onto State Route 40 North 117 West Continue north on Route 40 to where Route 117 splits off to the right. Travel on Route 40. When you reach the intersection of Route 40 and State Route 75, you will see a service station on your right and the Henagar Police Station across the road. Continue north on Route 40. At the first right, you will take the first of three quick turns. After turning right off Route 40, take another right at the red brick church and then take a left onto Liberty Road. Travel a couple of miles on Liberty Road to find Liberty Baptist Church. If you get lost, return to the Henagar Police Station and ask for directions. It's a small town and they will be happy to assist you.

To find the Ider Antioch Church, travel to the intersection of Route 40 and Route 75. Take Route 75 North to Ider. Continue north on Route 75 past Ider until you reach the small crossroads of Cartersville where you will see County Road 141. Turn left and you will soon come to a "Y" in the road where County Road 159 joins County Road 141. Look to your left and out in the field you will see two small churches. One will be Antioch Baptist Church.

To reach Old Shady Grove Baptist Church from Henagar, travel Route 40 West until you reach State Route 71 and turn left to travel south. The church is on County Road 408, just off Route 71 between the communities of Dutton and Section. Chestnut Grove Baptist Church is located on County Road 743, just off Route 117, three miles south of Ider.

BLOUNT COUNTY:
THE COVERED BRIDGE CAPITAL OF ALABAMA
by Verna Gates

Blount County's Swann covered bridge spans the Locust Fork of the Warrior River.

Walking into the cool shade of a covered bridge, you can almost hear the clip-clop of horses' hooves and the whispers of stolen kisses. The sheltered bridge hid the rushing water from the horse and the courting couple from the eyes of the world. Notice how the entrance resembles a barn – all the more to encourage a perhaps unwilling steed into the shelter of the bridge.

Also, In the 1800s, an uncovered bridge might last 10 to 12 years, but a covered bridge – well, it just might last for more than a century. Three of Alabama's 11 covered bridges can be found in Blount County, nestled into the curves of both roads and rivers, making this county the Covered Bridge Capital of Alabama.

All three bridges are listed on the National Register of Historic Places, with Horton Mill Bridge taking the honor of being the first Southern covered bridge to be added to the register. All have been restored to once again support car traffic – though with a single lane and a speed limit of 5 mph.

HORTON, OLD EASLEY AND SWANN: BRIDGES TO A SIMPLER TIME AND PLACE

Thurman Horton helped build the first of the bridges to bring Sand Mountain customers to his mill and general store. Rising 70 feet, Horton Mill Bridge stands as the highest covered bridge above any U.S. waterway.

ABOUT BLOUNT COUNTY

The Alabama Territorial Legislature created Blount County Feb. 6, 1818, from lands once owned by the Creek tribe. Named for Willie Blount, who was governor of Tennessee and helpful to the settlers, the county sits in the northeastern part of the state. It is bordered by populous Jefferson County, home to Birmingham. The county seat is Oneonta.

The original structure was built in 1894. Forty years later, another Horton, Talmedge this time, led the construction of the bridge we see today. A 15-man crew completed the 220-foot bridge in a year and a half with lumber bought for $714. Look for the bridge five miles north of Oneonta on Alabama Highway 75.

A tin roof kept the rain from dampening the spirits of many a traveler who crossed the Old Easley Covered Bridge. The smallest and oldest of the bridges, its single span is perhaps the most picturesque. Crossing the Dub Branch of the Calvert Prong of the Black Warrior River, Old Easley was used from 1927 until 2009, when it was restored. The Tidwell family built it, Zelmer and his uncle Forrest, undoubtedly to provide a shorter path home. The bridge sits three miles west of Oneonta, 1.5 miles off U.S. 231.

The third bridge was called Swann on one side and Joy on the other, depending on which community you called home. Perched over a scenic gorge, the bridge connected the town of Cleveland to the community of Joy. The triple spans of the Swann Covered Bridge stretch 324 feet, making it the longest covered bridge in Alabama and one of the longest in the U.S. It rises 27 feet above the rocky riverbed of the Locust Fork, a tributary of the Black Warrior River.

It lies one mile off Alabama Highway 79, near Cleveland.

OTHER AREA ATTRACTIONS

Travel from the river gorges to the mountain overlook. Palisades Park perches atop Ebell Mountain and offers views of a deep valley and forested ridges. The 1,300-foot elevation over limestone bluffs is a popular spot for rock climbing. More than 90 routes crisscross the 60- and 70-foot drops with ratings from 5.4 to 5.12. Bouldering invites those who enjoy climbing closer to earth. Eight nature trails guide you through trees and wildflowers.

Challenge the white water in Class III and IV rapids in the scenic Locust Fork of the Black Warrior River. Want a slower pace? Fishing, tube floats and swimming holes provide fun for families. The National Park Service has placed this wild and free river in the top 2 percent of all rivers nationwide for recreational uses. Challenge races to wildflower walks invite people to enjoy this stretch of water.

Descend beneath the earth's surface at

Fishing downstream from Childersburg's Kymulga Grist Mill and Covered Bridge

Rickwood Caverns to walk the miracle mile of 250-million-year-old limestone formations, complete with stalagmites, stalactites, blind cave fish and an underground pool bubbling up. The grounds offer visitors picnic tables, hiking trails, a playground and an Olympic-size swimming pool. You can also pan for gemstones.

ALSO ON THE ALABAMA COVERED BRIDGE TRAIL

In bordering Cullman, the Clarkson Covered Bridge built in 1904 is one of the largest covered bridges in the state. The bridge site is also a park that features picnic grounds, a dogtrot cabin, gristmill and hiking trails.

Talladega County is home to two covered bridges. The Waldo Covered Bridge was built in 1858 on the old Socapatoy trail, first used by Native Americans and then in the Civil War by Wilson's Raiders, a Union cavalry group. The Kymulga Covered Bridge (1860) once carried travelers along Old Georgia Road, a Native American trade route. It is located at Grist Mill Park. Both bridges span scenic Talladega Creek.

The Old Union Crossing Bridge near Mentone crosses the West Fork of the Little River with a 90-foot span. The Gilliland-Reese Covered Bridge dates to 1899 and was moved to Noccalula Falls in Etowah County.

Coldwater Covered Bridge was built by the hands of a former slave in 1850, making it Alabama's oldest covered bridge. It invites visitors from the Walking Trail at Oxford Lake in Calhoun County.

In west Alabama, the Alamuchee-Bellamy Covered Bridge was built of hand-hewn heart pine and wooden pegs in 1861. It can be visited in Sumter County on the University of West Alabama campus.

WHERE TO STAY

Capps Cove Bed and Breakfast continues the 19th-century theme of the covered bridges with its quaint cabins. Escape to 20 acres of babbling brooks, lush gardens and picket fences. Take the time to walk along the creek and enjoy a fire on a stone hearth.

WHERE TO EAT

Replacing a legendary dining favorite can be challenging, but Charlie B's The Lunch Place (300 Sixth St. S.; 205-274-7427) more than succeeds. Standing on hallowed restaurant ground of the old Round the Clock establishment, Charlie B's delivers Southern fried chicken, turnip greens, black-eyed peas and its predecessor's esteemed peanut butter pie.

Don't Miss This

THE COVERED BRIDGE FESTIVAL

The fourth weekend in October, Oneonta celebrates with a Covered Bridge Festival. On Saturday, vendors line the streets selling arts and crafts, homemade items and delicious festival food. Live entertainment sends toe-tapping music from the main stage through town.

Friends of the Locust Fork River, a river preservation society, lead a three-hour walk along the river from Swann Bridge to Powell Falls and back. A children's area provides plenty of play and activities.

The stunning Alabama Theatre opened on Christmas Day 1927

Birmingham was the Magic City during the 1920s, creating the downtown district that today offers culinary destinations, quaint shops, historic theater district and the Civil Rights District.

Five Points South is the state's number one neighborhood for fine dining, and chefs Frank Stitt and Chris Hastings have the James Beard awards to prove it.

One of Catholicism's most famous faces is Mother Angelica, whose EWTN broadcasts are seen around the world. Take a road trip to Irondale and then go north to Hanceville to see what the faith of one modest nun achieved.

Two of the state's college football teams have earned the nation's largest collection of consecutive championship trophies. See them on a road trip that links Tuscaloosa and Auburn.

Even visitors who've never played golf probably know that

Alabama is home to the world-class Robert Trent Jones Golf Trail. It stretches from Florence and Huntsville in the north to Mobile and Dothan in the south, with the longest course in Hoover.

If you find you have a need for speed, head for the Talladega SuperSpeedway, the Barber Motorsports Park and Tim Wellborn's MuscleCar Museum.

A town known now by the simple name of Moundville was the largest metropolis in the Southeastern U.S. in the 14th century. It's on the tentative list of UNESCO World Heritage Sites.

Cotton made kings of plantation owners in the 1850s. You can find that some of that heritage lingers today in the small towns of Eutaw, Marion and Greensboro.

There's still gold in the hills of Clay County in East Alabama. See if your luck pans out.

BIRMINGHAM:
DOWNTOWN STREET TOUR
by Grey Brennan

Get ready to travel to Birmingham, Alabama's largest city, for a stroll through historic downtown. On this walking tour, you will go to the place where hot peanuts have been sold for more than 100 years and through shops filled with memories. You will also visit important civil rights sites such as Sixteenth Street Baptist Church and the park that was the staging ground for protest marches during the Civil Rights Movement. You will stand at the very spot where buildings were constructed on each corner of the street that were so tall for their day they were called skyscrapers and the location became known as the "Heaviest Corner on Earth."

BIRMINGHAM'S OLDEST CHURCHES

The Tutwiler and Redmont are a block apart, close enough that in many of the rooms you can look out your window and see the other. From either of these historic hotels, walk south on Richard Arrington Jr. Boulevard North., where you will quickly come to First Presbyterian Church (2100 4th Ave. N.; 205-322-5469). Turn left and walk east on 4th Avenue to go past the front of the church.

First Presbyterian Church

First Presbyterian is one of Birmingham's first churches, dating to 1872. The present red brick, Victorian Gothic-style church building was built in 1888 with other enhancements being added through the years. Twenty-five bells manufactured in England were placed in the bell tower in 1924.

Continue east on 4th Avenue North to the corner of 22nd Street North, turn right and walk one short block to 3rd Avenue North

and turn right. By now you should have noticed another one of Birmingham's first churches, The Cathedral of St. Paul (2120 3rd Ave. N.; 205-251-1279). Known for its many elegant stained glass windows, The Cathedral of St. Paul, completed in 1893, has been called "the most highly developed Victorian Gothic structure in the South."

ENJOY UNUSUAL SHOPPING

From The Cathedral of St. Paul, continue walking west on 3rd Avenue North to find some unusual stores in the middle of the next block between Richard Arrington Boulevard North and 20th Street North.

First, you may notice the old Goodyear Shoe Hospital sign hanging outside that establishment (2016 3rd Ave. N.; 205-252-7346). Walk inside and ask for Rhonda Patton. She can tell you a lot about Birmingham and repair your shoes at the same time.

Across the street is Alabama's first fair trade store, Sojourns (2017 3rd Ave. N.; 205-323-5680). This store is filled with items from artists around the world and a pledge that they receive a living wage for their work. Meet owner Melissa Kendrick inside.

CHECK OUT THE LOFT DISTRICT

Walk back north to the corner of 3rd Avenue and Richard Arrington Boulevard, turn right and then turn left at the third block, onto 1st Avenue North. Walk east on 1st Avenue for a few blocks the Loft District of historic downtown Birmingham where you

Birmingham author Jim Reed inside his "Museum of Fond Memories"

will also find restaurants, night life and a small grocery. Rogue Tavern (2312 2nd Ave. N.; 205-202-4151), Urban Standard (2320 2nd Ave. N.; 205-250-8200), Pale Eddie's Pour House (2308 2nd Ave. N.; 205-297-0052), Yo Mama's Restaurant (2328 2nd Ave. N.; 205-957-6545) and EastWest Kitchen and Bar (2306 2nd Ave. N.; 205-202-4496) are on the same side of the block on 2nd Avenue.

STROLL DOWN COBBLESTONED MORRIS AVENUE

Walk back west to 23rd Street North and turn left. You will walk down a slight hill to Morris Avenue. Turn right and walk down Morris, where the lamp posts on the one-way cobblestone street take you to a different time and place. Continue west on Morris Avenue and just before you reach 20th Street, you will start to smell the aroma from the Peanut Depot (2016 Morris Ave.; 205-251-3314) where they have been roasting peanuts for more than 100 years using their time-honored method of not adding oils or preservatives. Next to the Peanut Depot, find The Essential (2018 Morris Ave.; 205-703-3012), a quaint café known for its baked pastries and Saturday and Sunday brunch. On the other

side of the Peanut Depot, satisfy your sweet tooth at the Honeycreeper Chocolate shop (2026 Morris Ave.; 205-290-5778).

"HEAVIEST CORNER ON EARTH" AND MCWANE CENTER

Continue from the Peanut Depot on Morris Avenue to 20th Street and turn right. At the next corner, 20th Street and 1st Avenue North, look around and you will see four buildings that were finished within a few years of each other: the Woodward Building (1902), Brown Marx Building (1906), Empire Building (1909) and the American Trust and Savings Bank Building (1912). At the time, the height and mass of the buildings were so impressive that the intersection was proclaimed the "Heaviest Corner on Earth." Today, the Elyton Hotel (1928 1st Ave. N.; 205-731-3600) occupies the Empire Building. The Elyton boasts premier amenities and one of the city's swankiest rooftop bars, Moon Shine. To experience what life must have been like when the skyscrapers were built, eat in the fine dining Café DuPont on 20th Street North near the corner (113 20th St. N.; 205-322-1282).

ABOUT BIRMINGHAM

Birmingham is Alabama's largest city. Rich in history, it is known for its industrial past and for its role in the Civil Rights Movement. Today, Birmingham is a center for the arts, entertainment, dining and shopping.

From 20th and 2nd Avenue, walk west to 19th Street and 2nd Avenue North, where you will find the the Pizitz Food Hall (1821 2nd Ave. N.; 205-939-3111). Located in the historic Pizitz building, the space houses restaurants, food stalls, a bar, and retail stores. Across 2nd Avenue North from The Pizitz Food Hall, visit the McWane Science Center (200 19th St. N.; 205-714-8300), located in the former Loveman's department store.

CHECK OUT THE THEATRE DISTRICT

On the same block as the McWane Center, you will see a large Alabama sign. You are now in the Theatre District of Birmingham. The historic Alabama Theatre (1817 3rd Ave. N.; 205-252-2262) has been beautifully restored, so check the marquee to see if a performance is scheduled during your stay. Across the street is the Historic Lyric Theatre (1800 3rd Ave. N.; 205-252-2262). Built in 1914, the Lyric was one of the first venues in the South where blacks and whites could watch the same show at the same time for the same price. The theatre was restored and reopened in 2016 and now showcases a variety of shows. The Red Mountain The-

Birmingham's historic Theatre District

atre Company (301 19th St.; 205-324-2424), with its Cabaret Theatre in the bottom floor of the historic Kress Building, is nearby.

4TH AVENUE AND THE CIVIL RIGHTS DISTRICT

Walk north on 18th Street for one block and turn left at 4th Avenue North and walk into Eddie Kendricks Memorial Park. It will be easy to find because you will hear Temptations music playing. Kendrick, who was born in Birmingham in 1937, added an "s" as his stage name and was a lead singer for The Temptations.

You are now in the 4th Avenue North Historic District, a place that was once the black business district. Walk inside the visitor's center at the Urban Impact non-profit agency (4th Ave. N.; 205-328-1850). They will be happy to provide you with the history of the district and tell you about the one-hour tour of the area.

Across the street is the Alabama Jazz Hall of Fame (1631 4th Ave. N.; 205-254-2731). This art-deco museum honors great jazz artists such as Nat "King" Cole, Duke Ellington, Lionel Hampton and Erskine Hawkins. From the Jazz Hall of Fame, walk cross the street to read the historic sign at the northeast corner of 17th Street North and 4th Avenue North.

Next, walk one block north on 17th Street and enter Kelly Ingram Park at the corner of 17th Street North and 5th Avenue North where you will see a limestone sculpture depicting three ministers – John Thomas Porter, Nelson H. Smith and A.D. King, kneeling in prayer. You are now in the heart of Birmingham's Civil Rights District. The four-acre park you are now in was the staging ground for large-scale demonstrations during the Civil Rights Movement in Birmingham. Bronze statues depict the historic events.

At the opposite corner of the park is a statue of Dr. Martin Luther King Jr. facing the Sixteenth Street Baptist Church (1530 6th Ave. N.; 205-251-9402), where four young girls died from a Ku Klux Klan bombing.

Sixteenth Street Baptist Church

In the church ask when the next tour starts. There are no tours on Sunday, but the congregation welcomes you to worship with them.

Across the street is the Birmingham Civil Rights Institute (520 16th St. N.; 205-328-9696). Go inside to see the cell where Dr. King was imprisoned when he wrote "Letter from a Birmingham Jail," part of the museum's Civil Rights Movement experience.

From this area, walk three blocks east on 6th Avenue North to the corner of 19th Street North. Here, you will pass by another of Birmingham's historic churches, First Church (518 19th St. N.; 205-254-3186).

SEE LINN PARK

At the corner of 19th Street and 6th Avenue North, turn left and walk the short block to Park Place. Walk east on Park Place where you will quickly see Linn Park. Walk diagonally through the park to the Birmingham Museum of Art (2000 Rev. Abraham Woods Jr. Blvd.; 205-254-2565). Consid-

ered one of the finest regional museums in the United States, you can spend half a day touring. If you have only one hour to visit, the museum has a list of the top 12 works of art that are a must-see.

GETTING AROUND

The Magic City Connectors are a group of buses that run along 20th street in downtown Birmingham, connecting travelers to the many restaurants, hotels, and other attractions in the area. Theses buses take a fixed route with turn-arounds at 14th Avenue South, near The J Clyde pub, on the south end and at 12th Ave North between 24th Street North and Carraway Boulevard on the north end. The cost one-way for adults is a quarter. There are also two other bus systems serving the Birmingham metro area. Call the Birmingham-Jefferson County Transit Authority (205-521-0101), or visit their website, MaxTransit.org, for more information.

WHERE TO STAY

Once you arrive in Birmingham, check into any of the downtown hotels such as the historic Tutwiler (2021 Park Pl.; 205-322-2100), Birmingham's oldest, or the Redmont (2101 Fifth Ave. N.; 205-324-2101), the oldest continually operating hotel and where Hank Williams' spent his last night in Alabama before his death on January 1, 1953.

THE ROBERT TRENT JONES GOLF TRAIL

by Bill Lang

View from "The Judge" at Prattville's Capitol Hill course

In Alabama, you can go for a drive on the RTJ Golf Trail, but these driving skills don't require a steering wheel. The premier set of 26 gold courses—including 468 championship holes—over 11 Alabama sites is the largest golf course construction project ever attempted. Celebrating 27 years of public golf in 2019, the courses are continuously receiving updates as needed. While the courses keep getting better, the Trail's commitment to serving and amazing value (most greens fees start at $65) will always be the same. For more information on the entire Trail, please visit the RTJ website at RTJGolf.com.

DAY 1 GOLF – OXMOOR VALLEY – BIRMINGHAM

Come see why *Golf Digest* called the state of Alabama "one of the top 50 golf destinations in the world."

Oxmoor Valley (100 SunBelt Parkway, Birmingham; 205-942-1177), a favorite on the RTJ Trail and a great place to start a road trip, is one of the many reasons *Golf Digest* called Alabama one of the top 50 golf destinations in the world. This 54-hole facility was built on former mining land owned by U.S. Steel. Sculpted from peaks and valleys of the

Appalachians, the courses offer scenic forests, numerous creeks and challenging elevation changes. The Ridge course, with its rollercoaster fairways and heavy tree cover, is incredibly photogenic. As a reminder of the site's former use, the green at the par-5 third hole is buttressed by a shelf of exposed shale rock.

The Valley course is dotted with picturesque lakes and beautiful rolling fairways, and stretches two miles downrange along a slender valley. The 18th hole, a 441-yard par-4, nicknamed "The Assasin," rises to a dramatic finish at the clubhouse just above the green.

WHERE TO STAY

Nestled into the gently rolling hills of Birmingham, the Renaissance Birmingham Ross Bridge Golf Resort & Spa (4000 Grand Ave., Birmingham; 205-916-7677) is less than a mile from Oxmoor Valley. Named one of *Travel + Leisure*'s "Top 500 Hotels in the

Check out the Short course at Oxmoor, a delightful collection of 18 pure one-shotters that offer severe elevation changes with almost every hole played downhill. It was listed by Golf Digest's "Places to Play" as one of the nation's great value public courses.

ABOUT THE ROBERT TRENT JONES GOLF TRAIL

Alabama's Robert Trent Jones Golf Trail is a collection of 468 holes at 11 sites and stretches from Muscle Shoals to Mobile and to every corner of the state.

World," this four-diamond property has 259 guest rooms, with balconies overlooking the third longest golf course in the world, which is also part of the RTJ Golf Trail. In fact, it will be the final course played on this road trip.

For an extra mile of fun, about 30 miles from the hotel is Barber Motorsports Park (6040 Barber Motorsports Pkwy., Birmingham; 205-699-7275), where you can access the Porsche Track Experience, a Porsche driving school. At the driving school, you'll sit behind the wheel of a Porsche to experience the track firsthand. The Spa at Ross Bridge offers the perfect refuge for relaxation at the end of the day.

WHERE TO EAT

You don't have to venture too far for incredible cuisine. Brock's restaurant downstairs at Ross Bridge provides an incredible atmosphere and Mediterranean-inspired dishes that promise to please every palate.

DAY 2 GOLF – CAPITOL HILL – PRATTVILLE

To be fully prepared for the day, stop by the breakfast buffet at Brock's before heading down I-65 to Prattville. Even though it's only a short one-hour drive to the course from Birmingham, it wouldn't be a proper trip without stopping in Clanton at either Durbin Farms Market (205-755-1672) or Peach Park (205-755-2065) at Exit 205 off I-65 to pick up some of their famous peaches (or peach ice cream).

Arrive at Capitol Hill in Prattville (2600 Constitution Ave., Prattville; 334-285-1114) to find three 18-hole championship courses, all of which offer unique challenges and dramatic landscapes. The Judge course, named by *Golf* magazine as one of the 10 public courses in America worthy of hosting the U.S. Open, begins with an intimidating first tee 200 feet above the fairway overlooking the Alabama River and Montgomery skyline.

With 14 holes adjoining the water and a stunning bulkhead green, the Judge is described as simply magnificent and was even ranked in the top 50 courses by the Zagat Survey of America's Top Golf Courses.

The Senator course, a Scottish-links style course with beautifully manicured bent grass greens, welcomes the world's best golfers at the Alabama LPGA Classic each fall. This course holds more than 160 pothole bunkers and mounds up to 40 feet in height, but it does not have a single tree. The secluded setting on this course will make you and your group feel as though you are the only foursome on the course. The Legislator, a more traditional course, plays in and out of pine trees and along the bluff. The natural landscape is impressive as the course leads back up the bluff to finish at the spectacular clubhouse. Stop in for a relaxing lunch or a quick snack before heading into Montgomery for the afternoon.

WHERE TO STAY

Conveniently located at the course, the Montgomery Marriott Prattville Hotel & Conference Center at Capitol Hill (2500 Legends Cir., Prattville; 334-290-1235) provides the perfect lodge atmosphere for a relaxing stay. The hotel's 96 guest rooms were renovated in 2017 and include flat-screen televisions and high-speed Internet access. Two eight-room luxury villas have living areas and are ideal for golf groups traveling together.

For something a little more adventurous, spend a luxurious evening at the Renaissance Montgomery Hotel & Spa at the Convention Center (201 Tallapoosa St., Montgomery; 334-481-5000), only a short distance from Prattville in downtown Montgomery. Renaissance Montgomery opened in 2008 bringing to the downtown area a great cultural and

Don't Miss This

THE BAGPIPERS AT SUNSET

In keeping with the Scottish theme of Renaissance Birmingham Ross Bridge Golf Resort & Spa, a traditional bagpiper wanders the golf course and grounds every evening at sunset playing a multitude of songs and calling golfers back to the clubhouse at the end of the day. Enjoy drinks or dinner on the terrace overlooking the gristmill and waterfall while the bagpiper serenades guests. Sometimes, the bagpiper even makes it to the lobby and the clubhouse where guests can request their favorites.

culinary hub. The hotel features 345 luxurious guest rooms and suites, several restaurants and bars and a European-style spa. Located near the Alabama River and across the street from popular Alley Station, Renaissance Montgomery is quickly becoming the city's social hot spot. The Montgomery Performing Arts Centre, an 1,800-seat theater connected to the hotel, hosts a variety of national and international acts from concerts to Broadway musicals to stand-up comedy and more.

WHERE TO EAT

Before dinner, stop by The Exchange (334-481-5165) for drinks and atmosphere. The Exchange is right off the lobby at the Renaissance, making it an extremely convenient option. Depending on the weather, enjoy the fire pits on the patio while listening to live music, scheduled nightly. If you're looking to stay in the hotel for dinner as well, visit The House

restaurant (334-481-5166) featuring an array of local cuisine with perfected Southern flavor.

DAY 3 GOLF – ROSS BRIDGE – BIRMINGHAM

After a visit to Montgomery, it's time to head back toward Birmingham. The ultimate golf trip would not be complete without playing the crown jewel of the Robert Trent Jones Golf Trail, Ross Bridge (4000 Grand Ave., Birmingham; 205-916-7677). The youngest of all the RTJ sites, Ross Bridge is beautifully carved into the rolling terrain of Shannon Valley. As mentioned previously, Ross Bridge is the third longest golf course in the world, making it a challenge for even the most seasoned golfers. It does offer multiple tees so that golfers of all levels can enjoy the course.

A gristmill on the waterfall reflects the history of the old mining site. Considerable elevation changes combine with water or other natural obstructions to get your attention. Large putting surfaces provide many tempting pin locations that will test golfers' approach shots.

The picturesque finishing hole leads back toward the resort, where lunch awaits at The Clubhouse. Don't leave without trying the breaded pickles or gourmet grilled cheese, and for the main course make sure to try the famous Ross Bridge burger with a side of homemade sweet potato fries.

To ensure the proper finish to the perfect trip, stop by the Spa at Ross Bridge for 9,000 square feet of relaxation. Enjoy a signature massage to soothe the muscles or simply spend time in the spa's sauna, steam room and whirlpool before heading home.

Relaxing beside the hot tub at Birmingham's Ross Bridge.

TUSCALOOSA TO AUBURN:
CHAMPIONSHIP TOUR
by Lee Sentell

Paul W. Bryant Museum on the University of Alabama campus

SEE WHY THE TIDE'S MAGIC NUMBER IS 17

Since the team from Tuscaloosa has won the most national championships, it is the logical starting point for your tour. Travel I-20/59 to exit 71 and follow the signs to the campus and Bryant Drive and park at the rear of the Paul Bryant Museum (300 Paul W. Bryant Dr.; 205-348-4668).

The museum is open seven days a week except for major holidays.

The first thing you notice is the museum is dark and quiet, like a chapel or a religious shrine. This is appropriate, since Tide fans believed that "Bear" Bryant, the most successful football coach of his era, could walk on water. His teams won six of the school's 17 national championships. Spotlights direct your attention to numerous displays of team and game photos and lots of trophies. During his 25-year tenure as Alabama's head coach, he amassed six national championships and 13 conference championships. When he retired in 1982, he held the record for most wins as head coach in collegiate football history with 323, a record that lasted until 1996.

The University of Alabama Crimson Tide and the Auburn Tigers are cross-state rivals in football, but together they've accomplished an incredible number of achievements that make their home state proud. To date, the two programs have achieved a combined 22 undefeated seasons, 22 division championships, 42 conference championships, 19 national championships, 5 Heisman Trophy winners and 35 College Football Hall of Fame inductions. By the time you're reading this, who knows how the numbers might have risen. While the records on both sides create much to boast about—and no doubt more than one Tide or Tiger fan will playfully argue the finer points—both teams will tell you it's not all about the numbers. School spirit runs deeper than the scoreboard, and both sides have it in serious supply. Visit Tuscaloosa's Byrant-Denny Stadium on a fall Saturday and witness Big Al bounding to the beats on the sidelines and the Million Dollar Band blasts classic cheers such as "Sweet Home Alabama" and "Yea Alabama!" A trip to Tiger town will lead you to Toomer Drug's to sip an iconic lemonade pre game, and inside Shug-Jordan Stadium, you'll get chills when the eagle circles the field before kickoff. Once the Tigers lock in a W, you'll return to Toomer's Corner to roll the trees in toilet paper.

Sports fans can visit the campuses at Tuscaloosa and Auburn to see the handsome Waterford crystal trophies that are surrounded by other awards, photos and athletic memorabilia dating back more than 120 years. In between is the Alabama Sports Hall of Fame in downtown Birmingham where stories of inducted athletes are showcased.

Alabama Sports Hall of Fame includes a bronze Bryant bust.

LEARN ABOUT NICK SABAN'S OWN DYNASTY

The number 17 also coincides with the year of Alabama's latest national-championship season, 2017. This time, the win was under another Alabama coaching legend Nick Saban. Saban and the Crimson Tide have amassed five national championship titles since Saban came to Tuscaloosa in 2007, thus solidifying Saban's reign in Bama football history. Currently, Saban and Bryant are tied for the most NCAA football championships by a head coach—the two Alabama greats each have six to their name. (Saban's first championship was during his head-coaching tenure at LSU.) The first of Saban's title take-overs for the Tide was in 2009, and as Saban himself said in a celebration after that victory, "This is not the end. This is the beginning."

True to his word, more championships followed in 2011, 2012 and 2015. Once again, one can only trust Saban's words uttered after the most recent national victory won on January 8, 2018 against Georgia: "We aren't finished"—and the crowd joined him in adding—"yet!"

Walk into the Paul Bryant Museum and you'll see trophies lined up like the place is a production plant. In 2009, running back Mark Ingram won the 75th Heisman Trophy, the first ever for a Bama player. (Coach Bryant promoted his teams, not individual players.) Perhaps by the time you arrive an identical twin trophy symbolizing the Tide's 18th championship win will be in the hushed halls of sports heaven, and there might just be another Heisman Trophy displayed there too.

WHERE TO STAY IN TUSCALOOSA

A classic place to stay overnight is the Hotel Capstone (320 Bryant Drive.; 800-477-2262) on the opposite side of the Bryant Conference Center from the museum.

Denny Chimes in Tuscaloosa

To see where many of the legendary football victories have taken place, walk four blocks over to Bryant-Denny Stadium (920 Paul W. Bryant Dr.; 205-348-3600).

STOP IN BIRMINGHAM

En route to see the state's other crystal trophy in Auburn, head east on I-59/20 for 56 miles toward Birmingham, where the Tide and Tigers played the "Iron Bowl" from 1948 through 1988 at the neutral site of Legion Field (400 Graymont Ave. W.; 205-254-2391). The ticket distribution was split 50/50.

When the park board managing Legion Field consulted Bama coaches – but not Auburn's – on installing AstroTurf, Auburn responded by expanding its stadium and took the 1989 game to Auburn, and upset the second-ranked Tide.

Head to downtown Birmingham to learn about many sports legends at the Alabama Sports Hall of Fame (2150 Richard Arrington Blvd. N.; 205-323-6665). The museum is housed adjacent to the Birmingham Jefferson Convention Complex.

Since 1967, the Hall of Fame has been the benchmark for other sports museums across the nation. More than 5,000 sports artifacts are elegantly displayed in the 33,000-square foot museum. When ESPN ranked the top 100 athletes of the past century, five out of the top 15 greatest ever were from Alabama and honored here. They are Jesse Owens, Hank Aaron, Joe Louis, Willie Mays and Carl Lewis. Allow a couple of hours to do your visit justice. When you leave, notice the headquarters of the Southeastern Conference across the street. Former SEC commissioner Roy Kramer is considered to be the "father" of the BCS.

DISCOVER THE AUBURN TIGER'S HISTORY

Auburn coach Ralph "Shug" Jordan guided his 1957 team through an undefeated season, beating Bama 40-0 in the season finale to win The Associated Press football championship title. Bama responded by hiring Paul Bryant away from Texas A&M and initiated the modern era of Southern football domination. Shug Jordan and Bear Bryant coached the rival teams for years, with Bama winning most of the time.

Tiger quarterback Pat Sullivan won the

Heisman Trophy in 1971. Coach Pat Dye amassed a 99-39-4 record from 1981 until 1992, along the way ending a nine-year drought against Bama, and Bo Jackson won the Heisman Trophy in 1985. Terry Bowden coached Auburn to an undefeated season in 1993 and Tommy Tuberville's 2004 team went undefeated, but neither won a championship.

Auburn had a museum tucked inside its athletics department headquarters for a number of years, complete with trophies and a replica of the famous Toomer's Drugs Corner where toilet paper hung in faux trees. (For decades, Auburn students have "rolled Toomer's" to celebrate important victories.) The museum was hard to find and the exhibits were removed.

A 9,121-seat basketball arena opened across the street from Jordan-Hare Stadium (251 South Donahue Dr.; 334-844-4040) in 2010 with space to house its trophies. The Auburn Arena (250 Beard-Eaves Ct.; 334-844-9750) is between Donahue Drive and Heisman Drive. It is set back from the street with the entrance facing a cluster of dorms, not the stadium or the street.

GET TO KNOW AUBURN'S THREE HEISMAN TROPHY WINNERS

The Lovelace Hall of Honor is not a freestanding museum, but a section between the lobby and the basketball arena's concession stand. Walk left up a ramp to see a trio of the school's legendary "Aubie" mascot suits behind glass. Pat Sullivan's Heisman is encased in a partition near a football from the

WHERE TO STAY

Want to stay in the official campus hotel? The Hotel at Auburn University (Corner of Thatch and South College, 241 S. College St.; 334-821-8200) is managed by a founder of the Ritz-Carlton chain and staffed by university hospitality students.

1957 season that is painted with the score of the Bama game. Look for an engraved silver cup that was presented to the API (Auburn) team for beating Bama 32-22 during their first game in 1893. A warrior statue was Auburn's prize for winning the second game, 40-16, later in 1893.

Under coach Gene Chizik, quarterback Cam Newton led the 2010 Tigers to an unexpected perfect 14-0 season, defeating Oregon in the championship game in Arizona and accepting the third Heisman for a Tiger. Coming back from a 24-point deficit,

Auburn's 28-27 win over Bama in Tuscaloosa in 2010 set a school record and was pivotal in the run for the BCS crown. Auburn's BCS trophy is housed in a circular glass case with the scores printed on the glass. Lots of parents stand their kids in front of the trophy for photos. Streamers overhead list titles or achievements in football and other sports, suggesting that those victories are also worth a celebratory rolling of Toomer's Corner.

Although there is a shop adjacent to the awards, the largest selection of Auburn merchandise is at J&M Bookstore (115 S. College St.; 334-887-7007).

Don't Miss This

TOOMER'S DRUGS

Toomer's Drugs (100 N. College St.; 334-887-3488) has been at the intersection of College and Magnolia streets for more than 130 years. It is the ideal place for a break to enjoy freshly squeezed lemonade. Toomer's Corner is "rolled" with toilet paper to celebrate athletic victories.

Visit Toomer's Drugs while you are in Auburn.

BIRMINGHAM:
THE CIVIL RIGHTS DISTRICT
by Lee Sentell

You may have read in history books about how Birmingham police used menacing dogs and fire hoses on civil rights marchers a half-century ago, and that racists bombed an African-American church, killing four little girls. You may have also heard of the Birmingham Civil Rights Institute, a world-class museum on human rights, but chances are you'll be surprised that they are together, side by side. Visiting Alabama's Civil Rights District, where some of America's most painful events took place, is a powerful and emotional experience you should not miss.

In the days leading up to Easter 1963, African-Americans, including many Miles College students and professors, organized a shopping boycott of department stores during the second busiest retail season of the year. One of the great myths of the Birmingham civil rights campaign is that African-Americans were simply trying to walk to City Hall to present their complaints over unequal access to public accommodations and education, and a shortage of meaningful jobs at department stores and in local government, including law enforcement. The marches, however, had a calculated purpose.

The Rev. Martin Luther King Jr. named his mission to Birmingham "Project C." The "C" stood for confrontation.

The marches from Kelly Ingram Park began as nonviolent events but were intended to goad public safety commissioner Bull Connor into arresting King and others to attract the attention of the national media. Connor responded on May 7 with police dogs and fire hoses. Because 2,000 children who marched were jailed, King got the headlines and media attention he wanted.

WHERE TO BEGIN: THE BIRMINGHAM CIVIL RIGHTS INSTITUTE

Begin your civil rights experience in Alabama's largest city at the Birmingham Civil Rights Institute. It's one of America's most outstanding museums dedicated to human rights issues. After a brief video that describes how this steel "boom town" became racially segregated, visitors walk past "white" and "colored" water fountains and exhibits that show the inequality of schools and living conditions in Birmingham and beyond.

ABOUT BIRMINGHAM

Nicknamed "The Magic City," Birmingham is Alabama's largest municipality. Rich in history, it is known for its industrial past and for its role in the Civil Rights Movement. Today, Birmingham is an eclectic center for the arts, entertainment, dining and shopping. In addition to the noted Civil Rights District, it is home to a number of other world-class attractions, including the Birmingham Museum of Art, Barber Motorsports Park, the Alabama Sports Hall of Fame and the Alys Stephens Center. Birmingham is centrally located and is within a two-hour drive of Atlanta, Montgomery and Huntsville.

A life-size bronze statue of minister and civil rights pioneer Fred Shuttlesworth stands guard. During the 1950s, he delivered fiery condemnations of the city's segregation laws from the pulpit of his small church, Bethel Baptist, without much impact other than to have his church and home bombed three times.

He traveled to Atlanta in early 1963 and persuaded King to bring the weight of his Southern Christian Leadership Conference – and his celebrity persona – to Birmingham.

Alabama was not the only Southern state involved in the Civil Rights Movement. But some of the most infamous scenes unfolded in the blocks surrounding the 58,000-square-foot institute.

The museum was built directly across the street from the 16th Street Baptist Church, where on Sept. 15, 1963, a bomb planted by segregationists killed four African-American girls. The block-long museum faces Kelly Ingram Park, where earlier that same year, the public safety commissioner, Bull Connor, blasted protesters with fire hoses and set dogs on them. Many of those marching in protest of racial segregation laws were children.

Installation at the Birmingham Civil Rights Institute

Exhibits include a stylized rendition of the heavily segregated city in the 1950s, replete with vintage water fountains designated for use by race, and a sobering side-by-side comparison of white and African-American classrooms of the time. The classroom for white students has a motion-picture projector and glossy textbooks while the classroom for black students is furnished with little more than beat-up wooden desks.

Many artifacts are on display, like one of the armored police vehicles used by Connor to attack the marchers and a replica of a burned-out Freedom Rider bus. There is also the actual door from the city jail cell in which King began his "Letter from Birmingham Jail" after being arrested on Good Friday, April 14, 1963, during the demonstrations. The 7,000-word letter is a defense of his tactics and is considered a definitive document in human rights literature.

Near the end of the museum exhibits, you'll see a massive photo of King speaking at the Lincoln Memorial and hear portions of his stirring "I Have a Dream Speech" in which he talks hopefully about how future generations of African-Americans will be "judged by their character and not by the color of their skin."

Chances are you'll not be prepared for what's around the corner: a large photo of the blown-out wall of the 16th Street Baptist Church basement and smiling photos of the four girls who died that Sunday. A wall clock is stopped at 10:22. Look to your right, and through a large window you'll see the front of the actual church, recently nominated as a UNESCO World Heritage Site.

Because the 16th Street church has an active congregation and isn't just a museum, the story of the bombing is housed in a small room in the basement. A poignant plaque features photos of the four girls: Addie Mae Collins, Carole Robertson and Cynthia Wesley, all age 14 at the time of their deaths and who are buried in a cemetery near the entrance of the Birmingham-Shuttlesworth International Airport, and Denise McNair, who was 11 and is buried in Shadowlawn Cemetery in southwest Birmingham.

An enlargement of a vintage postcard shows the exterior rear steps under which the bundle of 10 sticks of dynamite was hidden. No one was convicted in the bombing for 14 years. A third, and final, bomber was convicted in 2002, some 39 years after the savage crime.

Don't Miss This

TOUR OF 16TH STREET BAPTIST CHURCH

If you are visiting Tuesday through Friday, head across the street and walk through the glass doors to the basement of 16th Street Baptist Church for a tour. Pay the suggested donation of $5 and learn of the story that woke up the world.

The church was organized in 1873 as the first African-American church in the city. The present building was designed by Wallace Rayfield, the state's first African-American architect, and completed in 1911. Like other churches in the segregated South, it functioned as a meeting place, social center and lecture hall. Because of its central location four blocks from City Hall, it served as a headquarters for marches that began in the city park (where blacks were not allowed) in front of the church.

Tense negotiations continued for months in other areas of community life. Just a few days after African-American students began attending previously all-white schools, a group of Klansmen planted a time-delay bomb of 10 sticks of dynamite at the church. It exploded during Sunday School on Sept. 15, 1963. Four young girls died in the basement and 23 more people were injured. Before the terrifying day was over, police fatally shot one black boy who had been throwing rocks at cars. Another was murdered by a white mob.

The tragedy triggered shock and an outpouring of sympathy. About $300,000 in cash was sent to repair the church, which reopened June 7, 1964. From the front of the sanctuary, you can see a special memorial gift, a stained glass window of the image of a black crucified Christ, given by the people of Wales.

Created by artist John Petts, the window depicts Christ with his right hand rejecting oppression and his left offering forgiveness. The words "You do it to me" are part of the design and refer to Christ's parable of the sheep and goats.

In recent years, the U.S. Department of the Interior named Birmingham's 16th Street and Bethel Baptist churches as National Historic Landmarks. In 2008, both were given tentative status as UNESCO World Heritage Sites.

Statues honor the memory of the four young girls that died in the 1963 bombing

THE FREEDOM WALK THROUGH KELLY INGRAM PARK

Take time to wander through Kelly Ingram Park where a statue was unveiled on the 50th anniversary of the Birmingham Civil Rights movement to honor four girls killed during the bombing of 16th Street. A collection of sculptures along the Freedom Walk interprets events during the turbulent period. A statue of the Rev. Martin Luther King Jr. faces the church. The most photographed is a sculpture by Tuskegee artist Ronald McDowell of a young black man bravely facing down a policeman with a snarling dog. To hear a guided mobile tour of the park, call 205-307-5455 and follow the prompts.

FOURTH AVENUE BUSINESS DISTRICT

A few blocks from the Civil Rights Institute and 16th Street Baptist Church is the third element of Alabama's Civil Rights District. The Fourth Avenue North Historic District was the site of local entertainment for African-Americans and the place where many local leaders congregated during the Civil Rights Movement. A visitor's center inside

WHERE TO STAY AND EAT

Downtown Birmingham offers several places to rest after a long day touring the city. Check out The Westin (2221 Richard Arrington Jr. Blvd N; 205-307-3600), which opened its doors in 2013, or The Sheraton (2101 Richard Arrington Jr. Blvd N; 205-324-5000). Both are adjacent to Uptown Birmingham, a premier entertainment district featuring restaurants, bars and the Birmingham-Jefferson Civic Complex.

Stop by John's City Diner (112 Richard Arrington Jr. Blvd N; 205-322-6014) to experience the famous meatloaf and macaroni and cheese.

This stained-glass image of a black Christ was donated to 16th Street Baptist Church by the people of Wales after the 1963 bombing.

the nonprofit agency Urban Impact (4th Ave. N.; 205-328-1850) acquaints you with the history of the district and provides instructions on taking the one-hour tour of the area.

Across the street is the Carver Theatre (1631 Fourth Ave. N.; 205-327-9424), home of the Alabama Jazz Hall of Fame that honors great jazz artists such as Nat "King" Cole, Duke Ellington, Lionel Hampton and Erskine Hawkins. Today, the Carver Theatre is a popular venue for theatrical performances, jazz jam sessions and swing dance classes, as well as local comedy and presentations of the spoken word. Carver is also home to WAJH 91.1 FM Jazz Radio station.

WORTH THE VISIT

The renowned Rev. Fred Shuttlesworth's smaller historic Bethel Baptist Church, built in 1926, is restored and open for tours on a limited basis. Call 205-322-5360 for additional information.

About six miles west of Birmingham is historic Miles College. This historically black college, founded in 1898, has a unique place in civil rights history in that its brand of civic engagement and activism is credited with helping to jump-start the Civil Rights Movement in Birmingham and much of America.

During the planning stages of the Southern Christian Leadership Conference, when King and others were deciding in what test city to implement the Civil Rights Movement, Birmingham was proposed. At the time, Birmingham was considered one of the most racially segregated cities in America. And because students and professors at Miles College were already engaging in civic protests and boycotts against segregated public facilities, the city became the perfect staging ground for strategic activities at the height of the Civil Rights Movement.

Among the names recorded in the school's roster are Frank Dukes, Jonathan McPherson, Abraham Woods, Calvin Woods and others who strategized with King and were willing to take to the streets and be jailed for the cause of justice.

FOR MORE INFORMATION

Visitors wishing to experience the whole of Birmingham should contact the Greater Birmingham Convention and Visitors Bureau (2200 Ninth Ave. N.; 205-458-8000) for information on places to stay, dine and explore. Those interested in gaining a greater understanding of the Alabama Civil Rights Movement should download a free copy of the Alabama Civil Rights Trail brochure or request a free copy by calling 334-242-4169.

An official Alabama Civil Rights Trail mobile app covering Birmingham, Selma, Montgomery, Tuskegee, Scottsboro, Anniston and Greensboro is also available. To download for free, visit www.alabama.travel. Versions are available for Android and iOS devices.

MOUNDVILLE/ALICEVILLE:
SHARK TEETH, POWS & THE LOST REALM OF THE BLACK WARRIOR

by Grey Brennan

This road trip takes you on a journey through history. Visit Moundville Archaeological Park, one of the most important archaeological sites in the United States, and see artifacts dating back a millennium, then return to Tuscaloosa to eat, shop and see the sights. Journey to hunt prehistoric shark teeth left 70 million years ago. Then visit a museum in nearby Aliceville dedicated to one of the largest World War II German prison camps in America.

MOUNDVILLE: A JOURNEY OF EXPLORATION

Start your trip in Moundville, located a few miles south of Tuscaloosa. Here you will find the 26 flat-topped earthen mounds that gave the town its name. For almost 500 years, from around A.D.1000 to 1450, the Native Americans who predate the Creek and Choctaw lived, worshiped and created a large civilization in what would one day be called America.

Moundville is thought to have been the capital of a population of at least 10,000 men, women and children who were spread among smaller farming settlements along a stretch of the Black Warrior River and its tributaries. People continued to return to Moundville to bury the dead long after the site was mostly abandoned, leading to the theory that Moundville evolved into a location so sacred that the ancient natives considered it a portal to the "Path of Souls," the journey to the afterlife.

VISITING MOUNDVILLE

The minute you enter the Lost Realm of the Black Warrior inside the museum at the Moundville Archaeological Park (634 Mound Pkwy. 205-371-2234), you will begin to understand how important Moundville was to the people who inhabited the land 1,000 years ago. Inside the museum, near the halfway point on a drive that passes many of the mounds in the park, you can see

stunning displays that reveal and interpret artifacts found during digs at Moundville. Realistic, life-size figures and state-of-the-art technology bring this lost and ancient Native American civilization to life.

Moundville is known for the symbol of an eye in the palm of a hand that appears on many of the artifacts. An example of that symbol is found on the 12-inch sandstone disk displayed in the museum, commonly called the Rattlesnake Disk because of etchings of two rattlesnake-like creatures that surround a hand-eye symbol. As you walk through the museum, notice other artifacts that include the hand-eye motif. While no one knows the exact meaning of this important Moundville image, some believe it relates to Moundville's significance as a place of transfer to the hereafter.

Before you leave the museum, walk into the gift shop. Items for sale include river cane baskets and shell gorgets, reproductions of highly

The Museum at the Moundville Archaeological Park tells the story of the people who inhabited the land 1,000 years ago.

prized Native American pendants that were made from carved, polished seashells.

You can purchase Native American teas, coffees, chocolates, jellies and bread mixes in the gift shop, as well as crafts from Native Americans from other areas of the United States.

Once you leave the museum, be sure to explore the park. You can climb the largest of the more than two dozen mounds that dot the landscape and imagine how life was lived a thousand years ago. Nearby you can see many of the mounds where the different clan chiefs had their homes, each with their own smaller ceremonial mound nearby. While you are at Moundville, explore the area that extends to the Black Warrior River where you can enjoy a scenic view. Nature trails, including a boardwalk trail, are also on the grounds.

The largest event at Moundville is the annual Native American Festival (205-371-8732). Held Wednesday through Saturday during the first full week of October, the festival includes performers, artists and craftspeople who entertain and educate visitors. This culture and heritage event is extremely popular, attracting more than 12,000 people each year.

EXPERIENCE NEARBY TUSCALOOSA

Moundville is a half-day visit. Return to Tuscaloosa for dining, shopping and a visit to the Alabama Museum of Natural History (427 Sixth Ave. NE; 205-348-7550), located in Smith Hall on the corner of Sixth Avenue and Capstone Drive on the University of Alabama campus.

The first thing you will notice at this museum is the building itself. Meant to reflect the grandiose natural history museums built in Chicago, New York, and Washington, the Grand Gallery and mezzanine areas of the museum are smaller but beautiful.

A reconstruction of a complete skeleton of the large sea creature Basilosaurus cetoide hangs from the main hall. Most of what scientists know about this unusual prehistoric whale with hands, feet and double-rooted

teeth is based on fossils found in Alabama.

While at the museum, you will also see fossils spanning some 300 million years from the Coal Age, Dinosaur Age and Ice Age. Be sure to look for the Hodges Meteorite, also known as the Sylacauga Meteorite, which is on display and is said by the museum to be the only authenticated instance of a meteorite striking a human. This extremely rare incident occurred in Alabama in 1954.

ON TO ALICEVILLE

In the morning, head to Shark Tooth Creek Outdoor Adventures (24114 State Route 14; 205-373-2605) near Aliceville. You are about to hunt for souvenirs that were left 70 million years ago during the Earth's Cenozoic Period.

Much of Alabama was beneath an ocean full of sea creatures at this time. The area around Aliceville was a barrier island and over time thousands of ancient shark teeth were deposited on shore.

Gather at 9 a.m. near the entrance of Shark Tooth Creek Adventures (All visits must be scheduled in advance).

Here you will board the Shark Tooth Creek Express, an open-air trailer that can hold up to 50 adventure-seekers. The ride takes about 15 minutes. Once you are at the creek your hunt will begin. The shark teeth have been held in rock settlements for millions of years, but water from heavy rains dislodge the teeth, allowing them to be easily found near or in the creek.

It is hard to imagine how many teeth are in

ABOUT THE AREA

Moundville is located in southern Tuscaloosa and northern Hale counties while Aliceville is due west in Perry County. This area of Alabama is rural, with Tuscaloosa as the nearest city of size. Besides an abundance of timber, farming and hunting lands, the area is blessed with a network of waterways, including the Sipsey and Black Warrior rivers that flow into the larger Tombigbee River.

the creek. While people have been coming to this location and finding shark teeth for 50 years, there seem to be plenty more to be found. In an hour or two you may have more than 10 teeth, the limit each person is allowed to take home with them as souvenirs.

Aliceville Museum is home to many artifacts from the German Prisoner of War camp there during World War II.

CAMP ALICEVILLE

Across the road and one block away from the Plantation House Restaurant is the Aliceville Museum (104 Broad St.; 205-373-2363), where you can learn about Camp Aliceville, a World War II camp that held as many as 6,000 German prisoners of war.

During its time, Camp Aliceville was one of the largest POW camps in the United States. The camp has long since disappeared, but the Aliceville Museum's collection of camp artifacts is the largest of its kind in the country. You can see artwork and handmade objects made by the POWs, and view uniforms, sculptures and other artifacts from the camp's period of 1943-1945 on display at the museum.

The building housing the Aliceville Museum was once a Coca-Cola bottling plant. At the museum you can also see a bottling line, complete with machines that washed and filled the glass bottles. Other exhibits in the museum include cheerleading outfits from the local school that date back to the 1940s and American uniforms and memorabilia from past wars.

BIRMINGHAM'S FIVE POINTS SOUTH:
WALK TO JAMES BEARD-RECOGNIZED RESTAURANTS

by Grey Brennan

The Storyteller fountain in Birmingham's dining and entertainment center at Five Points South

Birmingham is home to great neighborhoods that are filled with a spirit that comes alive when you walk down the streets and step inside the boutiques and restaurants. For this road trip, visit one of the first (if not *the* first) Birmingham neighborhoods, Five Points South. You will want to overnight to experience breakfast, lunch and dinner the next day in restaurants that serve wonderful food and showcase the rich culinary traditions of Alabama's "Magic City."

THE FIVE POINTS SOUTH WALK

This is a one-mile walk around the Five Points South dining and entertainment district. Most of the restaurants and all of the night life establishments in this area stay open late, but shops mostly close at 5 p.m.

Start your walking tour after you have checked into the Hotel Indigo at Five Points

South (1023 20th St. S.; 205-933-9555), which began as an art deco-style medical office tower in the 1930s and was first renovated as a hotel in the 1980s, or stay at the historic home that is now Cobb Lane Bed and Breakfast (1309 19th St. S.; 205-918-9090). Of course, you can take this walk from any of the downtown accommodations by adjusting your starting point.

You can also start from the Five Points South public parking deck at 2012 Magnolia Ave. As you exit the deck, you will immediately see "The Storyteller" fountain that features a figure of a ram wearing human clothes reading to other animals gathered in a circle. Designed by Birmingham artist Frank Fleming, this landmark celebrates the deeply rooted Southern tradition of storytelling in a "peaceable kingdom" setting.

Look around the Five Points intersection to find the 1934 statue of Brother Bryan kneeling in prayer. James Bryan (1863-1941)

conducted large evangelistic and prayer gatherings in Birmingham and across the region but is most loved and remembered

Get the best photograph of "The Storyteller" by standing in front of the fountain with the church directly in background. If taken from other directions, the photo will include cars along the street that will distract from the beauty of the setting.

for his tireless work to help the homeless. His habit of calling everyone brother or sister got him the name Brother Bryan. Shortly before his death in 1941, the Brother Bryan Mission was formed to continue his work.

The Five Points intersection, for which the area is named, began as a turnaround for horse-drawn trolley cars that later were replaced by electric streetcars. This line was from downtown Birmingham to the city's first suburb called Highlands, which is why a church, restaurant and avenue bear this name. Here, you will see the elegant Highlands United Methodist Church (1045 S. 20th St.; 205-933-8751) that has been a part of the neighborhood for more than 100 years.

HISTORIC B&B

Look across the street from Renaissance Records and beyond the parking lot for Highlands Bar and Grill to see the back of the Hassinger Daniels Mansion Bed and Breakfast (2028 Highland Ave. S.; 205-930-5800). This Victorian mansion was built in 1898 and is named for its previous owner William Hassinger, who was the president of the Southern Iron and Steel Company during the city's iron and steel age. This B&B is on the National Register of Historic Places. It is open every day of the year and includes 10 rooms and suites.

WHERE TO EAT

Birmingham is home to some of the country's most celebrated restaurants. *The*

New York Times wrote in 2006 that, "With little fanfare outside the world of devoted gourmets, white-tablecloth establishments that rival New York's or California's have bloomed like azaleas all over Birmingham."

Rated one of the best restaurants in America, Highlands Bar and Grill (2011 11th Ave. S.; 205-939-1400) is across from Renaissance Records, just a few steps east from The Storyteller fountain. It is owned and operated by award-winning chef Frank Stitt. A signature item on the menu, which consists of a host of culinary delights, is his baked grits, listed on Alabama Tourism's popular "100 Dishes To Eat in Alabama Before You Die" brochure. Highlands Bar and Grill has been named one of the top restaurants in America by the James Beard Foundation for years. In 2018, the Foundation named Highlands Bar and Grill as the year's Outstanding Restaurant and the establishment's revered Dolester Miles won Outstanding Pastry Chef.

A word to the wise: since Highlands was honored with the title of America's finest restaurant, diners from across the nation have learned to make reservations well in advance of a trip to Birmingham.

Around the corner on Highland Avenue South are Stitt's Bottega Restaurants and Café (2240 Highland Ave. S., 205-939-1000). They are fine Italian restaurants housed in a historic limestone building.

A few blocks from Highlands are two top restaurants from the same chef in the Pepper Place design district where smart Birmingham residents flock on Saturday mornings to buy fresh vegetables and plants from local farmers.

Chef Chris Hastings operates Hot and Hot Fish Club (2901 Second Ave. S.; 205-933-5474) and OvenBird (2810 Third Ave. S.; 205-957-6686). In 2012, Hastings famously defeated Food Network star Bobby Flay on "Iron Chef America." Rob McDaniel of SpringHouse restaurant at Lake Martin was on the Birmingham team during the successful "Iron Chef" competition. Also

Frank Stitt, owner and chef at Highlands Bar and Grill

in 2012, the Beard Awards named Hastings as the Best Chef in the South. If you are visiting either Hastings restaurant during the summer, be sure to ask for Chris' legendary tomato salad that is stacked with bacon. It is enough for a meal.Back near the Five Points South fountain, you will find other great restaurants. You can enjoy burgers at Chez Fonfon (2007 11th Ave. S.; 205-939-3221), Thai at Surin West (1918 11th Ave. S.; 205-324-1928), and Asian and seafood at Ocean (1218 29th St. S.; 205-933-0999). Try one or more of over 30 craft beers and 8 keg-style wines on tap as well as oysters and pub fare at Five Points Public House and Oyster Bar (1201 20th St. S.; 205-918-0726), next door to Ocean. The Woolworth (1006 20th St S.; 205-518-6311) offers a menu of Southern-meets-Mediterranean fare, a rooftop bar, and a gaming area. A popular spot for barbecue is Jim 'N Nick's (1908 11th Ave. S.; 205-320-1060), one of several locations of the Alabama-based barbecue chain. Nick Pihakis, Jim 'N Nick's founder, has been repeatedly named a semifinalist in the James Beard Awards Outstanding Restaurateur category.

Walk west from "The Storyteller" on 11th

Avenue South to find Charlemagne Record Exchange (1924 ½ 11th Ave. S.; 205-322-5349). Gain entrance to the CD and vinyl record store through a doorway that leads you upstairs. You will see some boutique shops across the street. Continue west on that block and you will end up at an intersection where you will find the more-than 120-year-old Southside Baptist Church (1016 19th Street South; 205-933-8381) with its impressive 25 curved marble steps and six stately columns.

Also at this intersection on 11th Avenue South is the natural grocery and café, Golden Temple Health Foods (1901 11th Ave. S.; 205-933-6333). In the same building as Golden Temple is the Birmingham Festival Theatre (1901 ½ 11th Ave. S.; 205-933-2383), where plays have been performed since the 1970s. The theater is on the second floor of the building. From the theater, continue walking up the hill on 19th Street South to find St. Mary's-On-the-Highlands Episcopal Church (1910 12th Ave. S.; 205-933-1140), established in 1887.

COBB LANE

Southside has its own cobblestone street. To find it from St. Mary's-On-the-Highlands, walk east on 12th Avenue South one block to 20th Alley, turn right and walk one more block. Look for the brick-lined lane ahead and slightly to your right. This is Cobb Lane, a street narrow and short enough to make it fun to walk and discover several establishments including the Blue Monkey Lounge (1318 Cobb Ln.; 205-933-9222), which claims to be Birmingham's oldest martini bar. On one side of the Blue Monkey Lounge, visit The J Clyde (1312 Cobb Lane; 205-939-1312) and order from the menu of hundreds of craft beers. On the other side of the lounge, visit Delta Blues Hot Tamales (1318 Cobb Lane; 205-502-7298) for the best Cajun and Creole fare in town.

The Cobb Lane Bed and Breakfast (1309 19th St. S.; 205-918-9090), which gets its name from the street, backs up to Cobb Lane and fronts the street around the corner. This

B&B is a National Register of Historic Places property that was built in 1898. If you parked at the Five Points parking deck, it is a short walk back. Walk to 13th Street and turn right, walk two short blocks to 20th Street South and turn left. Walk two blocks north on 20th Street South to reach the five-point intersection and your beginning point.

MUSIC AND MORE

On your way back along 20th Street South, you will walk by Brennen's Irish Pub (1108 20th St. S.; 205-777-3089) where you can hear live music and get your fill of Guinness and Irish food. You'll also pass Dave's Pub (1128 20th St. S.; 205-202-4006), which routinely has live music and is listed in Alabama Tourism's "100 Places to Hear Live Music in Alabama." You will also walk by Mellow Mushroom, where you will find a large selection of pizzas, calzones and more.

NEARBY ATTRACTION

You are only a three-minute drive up the hill to Red Mountain and Vulcan Park and Museum (1701 Valley View Dr.; 205-933-1409). The view of Birmingham from this park is spectacular and even better if you go up to the pedestal on which the statue to the Roman god of fire and forge, Vulcan, stands. Vulcan is the largest cast iron statue in the world. A tour in the park's museum will explain Birmingham's past iron and steel history. Many other historic and interesting places to visit are included in the "Taking It to the Streets, Downtown" walking tour.

OTHER JAMES BEARD RECOGNIZED RESTAURANTS

For more dining experiences in the Birmingham area recognized by the James Beard Awards, visit Ollie Irene in nearby Mountain Brook (275 Church Street, Mountain Brook, 205-769-6034) named a semifinalist for Best New Restaurant in 2012. At Birmingham's

Vulcan Park

Pepper Place in the Lakeview District, you'll find Bettola, for which Chef James Lewis was named a 2012 and 2013 semifinalist for Best Chef: South (2930 3rd Ave. S..; 205-731-6499). Or experience an "American Classic" in Bessemer at The Bright Star. Opened in 1907, the Greek-style, Southern restaurant was honored with this title by the James Beard Foundation in 2010 (304 19th St. N., Bessemer; 205-426-1861).

PARKING IN BIRMINGHAM

The Birmingham Parking Authority (205-254-2330) operates 10 parking garages and two surface lots downtown, including the one at Five Points South. Some facilities will require payment in quarters to exit late in the evening when attendants are off duty. There is also metered street parking.

The Magic City Connectors are a group of six natural gas buses that run along 20th street in downtown Birmingham, connecting travelers to the many restaurants, hotels, and other attractions in the area. Theses buses take a fixed route with turn-arounds at 14th Avenue South, near The J Clyde pub, on the south end and at 12th Ave North between 24th Street North and Carraway Boulevard on the north end. The cost one-way for adults is a quarter. The bus services runs this route every 15 minutes from 10 a.m. to 6 p.m. on weekdays. The wait for the bus on weekday evenings is a little longer. You will wait up to

30 minutes to catch a ride Monday to Thursday from 6. to 9:53 p.m. and on Friday from 6 to 11:53 p.m. The bus is closed on Sundays but runs every 30 minutes on Saturdays from 10 a.m. to 11:53 p.m. To access the live-tracking system for the buses, download the MyStop Mobile app on any smart device and select MAX Birmingham. There are also two other bus systems serving the Birmingham metro area. Call the Birmingham-Jefferson County Transit Authority (205-521-0101), or visit their website, MaxTransit.org, for more information. For complete tourist information on the city, go to the Greater Birmingham Convention and Visitor's Bureau (2200 9th Ave. N.; 205-458-8000).

Spectacular view from the Vulcan pedestal

AVONDALE:
EAST BIRMINGHAM'S REVITALIZED HOTSPOT
by April Colburn

Avondale Brewing Company

No trip to the Magic City is complete without a trip to east Birmingham's hottest neighborhood, Avondale. The area was originally the home of Avondale Mills, where a small community formed around the company. That community became an incorporated town in 1887, and by 1910, the city was annexed into the city of Birmingham. From the beginning, Avondale was known for its natural spring, the namesake of Spring Street, the central street running through town that is now known as 41st Street. The Birmingham Zoo once was located in Avondale, in the area that is now Avondale Park. The zoo's most remarkable animal was a "Miss Fancy," a circus elephant that had been donated to the city.

EXPLORE AVONDALE

Though no longer home to a zoo, Avondale is not short on entertainment. Start your exploration at Avondale Park (4101 5th Ave. S.; 205-254-2391) a 36.5-acre space next to Avondale Library that features a rose garden, gazebo, outdoor ampitheatre, duck pond, walking track, and more. Cross over 5th Avenue South and walk down 41st Street, Avondale's main thoroughfare. Between 4th and 5th Avenues you'll discover Park Side (4036 5th Ave.S.; 205-595-0920), an eclectic neighborhood bar with a back patio that

houses the Asian-fusion Airstream eatery Hot Box (205-224-5632). Next door, you'll find The Marble Ring (430 41st St. S.), an art-deco-style speakeasy that's as secretive as it is suave. To access the hidden entrance, look for the blue phone booth labeled "Police Phone Call Box." Fancy's on Fifth (430 41st St. S.; 205-777-3662), named for the former Avondale Zoo's famous circus elephant, Miss Fancy, will serve you oysters, burgers, and other comfort foods. Further down 41 Street, find gourmet grilled cheese sandwiches at Melt (4105 4th Ave. S.; 205-917-5000). Past 3rd Avenue South, more delicious eats await. Saw's Soul Kitchen (215 4st St. S.; 205-591-1409) offers barbecue and other Southern soul-food classics. Post Office Pies (209 41st St. S; 205-599-9900), once the site of Avondale's Post Office, as its name suggests, is now home to some of the best pizza in Birmingham. Avondale Brewing Company (201 41st St. S.; 205-203-4546) is next door. This establishment's opening in 2011 essentially kicked off the rebirth of Avondale as an entertainment destination. Some of the brewery's beers, such as the Spring Street Saison and Miss Fancy's Triple,

are nods to Avondale's past. Across 41st Street from Avondale Brewery, is Saturn (200 41st St. S.; 205-703-9545), a live-music venue that includes the Satellite bar and café. Nearby, stop at Big Spoon Creamery (4000 3rd Ave. S.; 205-703-4712) for scoops of decadent seasonal ice creams, ice cream sandwiches, and sundaes.

WHERE TO SHOP

After you've finished your sweet treat at Big Spoon, peruse the vintage apparel next door at the Manitou Supply boutique (4000 3rd Ave. S.; 205- 907-7024). With graphic tees, rompers, and other boldly patterned and colored pieces, Manitou Supply offers clothing to satisfy your eclectic side. Go thrift shopping down the street at the upscale thrift marketplace, Sozo Trading Co. (4 41st St. S.; 205-703-0553). Not only will you find clothing, accessories, and home goods at Sozo, but the proceeds of your purchase will go towards helping neglected children in Africa.

EXPLORE NEARBY

A five-minute drive east of Avondale will take you to the heart of another east Birmingham treasure, the town of Woodlawn. Drop in Woodlawn Cycle Café (5530 1st Ave. S.; 205-224-4011) for brunch, an espresso, or a cup of coffee. This modern space also offers a selection of wine and beer, making it an excellent spot to unwind with a friend. Round the corner from Woodlawn Cycle Café and enter Club Duquette (17 55th Pl. S, 205- 202-4647). At this boutique, you'll find a carefully curated selection of the trendiest clothing, accessories, skin-care products, and gifts, including candles that are hand-poured on site.

WHERE TO STAY

Downtown Birmingham is only minutes away from Avondale and offers a large variety of accommodations, including the Redmont Hotel (2101 5th Ave. N.; 205-957-6828), SpringHill Suites by Marriott (2024 4th Ave. S.; 205-322-8600), and the Elyton Hotel (1928 1st Ave. N.; 205-731-3600).

TUSCALOOSA TO EUTAW:
ANTIQUES AND ANTEBELLUM MANSIONS
by Grey Brennan

Springtime azaleas grace the University of Alabama's historic Gorgas House.

With gracious antebellum mansions, wonderful art galleries, scenic waterways, landmark universities, a haunted bridge and a treasure-trove of antique shops, West Alabama offers the perfect road trip for lovers of antiquity, art and culture.

HISTORIC TUSCALOOSA

Start your adventure in Tuscaloosa, where vestiges of a rich heritage abound and the sound of "Roll Tide" echoes throughout. Tuscaloosa served as the state's capital from 1826 to 1846 and has been home to the University of Alabama (719 University Blvd.; 205-348-6010) since 1831. Here, history reverberates inside museums such as the Alabama Museum of Natural History (Smith Hall on campus, Sixth Avenue and Capstone Drive; 205-348-7550) and the Paul W. Bryant Museum (300 Paul W. Bryant Dr.; 205-348-4668) and throughout classic antebellum structures like the 1829 Gorgas House (UA campus; 205-348-5906). These museums are all located on the historic campus and featured as part of the University of Alabama Museums system (205-348-7550).

Highlighted on a downtown walking tour are the 1835 Greek Revival Battle-Friedman House (1010 Greensboro Ave.; 205-758-6138) and the Jemison-Van De Graaff Mansion (1305 Greensboro Ave.; 205-758-2906). Tuscaloosa's Riverwalk is situated near the beautiful Black Warrior River, home of the Bama Belle Riverboat (1 Greensboro Ave.; 205-275-0560). You can learn about the history of Black Warrior River at the Mildred Westervelt Warner Transportation Museum (1901 Jack Warner Pkwy.; 205-248-4931).

At the intersection of University Boulevard and Queen City Avenue, just across from the University Club, is The Downtown Gallery (408 Queen City Ave.; 205-752-6222) featuring wonderful sports art by Daniel Moore.

EXPLORE NEARBY

The Kentuck Art Center and Gallery (503 Main Ave.; 205-758-1257) in nearby Northport and the Moundville Archaeological Park (634 Mound Pkwy.; 205-371-2234) in Moundville are short drives away. Both attractions have gift shops offering unique gift selections and road trip souvenirs. A good time to visit is in October when two large festivals take place. During the first full week of the month, the Moundville Native American Festival is held. On the third weekend of October, the nationally recognized Kentuck Festival of the Arts takes place.

WHERE TO EAT

The original Dreamland Bar-B-Que is a can't miss. (5535 15th Ave. E.; 205-758-8135)

WHERE TO STAY

Plan on spending the night in the area traditionally referred to as "Bear Country" as Tuscaloosa is Alabama's fifth largest city, and you're guaranteed plenty of road trip adventure, including tall tales about football wins and barbershop talk about Tuscaloosa-born Dinah Washington, the "Queen of the Blues." Stay at Hotel Capstone (320 Paul W. Bryant Dr.; 800-477-2262), adjacent to the Bryant Museum, and walk to the University of Alabama campus. Or check into the boutique retreat, the Jack Warner Retreat at North River (2700 Yacht Club Way, NE; 205-343-4215) near Lake Tuscaloosa, 10 miles from downtown. Tuscaloosa also offers a variety of other accommodations with prices ranging from around $65 to $300. Advanced reservations are highly encouraged, especially on football weekends when rooms book early.

ABOUT WEST ALABAMA

Situated alongside the Black Warrior River, Tuscaloosa is Alabama's fifth-largest city and home to the University of Alabama.

The city is part of the area known as West Alabama, which is steeped in Native American and Civil War history. West Alabama includes other historic cities such as Moundville, Livingston, Demopolis, Gainesville, York and Eutaw.

SPEND THE MORNING IN LIVINGSTON

Drive 60 miles to Livingston and see one of the town's most treasured landmarks, the Bored Well on U.S. Hwy. 11. Historians say, beginning in 1854, an old blind mule pulled an auger around day after day until the artesian well was completed in 1857. When people began to claim the mineral water had medicinal value, Livingston's fame as a health spa spread far and wide. Located on the Courthouse Square and now covered by a brick pavilion, the iconic well remains as a longstanding piece of Livingston's history.

Across the street is a plaque honoring Vera Hall, who during the 1930s established one of the most stunning bodies of American folk music on record. She is perhaps best remembered for her song "Trouble So Hard" (1937). Today, Livingston is the location of the Sucarnochee Revue, a radio program of live music recorded over the course of several weekends each year beginning in late January, as well as the Sucarnochee Folklife Festival in April.

A "must do" in Livingston is enjoying the sites and scenes of the University of West Alabama (100 U.S. Hwy. 11; 800-621-8044), which dates back to 1835. A bronze tiger, symbolic of the school's athletic prowess, watches over students and visitors as they stroll through the storied campus.

On the north end of the campus and open daily to the public for picnicking, boating and fishing is Lake LU (pronounced Lake "El-Yoo") and the Sumter County Nature Trails. The lake and trails are popular destinations for observing the local plants and wildlife. While walking on the grounds of the university, you will see many outdoor sculptures that are placed from one end of campus to the other.

Near the Student Union Building, you'll find the Duck Pond and the Alamuchee-Bellamy Covered Bridge, one of the oldest remaining covered bridges in Alabama.

Many claim outlaw sheriff Stephen S. Renfroe's ghost haunts the bridge. If you see the lights blink on and off, you'll know he is there.

GAINESVILLE AND YORK

If you have the time, there are two communities that you may wish to visit before continuing your road trip to Demopolis. From Livingston, you can travel to Gainesville (16 miles north from Livingston), once the third largest city in Alabama. The town now boasts many historic homes and churches, a Confederate Cemetery which serves as the final resting place for hundreds of Civil War soldiers, the place where Lt. Gen. Nathan Bedford Forrest gave a farewell address to his troops (near the intersection of AL Hwy. 116 and Hwy. 39), and beautiful Gainesville Lake (560 Howell Heflin Lock Road), where you are invited to pull in, launch a boat, enjoy primitive camping or simply bask in the beauty of the area.

ALABAMA'S OWN "NEW YORK"

York (10 miles south from Livingston) was once called New York Station. The name was shortened when the community officially became a town in 1881. Located on York's historic Avenue A, the Coleman Center for the Arts (630 Ave. A; 205-392-2005) includes buildings that formerly served as an auto mechanic's shop, a general mercantile store, hardware store, and the original Bank of York.

Across the railroad tracks is the quaint downtown area. A great deal of freight train traffic continues to regularly pass through York as it is approximately the same distance from Mobile, Birmingham and Montgomery. Be sure to check and see if Larkin's Restaurant and Deli (1104 4th Ave.; 205-392-9988) is open on your visit. This local eatery is known for its home-style Southern comfort food, such as fried chicken, fried fish, wings, mac and cheese, dressing, collard greens, and large slices of cake and pie.

ANTEBELLUM MANSIONS

From Livingston, travel to Demopolis (28 miles east from Livingston), where you will find historic Bluff Hall (405 N. Commissioners Ave.; 334-289-9644), built by slaves in 1832.

The interior of this handsome structure has been restored to its pre-Civil War appearance. Also in Demopolis is Gaineswood National Historic Landmark (805 S. Cedar Ave.; 334-289-4846), often called the most unique antebellum mansion in Alabama. Tours are available Tuesday through Saturday from 10 a.m. to 4 p.m.

WHERE TO EAT

While in Livingston, be sure to eat at the Touch of Home Mennonite Bakery (90 North St.; 205-652-6561). This is one of the best places to eat in west Alabama. Get there early, as this is a breakfast and lunch-only destination. Open Monday through Friday until 3 p.m.

Don't Miss This

CELL PHONE AUDIO TOUR

There is an audio self-guided tour at Gaineswood that you will certainly want to hear, but be sure to take your cell phone with you. Unlike other audio tours where you are charged a fee and loaned a portable listening device, on this tour you take your cell phone, call a special telephone number that will be given to you at the property and punch in a location code. You will then hear a description and history of the exact location in which you are standing. There is no charge from Gaineswood for this service. The only charge for this helpful information may be from your mobile provider.

CHRISTMAS ON THE RIVER IN DEMOPOLIS

The annual Christmas on the River takes place here in late November/early December. Held since 1972, this festival has grown into one of the Southeast's leading events, attracting more than 40,000 attendees each year. People travel from coast to coast to see the "floats that really float," hear the reading of "The Christmas Story," enjoy candlelight tours, witness the crowning of St. Nick and celebrate during the famous barbecue cook-off.

ANTIQUES OF HISTORIC EUTAW

From Demopolis, travel to Eutaw (25 miles) on AL Highway 43. Just before you get to the sign that says Forkland community, you will see Jim Bird's Hay Bale Art in his open pasture. A pleasure for travelers for years, the collection of sculptures made of haybales can change from year to year. Once you get to Eutaw, you will find Eutaw Antiques (105 Boligee St.; 205-372-0943), in a former grocery store, and Courthouse Antiques (103 Boligee St.; 205-372-2022). Both are on the Courthouse Square. In addition, Eutaw boasts more than 40 residences and seven public buildings from the antebellum period and many others from the Victorian era. Twenty-seven are listed on the National Register of Historic Places. Each year, the Black Belt Folk Roots Festival – with handmade crafts, down-home cooking and old-timey blues and gospel music – takes place on the Old Courthouse Square on the fourth weekend in August, and the Historical Society hosts a tour of homes in October.

The historic Oakmont home in Eutaw is now a Bed and Breakfast.

Don't Miss This

THE GHOST OF "ALABAMA'S OUTLAW SHERIFF" AT ALAMUCHEE-BELLAMY COVERED BRIDGE

One of Livingston's more colorful characters was Stephen S. Renfroe, known as "Alabama's Outlaw Sheriff." According to many historians, he was a Confederate Army deserter who married three times. He killed his brother-in-law from his first marriage and his first two wives died unexpectedly from unknown illnesses. In 1878, he became sheriff of Sumter County but turned outlaw, committing crimes even while holding that office. He was repeatedly arrested only to escape. Luck ran out in 1886 when "Alabama's Outlaw Sheriff" was lynched by locals either from or near the Alamuchee-Bellamy Covered Bridge. During that time, the bridge spanned the Sucarnochee River.

Walk through the Alamuchee-Bellamy Covered Bridge at twilight as the lights first come on and you might meet "Alabama's Outlaw Sheriff." Many claim Renfroe's ghost haunts the bridge. If you see the lights blink on and off, you'll know he is there.

WHERE TO EAT

For authentic soul food, stop at South Fork Restaurant (1085 Co. Road 208; 205-372-9502). Catfish, ribs, fall-off-the-bone ribs, along with sweet tea and homemade pecan pie are on the menu.

WHERE TO STAY

Overnight accommodations in rural west Alabama include three hotels in Livingston and cabin rentals 25 minutes outside town at Mimosa Ridge Cabin Rentals (2684 McDowell Road; 334-289-4279) overlooking the Tombigbee River. In Demopolis, there are half a dozen hotels.

MARION AND GREENSBORO:
INTERESTING PEOPLE, PLACES AND FOOD

by Grey Brennan

Alabama's Black Belt region, so named because of its rich black soil, cuts a swath across the state that encompasses 22 counties, including Hale and Perry. Greensboro, the county seat of Hale County, boasts several National Historic Register sites, including a house museum honoring a hero of the Spanish-American War – Richmond Hobson. Standing guard over the town is a tall water tower proclaiming Greensboro's proud heritage as the "Catfish Capital of Alabama." Also downtown is a unique restaurant and local enterprise called Pie Lab, and in nearby communities are Rural Studio buildings, some of which are described as "the most beautiful in the world."

In Marion, the county seat of Perry County, you'll learn that this town is the site of the former Judson Female Institute (now Judson College) founded in 1838. Marion is also home to the once all-male Marion Military Institute established in 1842, and the birthplace of civil rights pioneer Coretta Scott King.

When you follow this road trip from Marion to Greensboro, you'll discover the historical and cultural richness of these two Southern towns. You'll visit antebellum mansions, explore the outdoors on a birding adventure and walk in the footsteps of civil rights leaders. You'll also meet newcomers who have opened quaint downtown shops,

In small towns, many businesses are closed several days of the week or have shorter hours than would be the custom in the big city. Some establishments may be cash only. Call ahead to make sure the locations you wish to visit will be open on the day and time of your visit.

cafes and bookstores and who are now sharing their stories and culinary delights with visitors.

EARLY MORNING BIRD-WATCHING

The best way to begin your road trip is with a bird-watching adventure in Marion just after sunrise when the Perry Lakes Park & Barton's Beach Cahaba River Preserve opens to visitors. For the best bird viewing, climb to the top of the 100-foot birding tower at the park. From this height, you will be above the tree canopy. The park comprises four swampy oxbow lakes, formed when the Cahaba River changed its course 150 years ago.

To get to the birding tower, you will first walk over a covered pedestrian bridge and then along a raised boardwalk that takes you by moss-covered trees and slightly over one

St. Wilfrid Episcopal Church in Marion, established in 1838 and site of Confederate cemetery

of the swampy oxbow lakes. This is a short and very scenic walk. In the opposite direction of the parking lot is a quarter-mile walk to Barton's Beach Cahaba River Preserve with a spectacular view of the Cahaba River.

Perry Lakes Park can be hard to find. Travel AL Highway 175 a few miles north of the AL Highway 14 intersection and look for the Aquatic Biodiversity Laboratory, which is marked by a sign on its building. Slow down and turn as if you were going to stop at the laboratory. You will find a road alongside the laboratory's parking lot. One hundred yards down the drive, you will see the Perry Lakes signs. Take the single-lane gravel road for approximately one mile until you reach a parking area.

HISTORIC MARION

From Perry Lakes travel to Marion, home to both the Military Hall of Honor, located on the campus of Marion Military Institute (1101 Washington St.; 800-664-1842), and the Alabama Women's Hall of Fame, located at Judson College (302 Bibb St.; 334–683–5110). While in the area, drive around town to spot the beautiful St. Wilfrid's Episcopal Church (104 Clements St.; 334-683-6562) and historic First Congregational Church (601 Clay St.; 334-683-8111). First Congregational Church was organized in 1871 by freed slaves. St. Wilfrid's cemetery includes graves of both Confederate and Union soldiers.

Judson College, the fifth oldest women's college in the nation, is one block from the courthouse square. The campus is also home to several state champion trees, including Leland cypress, Japanese flowering cherry, English oak and Japanese evergreen oak.

Park your car along the square in one of the many free parking spots. Look for Zion United Chapel's Methodist Church on Jackson Street. The Civil Rights Freedom Wall is a large black granite marker in front of the church honoring the many freedom fighters in Perry County, including pioneer Coretta Scott King who was born in Heiberger, a small settlement 10 miles north of Marion, on April 27, 1927. One of the other names listed is that of Jimmy Lee Jackson. He and others were attending a civil rights rally at the church on the night of February 18, 1965, when an Alabama state trooper shot him.

Walk around to the back of the church and look for a much smaller bronze plaque in the parking lot next door where Mack's Cafe once stood. This is where Jackson and his family fled after they had peacefully exited the church only to be met with hostile reactions from police and other law enforcement, including the trooper who shot the unarmed Jackson. Although the location is easy to find, the plaque can be missed if you are not looking carefully. Read the marker for more information about Jackson's death and the event that inspired the Selma-to-Montgomery marches, a major chapter in the American Civil Rights Movement of the 1950s and 1960s.

Marion's Reverie Mansion

MEET THE STORE OWNERS ON THE SQUARE

Walk inside Lottie's Restaurant (207 Washington Street, Marion; 866-409-0317) and find Southern–soul food the whole family will love. This family-owned restaurant started in 2005 and serves short-order lunch and dinner dishes. All meals come with two sides. Lottie's also offers take-out and catering options. Lottie's is open for lunch on Mondays and lunch and dinner every other day of the week.

The Shack (20555 Hwy. 183, Marion; 334-683-8966) is a local restaurant staple. Order burgers, barbecue, fish, chicken, fried pickles and other American comfort-food classics. The prices are great and the atmosphere is even better. They're open 11 a.m. to 9 p.m. Monday through Thursday and 11 a.m. to 10 p.m. Friday and Saturday.

Down the street is the town's bookstore and coffee house, As Time Goes By (418 Washington St.; 334-683-6757). Here you will find Charles Flaherty, who will sell you a book, pour you a cup of coffee, serve you a piece of pie and even spin records from the 20s, 30s, 40s, 50s or 60s depending on the time of day on his music clock. Flaherty opens the store on selected days and the hours are limited, so call ahead.

There are several antique stores on or near the square. As is the tradition in many small towns, most are closed the first couple of days of the week and open the latter part of the week. Just a block away from the square is Reverie (110 W. Lafayette St., 334-683-6320), a beautiful 1858 Greek revival home open for tours. While it is best to call a day ahead, attendants will try their best to accommodate a tour for a group or individual even on short notice.

Information on other attractions in Perry County can be found at the Old Marion Depot that serves as a Marion Welcome Center (1200 Washington St.; 334-683-9622). Marion was formed on land once known as Muckle's Ridge. It hosts the Muckle's Ridge Festival, usually in the spring.

Bookstore owner Charles Flaherty will sell you a book, pour you a cup of coffee, serve you pie and even spin records for you when you visit Marion.

SEE A WORKING PLANTATION

Seven miles west of Marion on AL Highway 14 is the site of one of Alabama's last active plantations, the Moore-Webb-Holmes Plantation (AL 14, Folsom; 205-292-6356). The land has been passed down for generations from William Moore, who came to Alabama and homesteaded the original 80 acres in 1819 shortly before Alabama gained statehood. Now operated by the sixth-generation descendants, the farm offers tours, which not only take you back in time, but also showcase the family's current practices of producing grass-fed beef, organic gardening and self-sustainability. While there is not a big white plantation home on the tour, most of the buildings are original to the site and include a log house, plantation store and tenant quarters. One of the owners of the Moore-Webb-Holmes Plantation, Cooper Holmes, offer tours of the Marion area. For a personalized tour, call Cooper (205-292-6356).

HISTORIC GREENSBORO

From Marion travel to Greensboro to visit Pie Lab (1317 Main St., 334-624-3899). This café located in the heart of downtown Greensboro and started by the

WHERE TO STAY

There are also two hotels in Marion located right next to each other: the Gateway Inn (1617 AL Hwy. 5; 334-683-9166) and the Sleep Inn & Suites (1605 AL Hwy. 5; 334-683-8600).

Between Marion and Greensboro you can stay at a quaint Airbnb on the grounds of the Moore-Webb-Holmes Plantation (AL Highway 14, Folsom; 205-292-6356). There you will have easy access to touring the working farm and historical sites on the property. In Greensboro, Blue Shadows Bed & Breakfast (11265 AL Hwy. 14; 334-624-3637) is a three-room secluded guesthouse.

Greensboro's Magnolia Grove flanked, of course, by magnolias.

HERO organization uses locally grown fruit in innovative recipes. Pie Lab teaches youths how to make pies, and then sells slices of their efforts. A small yet tasty menu allows you to have a wonderful lunch while watching passersby go in and out of buildings that line historic Main Street. Pie Lab has been featured in the *New York Times, Southern Living* and *Garden & Gun*. The success of Pie Lab has launched another innovative store on Main Street in Greensboro, HERObike. Here you can order a bike made with bamboo or make your own.

Magnolia Grove (1002 Hobson St., 334-624-8618), a house museum located in Greensboro's historic district, honors Spanish-American War hero, Richmond Pearson Hobson. The 15-acre grounds and home are open most days and operated by the Alabama Historical Commission. The knowledgeable staff will gladly take you on a tour.

The home is a relatively rare Alabama example of a full-scale pedimented temple-form two-story house in the Greek Revival style. This and other plantation-style homes combined with the avant-garde Rural Studio sites you can visit in nearby Akron and Newbern make for interesting contrast in architecture. Rural Studio is an off-campus design-

build program of Auburn University that's located in Hale County and focuses largely on community-oriented work. The students work within the community to define solutions, fundraise, design and, ultimately, build remarkable projects. Schedule a tour of the studio's work by calling 334-624-4419. The small Boys and Girls Club II in Akron was named by *Travel + Leisure* magazine as one of the most beautiful buildings in the world

Pie Lab's salad, pie and lemonade

in 2011. A short distance away from Magnolia Grove is the Safe House Black History Museum (2404 Davis St.; 334-624-4228) featuring 1860 slave auction documents. The historic structure served as a safe haven for Dr. Martin Luther King Jr. and others during the Civil Rights Movement. Auburn Univer-

sity's Rural Studio program has restored the museum and built a replica next door that functions as an interpretive center.

TAKE A GUIDED TOUR

For a personalized tour of the Marion and Greensboro area, call local tour guide and area expert Cooper Holmes (205-292-6356). In addition to helping run the Moore-Webb-Holmes Plantation, Cooper operates an Airbnb Experience called Discovering Alabama's Black Belt in which he gives tours that offer insight into the Antebellum and civil rights history as well as agritourism and ecotourism of the Marion and Greensborough area. On this personal tour, Cooper will take you to locations such as Reverie, Coretta Scott King's church and home, Courthouse Square, and The Greensborough Hotel, which houses Horseshoe Farms, a nonprofit organization dedicated to strengthening communities, improving the quality of life of our vulnerable neighbors, and preparing citizen service leaders for tomorrow's communities.

LINEVILLE & ASHLAND:
FROM ALABAMA'S HIGHEST POINT TO ITS HILLS OF GOLD

by Grey Brennan

Start your trip in the Talladega National Forest at Cheaha State Park (19644 Hwy. 281, Delta; 256-488-5111). Completely surrounded by the Talladega National Forest, the park is 2,407 feet above sea level and is the highest point in Alabama. As one of Alabama's resort state parks, accommodations include hotel rooms, cabins and chalets as well as sites for tent camping. Hiking is a popular activity at this 2,799-acre retreat. Cheaha State Park is home to the Cheaha Trailhead of the Pinhoti Trail, Alabama's long-distance hiking trail, as well as a series of smaller trails for day use.

LINEVILLE

As you travel from the Talladega National Forest area to the flatlands below, the first city you come to will be Lineville. Stop in at the Clay County Chamber of Commerce (88855 Hwy. 9, Lineville; 256-396-2828) for tourist information, maps and recommendations for dining and lodging. Highway 9 runs directly through the small city, and you'll see plenty of directional signs to get you to the office. For an overnight stay, try Chapman House (1440 Highway 48; 256-369-9396).

DRIVING TRAILS

At the information office, you will want to pick up a local map highlighting four scenic driving routes in Clay County. Together they are called the Tsalagi Trails and offer a less direct but very enjoyable way to reach many of the destinations on this road trip. Pick one or more of the driving routes and discover beautiful scenery.

The Wa Lo Si Trail starts in Lineville and goes past the turn-offs for both Flat Rock Park and the Alabama Gold Mine before taking you to Ashland and then back to Lineville.

The Wi Trail is popular with motorcyclists because of its twists and turns through the Talladega National Forest and rural Clay County. In fact, the route has 242 curves along a 75-mile stretch.

The No Tis Trail begins in the Talladega National Forest north of Cheaha State Park and includes both Lineville and Ashland.

Years before the California gold rush, prospectors were working their claims in Alabama. The peak of the Alabama gold rush was 1836. Several towns quickly grew, including Goldville, which reached a population of 5,000 at the height of the rush. On this road trip, you will start on a mountaintop at Cheaha State Park and travel down to the valley. Along the way you can ride horses, pan for gold and drive beautiful back roads to reach the small towns of Lineville and Ashland.

The route ends at a southern point in the Talladega National Forest.

The fourth trail is a mostly dirt road route called Gana Trail, which takes you past a waterfall and allows you to ford two creeks, water levels permitting. The Gana Trail is recommended for SUV-type vehicles.

GOLD IN THE HILLS OF CLAY COUNTY

Clay County is one of the locations of Alabama's 19th-century gold rush. Travel the short distance to the Alabama Gold Camp (1398 County Rd. 5, Lineville; 256-396-0389) where you can still prospect. The 200-acre site is located about 10 miles from Lineville at the Randolph County line near the community of Cragford. The on-site general store has a full line of prospecting supplies as well as groceries. If you want to stay overnight, you can camp or rent a prospecting shack.

HOW TO HAVE FUN PROSPECTING

Alabama Gold Camp is located along Crooked Creek and contains everything one needs for a gold-seeking adventure. Access to the gold hunting sites is easy. You can drive right to the edge of the creek in your car.

There are four ways of hobby gold-hunting: panning, sluicing, high-banking and dredging. Here are your choices:

Recreational panners still find gold in east Alabama streams.

Panning — Taking a cup of dirt, placing it in a pan and slowly letting the water flowing in the stream wash away the material until only the heavier gold remains can yield someone a flake of gold in just 15 minutes. A morning of this type of recreational gold prospecting should give you several flakes.

Sluicing — You can rent a tray called a sluice box. You put dirt in one end and let the water from the stream flow through, hopefully leaving you some gold.

High-banking — This is a more aggressive method of sluice box prospecting, and the Alabama Gold Camp includes several high bank stations.

Dredging — With dredging equipment, you get in the creek and suck up mud from the bottom of the creek. Bring a change of clothes as you will get very wet. The dredge will pump the dirt and water through a sluice box to leave heavier material. Constant dredging near one location will muddy the water, making it harder to see the bottom.

EXPLORING LINEVILLE AND WEDOWEE

Lineville is located between the Talladega National Forest and Lake Wedowee, both of which offer outdoor recreation opportunities. Just five miles east of Lineville in Randolph County is Flat Rock Park, known for its scenic views and 29 acres of granite (7115 County Rd. 870, Lineville; 256-396-2338).

A great time to visit Lineville is during its annual Heritage Day and old-fashioned street festival, held the first Saturday in November. Live music, historical displays, arts and crafts, an old-fashioned costume contest and an antique tractor parade are all part of the fall event.

The Clay County Car Show and Swap Meet, one of the largest one-day car shows in the Southeast, takes place the first Sunday in November in the Lineville Recreation Park. The show hosts thousands of antique cars each year.

Lake Wedowee events include the Card-

A road of color in Cheaha State Park

board Boat Regatta Races in early May and a Summer Jam in late May. The Fourth of July Boat Parade is held annually on the lake.

LAND OF REPUBLICAN GOVERNORS

Wedowee is home of Alabama's first Republican governor, William Hugh Smith. He served during the height of reconstruction. An opponent of secession, he left Alabama in 1862 and returned after the Civil War. An historical marker is located at the site of the former home of Alabama's 21st governor along North Main Street in Wedowee.

RILEY COUNTRY

Former Alabama Governor Bob Riley is one of Ashland's native sons. His family has resided in the town for six generations. Hugo Black, a native of Clay County, served as an associate justice of the United States Supreme Court. His first law office was on the square in Ashland. The century-old Clay County Courthouse on the town square was placed on the National Register of Historic Places in 1976.

WHERE TO EAT

Court Square Café (20 Court Square; 256-354-5000) is on the square in Ashland's

downtown. Eat at their famed hot bar that daily offers meat-and-three options. On Sundays, try their all-you-can-eat buffet. The café is open 11-1:30 Monday through Friday and on Sundays. One block west, Pizza Shack (114 Court Square; 256-354-4211) offers pizza and subs. Find Mexican food on the square at Monte Alban 2 Mexican Restaurant (County Road 31 Court Square; 256-354-2988).

ABOUT THE AREA

Cheaha State Park is a mountaintop retreat at Alabama's highest point. Taking the less traveled but scenic roads east and south of Cheaha, you will find a large portion of the Talladega National Forest and the Clay County cities of Lineville and Ashland. Lineville was founded largely as a result of Alabama's gold rush, which ended with the larger California gold rush. Just across the county line is Wedowee, the county seat of Randolph County and home to popular Lake Wedowee.

GETTING THERE

Cheaha State Park is just south of Interstate 20, at exit 191. Lineville and Ashland are both on Alabama Highway 9, which you can reach on the back roads from Cheaha or by going back to I-20 and taking exit 199 to travel south on Highway 9.

This area of Alabama is found south of Anniston and about halfway between Atlanta and Birmingham.

TUSCALOOSA AND NORTHPORT:
A FEAST OF ART AND FOOD

by Carolanne Roberts

In this football-crazed town, the official colors are crimson and white with a splash of Bear Bryant houndstooth. A passerby is as likely to greet you with a hearty "Roll Tide" as a mere "hello." You'll find that this head of steam for the team roars at fever pitch – enthusiastically so – no matter what month you visit. But when you do go, it's also easy (and rewarding!) to dive into a cultural calendar exploding with arts – visual, performing and culinary. The talents of University of Alabama faculty and students merge seamlessly with those of community artists and area restaurateurs, forging a unique and thriving scene. Paintings by John Singer Sargent and Mary Cassatt live here, dance and theater fill stages, colorful folk art is a local staple and farm-to-table eateries fuel you with flavor. Allow several days to see and savor the wonders of Tuscaloosa and Northport.

VIEW THE GALLERIES

Stroll collections by masters, see contemporary works (so recent the paint's still wet!) and visit retail collections where any piece might be yours to take home.

The Paul R. Jones Collection of American Art (2308 Sixth St.; 205-345-3038) offers frequently changing exhibits drawn from an extensive body of 20th-century African-American works donated to the University's College of Arts and Sciences by the premier collector

in the field. Three additional university spaces – the Sarah Moody Gallery (205-348-1891), Sella-Granata Gallery (205-348-5967) and the Ferguson Center Art Gallery (205-348-5967) – feature faculty and student work as well as permanent collection pieces.

Collector Jim Harrison, III fills his Harrison Galleries, LLC (2315 University Blvd.; 205-464-0054), with 19th- and early 20th-century drawings, sculpture and contemporary photography. It's artfully housed in the original Central Drug Company, a pharmacy founded by Jim's grandfather in 1926.

On the first Friday of the month, be sure to take advantage of the Frist Friday art walk in downtown Tuscaloosa, in which local art galleries, businesses, and restaurants are open in the evenings for the community to experience what downtown Tuscaloosa has to offer. Galleries on the art walk include the Arts Council and the University of Alabama galleries at the Dinah Washington Cultural Arts Center, The Paul R. Jones Gallery, Harrison Galleries, O'Connor Art Studios and Grace Aberdean Habitat Alchemy.

THEATER & DANCE PERFORMANCES

Hum along, laugh out loud, ponder weighty issues or appreciate the skillful leaps of grace on the stages of Tuscaloosa. Community groups include Theatre Tuscaloosa (9500 Old Greensboro Road.; 205-391-2277), performing musicals, plays and one-person shows at Shelton State Community College; Actors Charitable Theatre (ACT), offering mostly musicals at the historic Bama Theatre; Tuscaloosa Children's Theatre, also at the Bama Theatre; and the Rude Mechanicals, a summertime rendering of Shakespeare favorites, performed free on the Tuscaloosa Riverwalk.

Tuscaloosa Community Dancers present various programs, including an annual presentation of The Nutcracker, at the Bama Theatre. The University of Alabama's dance season falls within the academic year with a variety of classical and contemporary works.

"Tuscaloosa is much more than a football town. Come for a game and you'll find a lot of reasons to stick around … with more to come in the near future," says Jim Harrison, III, chair of the Alabama State Council on the Arts.

MAKE SOME MUSIC

From big names to aspiring ones, Tuscaloosa's got the sounds. At the waterfront Tuscaloosa Amphitheater, Red Mountain Entertainment brings national acts to the stage – Brad Paisley, Avett Brothers, Counting Crows, Kelly Clarkson and Crosby, Stills and Nash among them. The Tuscaloosa Symphony Orchestra draws musicians from Atlanta, Nashville and Memphis in addition to Alabama artists; more classical sounds come from the String Quartet Society. The Bama Theatre's pop-up Acoustic Nights, set in the Greensboro Room of the 1938 facility, feature singer-songwriter shows. Faculty, students, and featured guest artists at UA, Shelton State Community College and Stillman College, all located within a 10-mile radius, enrich the offerings.

WAGE A BARBECUE WAR

When you hear the term "barbecue wars," it's a reference to the personal battle you'll wage on any visit, trying to taste the different styles and proclaim your own winner. Try Dreamland, the most famous of them all. The original location (5535 15th Ave. E.; 205-758-8135) serves the rib sandwich, full slabs, white bread and banana pudding. Or head to the Northport Dreamland location (101 Bridge Ave.; 205-343-6677) for an expanded menu including a half chicken, Brunswick stew and salads.

The other must is Archibald's in Northport (1211 Martin Luther King Jr. Blvd.; 205-345-6861) for tangy vinegar-based sauce on ribs or sliced pork. Archibald & Woodrow's (4215 Greensboro Ave.; 205-331-4858) offers its thin-but-spicy sauce on chopped pork, plus great mac and cheese.

GET A TASTE OF THE TOWN

The food scene in Tuscaloosa and Northport includes old favorites and popular new spots alike. You must do breakfast at The Waysider (1512 Greensboro Ave.; 205-345-8239) – a Tuscaloosa tradition – for eggs, grits and sports memorabilia. For meat-and-three plates (and reasonable prices), Northport's City Cafe (408 Main Ave.; 205-758-9171) and The Blue Plate (450 McFarland Blvd.; 205-462-3626). For seafood as well as beef and poultry, visit Northport's The Levee Bar and Grill (One Bridge Ave.; 205-632-3136). Tuscaloosa's Avenue Pub (405 23rd Ave.; 205-759-4900) offers top-notch burgers, sandwiches, happy hour specials, and live music on Sundays from noon to 4. Also while in Tuscaloosa, visit River (1650 Jack Warner Pkwy NE Unit 1005; 205-632-3801), where you'll find a casual-upscale eatery on the banks of the Black Warrior River. The restaurant has patio seating overlooking water, complete with a fire pit for cooler evenings. On the menu, you'll find dishes such as shrimp and grits, catfish tacos, steaks, fish, an extensive wine list and Saturday and Sunday brunch items. For a quality cup of joe, Monarch Espresso Bar (714 22nd Ave.; 205-210-8751) is your place.

Just-for-fun spots include 5 (2324 Sixth St.; 205-345-6089), with coffee by day and a late-night culture, too. Go to Chuck's Fish (508 Greensboro Ave.; 205-248-9370) for fresh-catch and sushi bar and Nick's in the Sticks (4018 Culver Road.; 205-758-9316) for the wait-in-line experience of steak and the sweet-but-strong Nicodemus drink. Ever-popular are Buffalo Phil's (1149 University Blvd.; 205-758-3318) for wings, pitchers and patio dining; Baumhower's of Tuscaloosa (500 Harper Lee Drive; 205-556-5658) for more wings before, during or after any game.

An upscale dinner awaits you at Evangeline's (1653 McFarland Blvd.; 205-752-0830), a local favorite with a fine wine list and great crab cakes and shrimp-and-grits. DePalma's (2300 University Blvd.; 205-759-1879) serves up a long list of over-the-top pastas and Italian specialties (including the Lasagna of the Day.

Another must in Tuscaloosa is The Cypress Inn (501 Rice Mine Road N.; 205-345-6963). The combination of family recipes and local ingredients – from the smoked chicken with white barbecue sauce to the bran muffins and yeast rolls – makes this eatery popular with locals and visitors. Built with cypress wood, the restaurant blends in perfectly with the landscape along the Black Warrior River.

Don't leave town without strolling The Strip on University Boulevard, just a short walk from both The Quad (a sprawling green space in the center of campus) and the hallowed Bryant-Denny Stadium. The Strip is dotted with small student bars and restaurants – chain and non-chain – and makes you feel officially collegiate. Want the truly quintessential Tuscaloosa experience? Go to Gallette's, a true UA watering hole, to sample the citrus-vodka-rum combo called the Yellow Hammer (named after the state bird and a popular Bama victory chant). It's said Gallette's dispenses as many as 5,000 cups on a game day – but it only takes one to check the Yellow Hammer off the bucket list of Tuscaloosa musts.

A plate of ribs at the Original Dreamland in Tuscaloosa.

ABOUT TUSCALOOSA & NORTHPORT

Tuscaloosa, the fifth largest city in Alabama, is home to the University of Alabama and the National Championship Crimson Tide football team; the city served as the state capital from 1826-1846. Located in the west-central sector of the state, Tuscaloosa sits along the Black Warrior River (the warrior, legendary Chief Tuskaloosa, is the source of the town's name). Neighboring Northport, across the Black Warrior, dates to the river traffic of the late 1700s when it was indeed a North port. Today, Northport's charming downtown is a mecca for diners and shoppers, particularly during the annual Kentuck Festival of the Arts each October.

IRONDALE-HANCEVILLE-CULLMAN:
A PILGRIMAGE FOR THE SOUL

by Carolanne Roberts

One cloistered nun – a determined soul who acted on miracles – paved the way for the spiritual journey you can experience today in Alabama, starting with the Eternal Word Television Network in Irondale and continuing north to The Shrine of the Most Blessed Sacrament in the rolling countryside outside Cullman, near Hanceville. Just 20 minutes farther along in Cullman, a German-born immigrant known as Brother Joseph left a legacy of miniature buildings at Ave Maria Grotto, a walking trail on the grounds of a Benedictine abbey. Pilgrims of all faiths journey from far corners of the globe to nourish spirits and deepen understanding at the three Alabama locations. You can travel with an organized pilgrimage group (special programs are available for 10 or more visitors) or merely drop by as an individual. Each stop is an easy drive from major interstates, but you'll feel transported to spiritual realms in your heart.

SEE EWTN IN ACTION

The first thing you notice are the satellite dishes – a fenced-in collection of huge white dishes behind the world headquarters of the Eternal Word Television Network. Those big transmitters mean EWTN is broadcasting from this very spot 24 hours a day, in four languages, on 11 channels, and to more than 200 million viewers in more than 140 countries. On the daily tour here, you hear how Mother Angelica, who died in 2016, was a feisty Franciscan nun who started EWTN with a mere $200 in 1981. It is now one of the biggest religious media networks in the world – programming also beams out on satellite and shortwave radio and EWTN also operates a newspaper and two wire services.

After seeing the welcome video, you're guided through the studios themselves, peering into production bays and at banks of monitors showing what's being seen in the Pacific Rim, Africa, South America, Europe or the U.S. at that exact moment. All visitors are invited to attend a live mass as it is televised in the EWTN Chapel (also open for personal prayer and contemplation). Faithful viewers who visit here will often see – and can engage with – favorite on-air friars as they move about the complex.

Access EWTN off Interstate Highway 20, Exit 133 (Kilgore Memorial Drive). Turn right at the foot of the ramp, continuing about a mile to Grants Mill Road. Turn right to 5817 Old Leeds Road and pass through a friendly checkpoint station.

CONTEMPLATION AT THE SHRINE

In contrast to EWTN's constant activity, Mother Angelica set out to create a place – a more solitary place – for prayerful pilgrims to experience their faith. That site, a mere hour from the TV studios, is The Shrine of the Most Blessed Sacrament. The pastoral 18-mile drive off Interstate Highway 65 North helps you slow down – both physically as well as mentally. You follow several miles of pristine white fence past pastures of grazing horses and officially arrive at the shrine, consecrated in 1999.

Park in the ample lot and go directly into the shrine itself, walking across a circular stone piazza inspired by St. Peter's Basilica in Rome. Mother Angelica purposely planned the serene and scenic approach with the intention of shifting the pilgrim's mind from the temporal world to the spiritual one. As you near the entrance, notice the clay roof tiles, molded and fired in Colombia, and hear the 14 bells (more than 100 years old) chime from the 110-foot campanile.

Then push the doors open gently – and

Don't Miss This

You can reserve free tickets for live shows in advance at www.ewtn.com/pilgrimage/ticketsopens in new window or work with the pilgrimage department to customize a group visit, which can include catechetical talks by friars, healing services, and other activities.

Interior of Hanceville's Shrine of the Most Blessed Sacrament

gasp. Almost everyone does. No photos, no words can prepare you for the reality and beauty of the sanctuary with its gleaming 24-karat gold leaf over cedar. The interior is simply stunning and it's easy to utter a prayer of thanks for those who labored across the world to create it.

Much of what you see – from the sanctuary to sacred vessels, altar rail, crucifix, confessionals and Stations of the Cross – was designed and constructed in Madrid, Spain. Inspired by the Romanesque-Gothic architecture of the great 13th-century Franciscan churches, the shrine rises from Italian marble floors inlaid with crosses of red jasper from Turkey. The altars are inlaid with mosaics of glass and gold, created using a 400-year-old method of hand chiseling and fitting. You'll notice light dappling the room from stained glass windows custom-made in Munich, Germany. Much of the marble work itself, however, was accomplished by the Alabama firm of Masonry Arts.

There's no bad time to visit. Life here begins early, at 6:05 a.m., with Divine Office (morning prayers) followed at 7 a.m. by the Nun's Mass. There's yet another mass at noon (10 a.m. on Sundays only) in the more intimate Lower Church, embellished with marble columns. Just outside this area is an exhibit based on the Shroud of Turin, worth the time either before or after the service.

To access the shrine from I-65, take Exit 291 onto State Route 91 for 14 miles. Turn right onto County Road 747 (0.9 miles) and right again onto County Road 548 (0.4 miles) and follow to the shrine. Well-placed signage helps.

MORE TO SEE ON THE GROUNDS

Across the piazza, on the left as you leave the shrine itself, stop in the Crèche, a year-round depiction of the Nativity scene in a cavelike setting swelling with the choral sounds of Christmas. The lifelike figures are captured in the radiant joy of Christ's birth; rows of seats invite you to linger. Back outside, head to the Castle San Miguel, a medieval-inspired

building whose major draw, beyond its embellished interior, is the expansive Gift Shop of El Nino (books, rosaries and other items). A refreshment area with vending machines is located on the lower floor.

Before you leave, follow the curving path down to the Lourdes Grotto by the rippling Warrior River. The replica depicts the setting where 14-year-old Bernadette lit a candle and prayed with a holy apparition in 1858 Lourdes, France. The tradition of candle lighting continues in this Alabama re-creation.

> *"I never in my wildest dreams thought it would be so beautiful ... At every turn [Our Lord] would change it. It got bigger and bigger, and more and more beautiful."*
> *– Mother Angelica, reflecting on building the shrine.*

AVE MARIA GROTTO

The Ave Maria Grotto consists of 125 small stone and cement structures on a hillside at St. Bernard Abbey, built over a 40-year period by a Benedictine monk, Bavarian-born Brother Joseph Zoettl.

The monk, working from books and postcard images, reproduced Gethsemane, the resurrection, the Ten Commandments, Spain's Montserrat Abbey, Bethlehem and various other world missions; he also rendered Noah's Ark, the Tower of Babel, scenes from the Holy Land and graceful guardian angels. Brother Joseph forayed into such secular themes as Hansel and Gretel, a Temple of the Fairies (using cold cream jars), and the Statue of Liberty as a tribute to his adopted land. His most breathtaking piece is the Ave Maria Grotto itself, a rendition of a cave with stalactites of colored glass and stone; a marble altar, encrusted with glass, pebbles and shells, sits beneath a statue of the Virgin Mary and the Christ Child.

To reach Ave Maria Grotto from The Shrine of the Most Blessed Sacrament, take County Road 548 from the gate, turning left onto County Road 278 West. Continue nearly eight

Ave Maria Grotto architecture in miniature

miles to the intersection of U.S. 278 West, turn left and travel three miles. To access from I-65 North, take Exit 308 (Cullman) onto U.S. 278 toward the city of Cullman. Turn right onto State Route 74 East/U.S. 278 (which is also Fourth Street). After three miles, turn right onto St. Bernard Drive. Admission is charged.

EATING AND LODGING ON YOUR DRIVE

While St. Bernard Abbey offers both food and rooms, your stops in Irondale (suburban Birmingham) and Hanceville take you off the grounds of the pilgrimage sites for sleep and food.

Irondale offers a selection of popular chain properties (Holiday Inn Express, Hampton Inn, Quality Inn) within 10 minutes of ETWN.

Enjoy the famous fried green tomatoes at the Irondale Cafe (1906 First Ave. N.; 205-956-5258). This down-home eatery, which inspired Fannie Flagg's novel and film *Fried Green Tomatoes*, turns out 600 to 800 slices a day.

A smattering of guest houses sits near the gates of The Shrine of the Most Blessed Sacrament in Hanceville; request a listing from the Pilgrimage office or search online for selections. You can also opt for chain motels in either Hanceville or Cullman, some 20 minutes away.

One of the closest food establishments to the Shrine is Luna's BBQ (105 Main St. NW; 256-352-1950).

RACING, RIDING AND BUILDING AMERICA'S WHEELS

by Verna Gates

Panoramic photo of Talladega fans at a race

From the first crank of an engine, America fell in love with the automobile. Throughout Alabama, testimonials to our devotion abound in museums, on racetracks and in manufacturing facilities. Alabama is geared to show you vehicles from early Civil War motorcycles to the next new SUV to come off the assembly line.

Five museums dot the state with displays of vehicles ranging from two-wheelers to race cars. In Alabama, you can find one of the world's largest collections of motorcycles, along with an exhibit of iconic Dodge Chargers. Both collections are privately owned but shared with the public. In Talladega, race fans can see another famed Dodge Charger – the one driven by legendary Richard Petty – along with other racing machines. Alexander City's Wellborn Musclecar Museum has one of the finest collections of American Muscle Cars in the country.

Ranked fifth in automobile production in the nation, Alabama is home to four auto factories. Three of these, Mercedes-Benz, Hyundai, and Honda, open their doors to show the steps it takes to put a driver behind the wheel. In January 2018, Mazda and Toyota announced they would be opening a joint car plant in Hunstville to be ready in 2021, which will be auto factory number five for the state.

TALLADEGA SPEEDWAY

Tour Bill France's masterpiece. Still the undisputed largest and one of the fastest tracks in NASCAR, the Talladega Superspeedway is the true test of driving skill. On the 2.66-mile track, you can see the steep banking, the unusual start/finish line that hugs turn one, and where "the big ones" – the infamous multicar pileups – have happened. The speedway completed a $50 million renovation project in 2019 as part of its 50th anniversary. Bus tours of the track are available seven days a week (during non-racing weeks) through the adjoining International Motorsports Hall of Fame and Museum (3366 Speedway Blvd., Lincoln; 256-362-5002).

To experience the thrill of the track from a driver's point of view, the NASCAR Racing Experience (3366 Speedway Blvd., Lincoln; 888-467-2231) will take you full throttle. At this race-car-driving program located at the Talladega Superspeedway, you

WHERE TO STAY

Few cities can offer the lovely small-town nostalgia that envelops Talladega. Looks for the Somerset House on Airbnb.com. This 1905 home, which listed in the National Register of Historic Places, is a few blocks from the historic Talladega town square and welcomes visitors with 12-foot ceilings and gas fireplaces. For a peaceful, river-front stay on Logan Martin Lake that's within easy range of the Talladega Superspeedway, choose the spacious River Rest Bed and Breakfast (3883 Griffitt Bend Road, Talladega). Book through BedandBreakfast.com.

WHERE TO EAT

Meat-and-veggie lunch specials, homemade peanut butter pie, and, of course, the steaks are favorites at Stampede Steakhouse (710 Battle St E., Talladega; 704-886-2400), which is located just a block from the Somerset House B&B. You'll want to try the Bloomin' Onion appetizer as well.

can drive a real NASCAR race car or take a NASCAR ride along. Personal racing instructors will teach you the ropes.

Within the International Motorsports Hall of Fame and Museum sits millions of dollars' worth of race cars and memorabilia. The displays celebrate the greats: Dale Earnhardt, Al Unser Jr., "Fireball" Roberts, Buddy Baker, Richard Petty, Bobby and Davey Allison, Bobby Isaac, Dale Jarrett and "Big Daddy" Don Garlits. Along with the stars are the cars and the boats: the Budweiser Rocket Car that broke the sound barrier, and Tom Gentry's Superboat that set a record speed of 148 miles per hour.

HISTORIC TALLADEGA

The historic square leads to a broad avenue of antebellum- to Victorian-era homes beautifully preserved. Along the main street lies the Alabama Institute for Deaf and Blind. Opened in 1858, the historic school has served hundreds of students and adults throughout the state with vision and hearing loss. The Helen Keller School serves students with multiple sensory impairments. As a result of the institute's strength in the community, Talladega is one of the most advanced cities in the U.S. for handicapped accessibility, with talking street corners, public text phones, and sign language as the city's second language.

Towers of bikes at Barber's Vintage Motorsports Museum

BARBER VINTAGE MOTORSPORTS MUSEUM

Entrepreneur and former Porsche race car driver George Barber Jr. sped into motor history on two wheels.

Noticing that there were no museums dedicated to preserving vintage motorcycles, he began a collection and even formed a team to race the classic bikes.

Now his collection is housed in the largest motorcyle musuem in the world, the Barber Vintage Motorsports Museum (6030 Barber Motorsports Pkwy.; 205-699-7275) between Birmingham and Leeds.

Showcasing more than 900 motorcycles from the collection of 1,600 motorcycles, the museum displays bikes dating from the Civil War all the way to today's best designers. More than 200 manufacturers from 20 countries are represented. The museum also holds the largest known collection of Lotus race cars.

The museum is only one of the jewels of the Barber Motorsports Park, a beautifully manicured park resting on the banks of the Cahaba River. The technically complex racetrack which is located at the heart of the site hosts frequent events for both cars and motorcycles.

Located on the grounds is the Porsche Track Experience (6075-B Barber Motorsports Parkway, Leeds; 770-290-7000), the industry's premier driving school.

WHERE TO STAY

The luxurious Grand Bohemian Hotel in Mountain Brook is the official partner of Porsche Track Experience (2655 Lane Park Rd.; 205-414-0505). Another favorite is Renaissance Birmingham Ross Bridge Golf Resort & Spa (4000 Grand Ave.; 205-916-7677). As a four-star resort, it offers a full range of amenities from a spa to gourmet restaurants to a bagpiper playing at sunset. Perched on a Robert Trent Jones championship golf course, players can experience the fourth longest course in the world. offers amenities, such as a spa, a rooftop restaurant and bar, cooking classes, wine blending experiences, and a heated outdoor pool.

WHERE TO EAT

Dine at two of the James Beard award-winning restaurants that call Birmingham home: Highlands Bar and Grill (2011 11th Ave. S.; 205-939-1400) received the James Beard award for America's best restaurant in 2018. Chef Frank Stitt gained fame for his French twist on Southern ingredients.

Hot and Hot Fish Club's (2901 Second Ave. South.; 205-933-5474) owner/chef Chris Hastings beat challenger Bobby Flay in Food Network's "Iron Chef America" competition. Hastings chooses only the freshest local ingredients for his exquisite cuisine.

The Barber Motorsports Park

HONDA MANUFACTURING IN ALABAMA

Since 2001, the Honda Manufacturing Plant in Lincoln (1800 Honda Drive; 205-355-5000) has been producing top-quality vehicles and V-6 engines—about 340,000 a year to be exact. The plant is more than 4.2 million square feet and currently produces models such as Honda Odyssey, Pilot, and Ridgeline. Tour this facility and see how these models and engines are produced. Plant tours are available on Tuesdays and Wednesdays at 8:45 a.m. and 12:30 p.m. Though the hour-long tours are free, advance reservations are required.

MERCEDES-BENZ U.S. INTERNATIONAL

In 1886, Carl Benz took the horse away from the carriage, inventing the first automobile that could run on a different type of horsepower. The Mercedes-Benz Museum (11 Mercedes Dr., Vance; 205-507-2252) traces the history of his invention all the way forward to the modern cars issuing daily from the adjoining factory. The exhibit showcases the design and craftsmanship that shaped the iconic cars through the years, making the company a world leader in quality and engineering. From antique "horseless carriages" to modern race cars, this museum displays style, beauty and performance.

Twice weekly, the Mercedes-Benz U.S. International plant offers two-hour tours that take visitors through the production of the autos here.

This insider's view of the state-of-the art plant shows how Mercedes brought its vision for a new plant in a new country to Alabama.

HYUNDAI MOTOR MANUFACTURING

Watch a Hyundai as it is being made during a tram tour of the company's production facility in Montgomery. Hyundai Motor Manufacturing in Alabama (700 Hyundai Blvd, Montgomery; 334-387-8019) produces 1,500 cars per day.

Tour guides explain how during the 1.5-hour tour that explores every step of the process. Tours leave on scheduled times Monday, Wednesday and Friday.

WHERE TO STAY

Located in the heart of downtown Montgomery, the Renaissance Montgomery Hotel & Spa at the Convention Center (201 Tallapoosa St.; 334-481-5000) is convenient to the Capitol, Old Alabama Town and the riverfront. Enjoy the spa and events at the performing arts center. For a complete list of accommodations, contact the Montgomery Visitors Center (334-261-1100).

WHERE TO EAT

For Southern cooking, the Farmers Market Cafe (315 N. McDonough St., Montgomery; 334-262-1970) serves up authentic country cooking from its meat-and-three steam table. The historic cafe gained fame from its fried chicken.

WHERE TO STAY

There are many hotels available in Tuscaloosa, home of the University of Alabama and its Crimson Tide championship football team. If you visit during the non-football season, book a room at Tuscaloosa's only bed and breakfast, the Bama Bed and Breakfast (46 Sherwood Drive; 205-750-0990). This antebellum home built in 1823 is just two blocks from the University of Alabama's Bryant-Denny Stadium and offer five suites.

WHERE TO EAT

John "Big Daddy" Bishop started his business the same year another legend, Paul "Bear" Bryant, came to town. Both of them served football fans, one with victories, the other with barbecued ribs. While Bishop's Dreamland Bar-B-Que (5535 15th Ave. E., Tuscaloosa; 205-758-8135) has expanded into other menu items such as sausage, chicken and sides, it is the ribs that customers dream about.

WELLBORN MUSCLE CAR MUSEUM IN ALEXANDER CITY

In the 1960s and early 1970s, the music was rocking and muscle cars were rolling. With light bodies and big engines, these mighty machines gave tire-burning performances. They were the "pony" cars: the Mustangs, Chargers and Challengers, along with the Barracuda, GTO and Camaro. America was young, rebellious and running life at top speed.

Tim and Pam Wellborn fell in love in a Dodge Charger and have celebrated ever since – amassing the country's largest collections of Chargers, including the original love machine. The Wellborn Muscle Car Museum (124 Broad St., Alexander City; 256-329-8474) celebrates the brief and glorious era of fast times and faster cars. The museum is open on Saturdays from 10 a.m. to 3 p.m., with no appointment needed, and Tuesday through Friday by appointment only. Admission is charged. Private tours can also be arranged.

SpringHouse offers fine dining on Lake Martin

WHERE TO STAY

After your speedy trip through the muscle cars, slow down at the Mistletoe Bough Bed & Breakfast (497 Hillabee St., Alexander City; 256-329-3717). Sit on the broad porch or stroll through the gardens of this charming Queen Anne mansion, complete with a corner turret. Enjoy 1895 elegance with 21st century conveniences.

WHERE TO EAT

For fine dining, SpringHouse (12 Benson Mill Rd., Alexander City; 256-215-7080) brings the farm and sea to the table with fresh ingredients and Southern flair.

Chef Rob McDaniel has been a James Beard semifinalist for Best Chef: South each year from 2013 to 2017. SpringHouse, is located in the Russell Lands on Lake Martin residential community, has an elegantly rustic look with exposed stone and rough-hew beans and overlooks stables, pastures, and Lake Martin. The restaurant has a private 12-seat dining room called the Well House that is accessed via an underground wine cellar.

The Wellborn Muscle Car Museum

CHILDERSBURG AND SYLACAUGA:
FAMILY FUN
by Grey Brennan

Take your family to explore a cave that's 12 stories deep. Eleven miles away, amaze them as your car rolls uphill, seemly defying the law of gravity. Along the way, you can see how ice cream is made and the location where "stars fell on Alabama." This road trip takes you along U.S. Hwy. 280 between Sylacauga and Harpersville and includes a stop at a 100 year-old farm as well as a vineyard, where each September contestants dress up as if they are in an "I Love Lucy" television episode and participate in an annual grape stomp.

CHILDERSBURG — COVERED BRIDGE AND CAVERN

Childersburg is believed to be the location of a Coosa Nation village visited by the Spanish explorer Hernando de Soto in the fall of 1540. Childersburg calls itself "The Oldest Settlement in America." Named for the explorer, DeSoto Caverns Family Fun Park (5181 DeSoto Caverns Pkwy.; 256-378-7252) is a magnificent 12-story cave. Guided tours of the cave include a light, sound and water show on every tour. The more than 20 attractions outside the caverns include a maze and wacky water golf. Be sure to stop by the gift shop for some delicious DeSoto Caverns fudge. This stuff is so good that it's featured as a "must taste" on Alabama Tourism's list of "100 Dishes To Eat in Alabama Before You Die."

Also on the outskirts of Childersburg are the historic 1864 Kymulga Grist Mill and the adjacent Covered Bridge built in 1860 (7346 Kymulga Grist Mill Rd.; 256-378-7436). Visit the mill site, walk across the covered bridge that spans Talladega Creek and then explore the nature trails. The Kymulga Grist Mill grounds are the home of the annual Coosa Fest held in late September.

The gristmill is also home to the Butler-Harris Rainwater Museum (205-378-5521), an historic home that overlooks the city of Childersburg. The Victorian home, called the Rainwater House, was given to C.H. Butler as a wedding gift in 1894. It is now home to artifacts from the city. It's open to visitors and free to visit.

WHERE TO EAT

If you want to eat where the locals eat, then go where the locals go. In this case, that is Old Town Grille (50 River Run Road; 256-378-5022). This restaurant has high recommendations for its homemade pizza.

VINEYARD & FARM

Drive on U.S. Hwy. 280 across the Coosa River and as you head north toward Harpersville (less than 10 miles), you will reach Morgan Creek Vineyards (181 Morgan Creek Lane, Harpersville; 205-672-2053). This family-owned vineyard and winery offers free guided tours and wine tastings. During its annual Grape Stomp, held the third Saturday in September, you can crush grapes with your bare feet while listening to live music and watching the "Lucy Look-A-Like" contest recognizing the best Lucille Ball costumes. Morgan Creek is also a great spot to stop in early summer to pick berries. The whole family can enjoy the activity, and you can purchase what you pick for a small fee. The vineyard has blueberries and blackberries. When the days are hot, it's a good idea to go in the morning.

A family road trip to this part of Alabama wouldn't be complete without going to the Harpersville Old Baker Farm (184 Furrow Lane; 205-762-7209). This farm, which was established in 1899, has raised cotton, soy beans, corn, pumpkins, watermelons, as well as the garden that feeds the entire family. Now, in addition to farming and raising livestock, the farm is open to the public

for seasonal special events and activities. In October, pick your own pumpkins, ride horses, and see the farm animals, and attend the Cotton Pickin' Celebration, where you'll learn about cotton picking, witness a Civil War reenactment, and peruse arts and crafts from local vendors. The farm also includes a Christmas tree farm. From Thanksgiving through Christmas enjoy complimentary apple cider and hayrides through the trees.

Visitors at Morgan Creek Vineyard's gift shop and tasting room

WHERE TO STAY

There are more than a half-dozen hotels in the Childersburg/Sylacauga area. Choose the Holiday Inn Express and Suites in Sylacauga (40743 US-280; 256 2071511), or stay at the 3,500-acre Pursell Farms (386 Talladega Springs, Sylacauga; 877-292-3276). Located less than 30 minutes from either Sylacauga or Childersburg, the farm offers an estate-style inn as well as a lodge, cabins, and cottages. In addition to lodging, the farm offers horseback riding, a spa, dining options, and even meeting spaces for business and social events. The farm's golf course, FarmLinks, is the world's only research and demonstration golf course, and includes on-site hunting and fishing as well.

WHERE TO EAT

If you're hungry, try Giovanni's Italian (42490 US Hwy. 280; 256-208-0351) known for their authentic Italian pizzas, lasagna and pasta. Or try Buttermilk Hill Restaurant and Bar (300 East Third Street; 256-207-1001), located in downtown Sylacauga. It offers upscale Southern comfort food, such as buttermilk-battered chicken breasts topped with goat-cheese cream and bread pudding with chocolate whiskey sauce, in a 1904 Victorian frame-home setting.

SYLACAUGA'S MAGIC MARBLE

Since you are in Sylacauga, which sits atop a bed of mostly white marble, take time to visit the Isabel Anderson Comer Museum and Arts Center (711 North Broadway, 256-245-4016). This museum, containing works of art by the Italian sculptor and quarry investor Giuseppe Moretti, is a great place to learn about Sylacauga's marble history. It also has a "Nabors Room," which celebrates native son Jim Nabors, who gained national fame as both an actor and a singer. Nabors was discovered by Andy Griffith and played the garage attendant Gomer Pyle on the "Andy Griffith Show." Be sure to tour the upstairs gallery inside the museum, where you will see a copy of the Hodges Meteorite and newspaper clippings that tell the story of the 8.5-pound rock that fell from the sky and struck Ann Elizabeth Hodges as she napped in a farmhouse in Oak Grove just outside of Sylacauga.

You can also view Sylacauga marble sculptures at the B.B. Comer Memorial Library (314 N. Broadway; 256-249-0961) where the sculptures from visiting Italian artists are on permanent display. They can be found in the lobby around the stairwell. Another must-see are the 17 paintings that ran as advertising for Avondale Mills in *The Saturday Evening Post*. These paintings by Douglass Crockwell reflect the American way of life in 1948 and are in a similar style to that of Norman Rockwell. Look for the Crockwell painting that includes a very young Doug Layton before he became the longtime color commentator for the University of Alabama Football Radio Network. Layton was born in Sylacauga.

TRAIL'S END

Sylacauga is also the ending point of the Pinhoti 100, so for avid runners, fall is also a great time to visit. Held annually in November, the Pinhoti 100 is a point-to-point trail run starting in Heflin, AL on the unspoiled Pinhoti single-track trail. Runners make their way over the highest point in Alabama while navigating over rocks, through creeks and across beautiful ridgelines of the Talladega National Forest.

OAK GROVE – WHERE "STARS FELL ON ALABAMA" AND YOUR CAR ROLLS UPHILL

From Sylacauga, travel north on U.S. Hwy. 280 to the adjacent community of Oak Grove, the site of a rare occurrence. An 8.5-pound meteorite crashed into the home of the Guy family on November 30, 1954, striking Elizabeth Ann Hodges. A farmer found another meteorite nearby. These two Oak Grove rocks from the sky are the only known meteors from that day.

To find the location of this unusual event and see the "Stars Fell on Alabama" historical marker commemorating the occurrence, travel U.S. 280 N. from Sylacauga. When you see the Nissan automobile dealership, exit to the right onto the Old Birmingham Highway. The historical marker will be on your right just before you reach Odens Mill Road.

GRAVITY HILL

Seeing the site where a meteorite struck a human is bound to be an exciting experience, but what will baffle you about your trip to Oak Grove is Gravity Hill, where, oddly enough, cars appear to coast uphill. This last adventure is a great way to end your road trip to the area.

This oddity happens on a section of Old Hwy. 280, now officially named Gravity Hill.

For those with a GPS, it should be easy to find; simply type in Gravity Hill. If your GPS doesn't have the road listed or you're traveling using a map only, closely follow the directions included here.

DIRECTIONS TO GRAVITY HILL

If you have driven to the "Stars Fell on Alabama" historical marker, return to U.S. Hwy. 280. From the Nissan dealership, travel U.S. Hwy. 280 N. for 1.3 miles where you will see Ogletree's Garage on your right. Directly on the other side of U.S. Hwy. 280 from Ogletree's is Kimberly Road. Exit U.S. Hwy. 280 onto Kimberly Road and then immediately turn onto a small paved road. This will be Gravity Road. If you reach mile marker 38 going north on U.S. Hwy. 280/231, you have gone too far. Turn around and look again for the road that is directly across the divided highway from Ogletree's Garage. Once you've turned onto Kimberly, you will immediately take a left onto Gravity Hill. Please note there's not a road sign for Kimberly Road or Gravity Hill, so the site might be a little difficult to find. Once on Gravity Hill, you will be headed south, parallel to U.S. Hwy. 280. This is a short half-mile road. You will soon reach a stop sign where Gravity Hill intersects with U.S. Hwy. 280. This is where the fun starts.

HOW TO EXPERIENCE GRAVITY HILL

You will have the most fun if you position your car south on Gravity Hill so that your car goes uphill backward. Drive to the stop sign on Gravity Hill at the U.S. 280 intersection. Pull up to the stop sign. U.S. 280 should be in front of your car and the rest of Gravity Hill in your rearview mirror. Make sure no one is behind you. Put your car in neutral and take your foot off the brake. Your car should start to roll backward and uphill. Be sure to keep your foot close to the brake pedal, as you will pick up speed as you coast uphill. This little adventure is so amazing that you'll find yourself driving back to the stop sign to try it again.

Montgomery is a city where layers of history run deep. You can stand on the bronze star where Jefferson Davis was sworn in as president of the Confederate States of America and look straight ahead one block to the church where a century later the Rev. Martin Luther King started the Civil Rights Movement.

Alabama's historic State Capitol, completed in 1851, is the fifth seat of government. Visit the others at St. Stephens, Huntsville, Cahawba and Tuscaloosa.

In 1965, state troopers attacked African-Americans attempting to walk across the Edmund Pettus Bridge for the right to vote. Take a road trip to Selma and park your car and walk across. It's a highlight of the Alabama Civil Rights Trail.

Visit Tuskegee where blacks earned the right to pilot planes during World War II and became heroes in Europe, but faced the old

Shorter Mansion, Eufaula

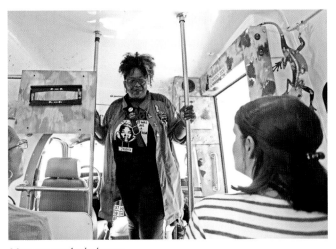

Montgomery civil rights bus tour

familiar enemy of racism when they came home. The National Park Service's new Tuskegee Airmen Museum tells their story in Lionel Richie's hometown.

Take the pilgrimage to Nelle Harper Lee's hometown of Monroeville in the spring to watch the theatrical version of "To Kill a Mockingbird." It's in the courtroom where her father practiced law and inspired her courageous coming-of-age story.

Buy a colorful Gee's Bend original at the Quilters Collective in the isolated community about an hour south of Selma. The *New York Times* called them "miraculous works of modern art."

Eufaula, bordered by the Chattahoochee River, boasts the state's most popular pilgrimage of houses. Walk among the richly detailed Italianate homes when the azaleas are in bloom in early April.

Selma's Old Live Oak Cemetery

EUFAULA:
PICTURE-PERFECT AND PILGRIMAGE-READY
by Marilyn Jones Stamps

If you're looking for the warmest hospitality and a unique collection of Italianate architecture, head to Eufaula. The southeastern Alabama town on the west bank of the Chattahoochee River is one of the most picturesque and historic in the South. It's no wonder that Eufaula boasts the state's oldest and largest tour of homes, the Eufaula Pilgrimage, each spring. The pilgrimage features some of the South's grandest structures in the Seth Lore-Irwinton Historic District.

You'll know you have arrived in Eufaula when you drive down beautiful Eufaula Avenue. This street is perhaps as pretty as any street anywhere. Lined with dogwoods and magnolias, it is flanked by gracious antebellum mansions that "rise like ornate wedding cakes," as described by Lee Sentell, author of *The Best of Alabama.*

During your nostalgic return to the Old

South, you are invited to step inside grand structures built by 19th-century planters and merchants that still house period heirlooms and family treasures. Sit and enjoy an afternoon tea on the front porch of one of the grand mansions in the Seth Lore-Irwinton Historic District. At an old cemetery, listen to stories about Eufaula's former residents as told by local tour guides. And explore treasures of the past at the Eufaula Pilgrimage Antique Show.

Most of the homes on tour are private residences, open only during the annual Pilgrimage. As you stroll from Greek Revival cottages to Italianate showplaces, enjoying tours by daylight and candlelight, you'll find yourself spellbound by Eufaula's colorful trail of floral beauty and the warm hospitality of the people you meet along the way.

WHERE TO BEGIN: SHORTER MANSION

Begin your Pilgrimage experience at Shorter Mansion (340 N. Eufaula Ave.; 334-687-3793). By far one of Eufaula's finest homes, this 1906 Classical Revival-style house museum serves as the town's welcome center and is headquarters for the annual tour of homes weekend.

Shorter Mansion, located in the Seth Lore Historic District, is graced with bold Corinthian columns that support an entablature extending around three sides of the structure. It was originally built in 1884 by Eli Sims Shorter II, a wealthy cotton planter, and his wife, a Georgia-born heiress to the SSS Tonic fortune. When the mansion was put up for auction by the builder's granddaughter in 1965, it was purchased by a group of civic-minded citizens who organized the Eufaula Heritage Association. They held the first pilgrimage in 1966. Now, decades later, the

Young women in period dress greet visitors at Eufaula's Shorter Mansion

Pilgrimage continues to be the No. 1 drawing card for Eufaula each spring.

EXPLORE SETH LORE-IRWINTON HISTORIC DISTRICT

The Seth Lore-Irwinton Historic District, the largest historic district in east Alabama and one of the largest in the state, encompasses much of the oldest part of Eufaula. In 1834, Capt. Seth Lore and others founded what is today known as the downtown area. They named the four main avenues Livingston, Orange, Randolph and Eufaula. The first letter of each avenue together spelled the captain's last name. Many of the historic homes and buildings in the district can be found along these streets. In addition to Shorter Mansion, where scenes from the movie *Sweet Home Alabama* were filmed, the district – listed in the National Registry of Historic Places – showcases more than 700 significant sites, including an extensive collection of domestic Italianate architecture and other homes and churches built between 1834 and 1915.

Maps for self-guided walking or driving tours of the district, as well as information on other attractions in the county, are available at the Eufaula Chamber of Commerce (333

ABOUT EUFAULA

Situated high upon a bluff overlooking scenic Lake Eufaula on the west bank of the Chattahoochee River, Eufaula has an intriguing past dating as far back as 1733, when it was occupied by Creek tribes of the Muscogee Nation.

It was settled in 1823 as Irwinton. In 1843, the town was renamed Eufaula in honor of its Creek heritage and because the postman kept misdirecting mail to the Georgia town of Irwinton. Incorporated in 1857, Eufaula prospered as a river town serving first as a port for cotton distribution and a business hub for Alabama and Georgia in the 1800s then as an agricultural stronghold for supplying cotton to textile mills in the 1900s.

E. Broad St.; 334-687-6664). The chamber is located in the James S. Clark Center, which was built in 1892 as a Central of Georgia freight train depot.

Fendall Hall (917 Barbour St.; 334-687-8469), also located in the Seth Lore-Irwinton Historic District, is a state-owned house museum and one of Alabama's outstanding Italianate houses. Crowned by a cupola and aptly nicknamed the "groom's cake" because of its Victorian chocolate-and-tan color scheme, the heavily detailed house was completed in 1860 by Edward and Anna Young and was home to five generations of the Young family. Among its many treasures are family and period furnishings, marble mantles, and a black and white marble tiled entry. In 1973, it was purchased by the Alabama Historical Commission and later restored for preservation as a house museum.

The Hart House (211 N. Eufaula Ave.; 334-687-9755), built by John Hart around 1850, is recognized as an outstanding example of pure Greek Revival architecture. It features Doric columns, an entablature with dentils, and a center doorway with sidelights and transom. It was purchased by the Historic Chattahoochee Commission in 1985 for use as its headquarters.

Following a preplanned driving route, you can see many other structures and sites that are part of the Seth Lore-Irwinton Historic District, including Shorter Cemetery where Alabama Gov. John Gill Shorter and his family are buried.

Also see the 1869 First Presbyterian Church, featuring a gothic vaulted ceiling made of brick from Holland and fashioned after English parish churches, and historic Fairview Cemetery, where many of Eufaula's black citizens were interred until 1870. In addition to the "Old Negro Cemetery," there are at least five other graveyards, including the Jewish, Presbyterian, Masonic, Odd Fellows and Public sites, which are part of present-day Fairview Cemetery. During the Pilgrimage weekend, live performances of Tales from the Tomb take place here.

FROM "WEDDING CAKE" HOUSES TO ANTIQUES

In addition to the homes tour, you can also enjoy the Eufaula Athenaeum Tour of a private collection featuring items of historic significance to Barbour County and relics associated with the American Revolution, early presidents and founding fathers; Civil War reenactments; Civil War period music; professional and children's art exhibits; garden tours; and carriage rides, as well as the annual antique show and sale. Held at the Eufala Chamber of Commerce (333 E. Broad St.; 334-687-6664), the Eufala Pilgrimage Antique Show is one of the most prestigious in the Southeast. Dealers offer linens, silver, china, furniture, glassware and collectibles for show and sale throughout the weekend.

WHERE TO STAY AND EAT

If you are worried about what to eat while visiting Eufaula, don't. Throughout the weekend, you can experience everything from sitting on the porch of a historic home enjoying snacks and good conversation with homeowners and feasting on buffet lunches provided by the local country club to enjoying appetizers and desserts during an afternoon tea. Of course, there are also several local eateries for you to enjoy.

Eufaula offers several chain hotels for overnight lodging and one bed and breakfast facility. A recommended choice for both lodging and dining is Lakepoint State Park Resort (104 Lakepoint Dr.; 334-687-8011). This picturesque 1,220-acre park provides a great place for photographing a wild heron at sunset, watching the sun rise over Lake Eufaula from your hotel room or cottage or enjoying the many activities that include fishing, camping, golfing, swimming, bird watching, and walking or biking along scenic trails.

Costumed musicians play at Fendall Hall during the spring pilgrimage.

THE EUFAULA PILGRIMAGE

For a breathtaking view of the town, plan your visit in late March and early April to coincide with the annual Eufaula Pilgrimage (334-687-3793). This is when colorful red and pink azaleas blanket the area and Southern belles in hoop skirts and white bonnets turn out to welcome you and hundreds of other visitors to their historic hometown.

NEARBY HISTORIC ATTRACTIONS

In nearby Clayton (about 20 miles away), you will find Alabama's only remaining eight-sided antebellum house. The two-story structure, featuring a flat roof with a cupola, served as Union Cavalry Cmder. Benjamin H. Grierson's headquarters in April 1865. While visiting Clayton, be sure to stroll through the historic Clayton Cemetery. Among the many gravestones you'll find is one that's shaped like a whiskey bottle. It marks the gravesite of W.T. Mullen, who "drank himself to death." According to his wife, who commissioned this unique headstone, Mullen died in 1863 at the age of 29.

MONTGOMERY:
WHERE HISTORY RUNS DEEP
by Marilyn Jones Stamps

History is woven into the very soul of Montgomery. It spirals down grand staircases, like the one inside the 1847 State Capitol building. It descends from lofty places, such as Dexter Avenue King Memorial Baptist Church, where a humble preacher rose to prominence as the leader of the Civil Rights Movement. And it bubbles up from streets such as historic Dexter Avenue that bustled with merchants in the 1800s, served as an auction block for slaves during the Civil War and was later pounded by foot soldiers during the 1965 Selma to Montgomery march. Captured between the brick and mortar of historic churches and notable dwellings and inside museum after museum in downtown Montgomery, you'll hear epic stories of a past that is unparalleled by that of any other city in America.

WALK OR RIDE THE TROLLEY TO EXPLORE MONTGOMERY'S HISTORY

Begin your tour at the Montgomery Area Visitor Center (300 Water St.; 334-262-0013) at Union Station. Park your car and go inside for brochures and information on what to see and do in the city. Be sure to purchase a piece of history or a souvenir at The Stop at Union Station gift shop. You can walk to many of the downtown attractions and museums, but to get to others, you'll want to drive. If you choose to walk or take the trolley, there are metered parking spaces in and around the train shed and The Alley, Montgomery's thriving downtown entertainment district.

SITES SHOWCASE BIRTH OF THE CIVIL WAR AND THE CIVIL RIGHTS MOVEMENT

One of the fascinations of downtown Montgomery is the fact that there are so many museums and attractions dedicated to telling the story of the city's role in the Civil War and the Civil Rights Movement that occurred nearly a century apart. With Jefferson Davis as its leader, Montgomery served as the cradle of the Confederacy from February 4, 1861, to May 29, 1861. A century later, congregations in African American churches conducted peaceful protests to overturn laws allowing segregation. In 1955, when seamstress Rosa Parks was arrested after boarding a Montgomery bus at Court Square and refusing to give up her seat to white passengers, the modern Civil Rights Movement was born. A new Montgomery minister, Martin Luther King Jr. was recruited to organize a boycott of city buses. The Montgomery Bus Boycott lasted a year and ended when a U.S. Supreme

A view of Dexter Avenue

The United States and Alabama flags drape the entrance to Alabama Governor's Mansion.

bama State Capitol (600 Dexter Ave.; 334-242-3935) building, where Jefferson Davis took the oath of office as president of the Confederacy in February 1861 and where civil rights activists ended the historic Selma to Montgomery march in 1965. You can enter the Capitol by way of the entrance on Dexter Avenue unless you are traveling with an organized tour group or visiting on Saturday, in which case you must enter

Inside the more than 130-year-old Dexter Avenue church, a giant mural in the basement highlights the emergence of Dr. King as the leader of the Civil Rights Movement and the journey that took him to his death at the Lorraine Motel in Memphis.

Adjacent to the State Capitol is the First White House of the Confederacy (644 Washington Ave.; 334-242-1861) where Jefferson Davis and his family lived during the brief period when the capital of the Confederacy was in Montgomery. Go next door to the Alabama Department of Archives & History (624 Washington Ave; 334-242-4364). Inside, the Museum of Alabama chronicles three phases in the state's history, including its Native American heritage, the Civil War and the Civil Rights Movement.

Located a block west of the Capitol is the Dexter Avenue King Memorial Baptist Church – the only church where Dr. Martin Luther King Jr. ever served as pastor (454 Dexter Ave.; 334-263-3970). The meeting to launch the Montgomery Bus Boycott was held at the church on December 2, 1955. The handsome red brick building was designated a National Historic Landmark on June 3, 1974.

Court decision stopped segregated public transportation in 1956.

A must visit in Montgomery is the Rosa Parks Museum and Children's Wing (252 Montgomery St.; 334-241-8615) located on the very site where Mrs. Parks was arrested. The museum chronicles the history of the Civil Rights Movement and the Montgomery Bus Boycott through presentations, newspaper clippings and exhibits, including a replica of the bus on which the civil rights pioneer was riding.

A block away is the Freedom Rides Museum at the historic Montgomery Greyhound Bus Station (210 S. Court St.; 334-414-8647). Interpretive panels on the outside and contemporary artwork on the inside of the museum tell the story of young Freedom Riders who faced mob violence with non-violence and courage in May 1961. The museum is located in the Court Square Historic District, which includes the Court Square Fountain and more than two dozen buildings that have stood long past many of the businesses that once occupied them.

From the Freedom Rides Museum on Court Street, take the first left on Alabama Street; turn left onto South Perry Street and then right on Dexter Avenue. Standing gallantly at the top of Dexter Avenue is the Ala-

The first White House of the Confederacy

via the rear entrance at 1 North Union Street. Once inside, be sure to ask to go upstairs to see the grand spiral staircases illuminated by beautiful chandeliers. Before departing the Capitol, stop by the Goat Hill Museum Store for unique gift items and Alabama-related books and other memorabilia.

The Dexter Parsonage Museum

Dexter Avenue King Memorial Baptist Church

A block behind the church is the Civil Rights Memorial designed by renowned sculptor Maya Lin. Etched into a granite table overflowing with water are the names of 40 martyrs who died between 1954 and 1968 during the struggle for civil rights. After you read the names of the martyrs and a timeline of landmark events, walk up the entrance at mid block to enter the Civil Rights Memorial Center (400 Washington Ave.; 334-956-8439) and learn more about this period in American history. The "Here I Stand" exhibits and videos chronicle important events that occurred downtown during the Civil Rights Movement. Before leaving, you'll be given an opportunity to sign a pledge to work for justice on the Wall of Tolerance.

Less than five minutes from the Dexter Avenue Baptist Church and the Civil Rights

Your best bet for parking would be to find one of the decks where you can park for a small fee or look for a lot where you can pay for extended day parking. Signage is visible for designated public parking.

Memorial is the Dexter Parsonage Museum (309 S Jackson St.; 334-261-3270), where Dr. King and his wife Coretta lived from September 1, 1954 until late 1959 when they moved to Atlanta. Mrs. King and their baby, Yolanda, were home when a bomb damaged the front porch of the parsonage one night during the bus boycott. Nearby is the 1853 Jackson Community House (409 S. Union St.; 334-221-1973) which has served many functions, including being home to Montgomery's first public library open to African Americans beginning in 1948.

Located a few minutes away from the Dexter Avenue Parsonage Museum is historic Alabama State University. The National Center for the Study of Civil Rights and African American Culture (915 S. Jackson St.; 334-229-4876), located on the campus, documents the Civil Rights Movement and Montgomery's role in it. Also on campus are two historic homes: the childhood home of singer Nat "King" Cole and the former home of civil rights pioneer Ralph David Abernathy, both strategically located across from the proposed site of the Montgomery civil rights interpretive center.

THE LEGACY MUSEUM

This moving museum and memorial, which opened in April 2018 and was a decade or more in the making (115 Coosa Street, Montgomery, AL 36104; 334-386-9100). Located on the site of a warehouse where tens of thousands of black people

were enslaved, a block from a dock and rail station where they were trafficked in the 19thcentury, the museum offers an immersive experience with the sights and sounds of "Enslavement to Mass Incarceration."

The indoor museum states its mission this way, "EJI (Equal Justice Initiative) believes that the history of racial inequality and economic injustice in the United States has created continuing challenges for all Americans, and more must be done to advance our collective goal of equal justice for all."

Extensive research informs every display at the museum, making the sculptures, videography and animated content come to life to narrate the racial terrorism of lynching and the humiliation of the Jim Crow South. Researchers can access the museum's comprehensive collection of data on lynching.

The iconic Montgomery Court Square Fountain

The museum and the nearby memorial have garnered national attention welcome thousands of visitors weekly. It uses a multimedia approach to storytelling, offering firsthand accounts from ex-slaves. Photos, art, audio, video and other media are used to relay to story to visitors. There are fine art pieces from Elizabeth Catlett, John Biggers, Yvonne Meo and Kay Brown.

The museum is open Wednesday through Monday, starting at 9 a.m. and ending at 7:30 p.m. every day except Saturday, when it closes at 6 p.m. Museum tickets are $8 for adults, $5 for students and seniors and free for children age 6 or younger. Be sure to visit National Memorial for Peace and Justice.

Dexter Avenue King Memorial Baptist Church in Montgomery

NATIONAL MEMORIAL FOR PEACE AND JUSTICE

The outdoor Peace and Justice memorial is the first of its kind – designed to honor the legacy of the enslaved and terrorized by lynching. Statues and other art throughout the six-acre property narrate the story. More than 800 steel monuments—one for each county in the U.S. where a lynching occurred—is at the center of the site. The names of the lynched are engraved on the columns. Similar columns have been created for the counties. The EJI provides those to the appropriate groups for them to display locally.

The entire campus is operated by the EJI, which is "committed to ending mass incarceration and excessive punishment in the United States, to challenging racial and economic injustice, and to protecting basic human rights for the most vulnerable."

Visitors should plan to spend three or four hours at the site to tour both the indoor and outdoor displays. Families who are concerned about the subject matter for younger children should visit museumandmemorial.eji.org for assistance. Group visits are available. Because of the intense interest in the museum and memorial, it is probably best to purchase your tickets in advance.

Landmarks in Birmingham, Montgomery, Selma and Tuskegee form the nucleus of the U.S. Civil Rights Trail.

The memorial structure includes 800 corten steel monuments

The memorial is open Wednesday through Monday from 9 a.m. to 5 p.m., with last entry starting at 4:30 p.m. Memorial tickets are $5 or free for children age 6 or younger." Both sites are handicap accessible, and wheelchairs are available upon request.

OLD ALABAMA TOWN

Continue your tour through Montgomery history with a visit to Old Alabama Town (301 Columbus Street, 334-240-4500). The six-block village includes authentic homes and buildings from the 19th and early 20th centuries. The buildings are restored and open to the public so visitors can learn how early Alabamians lived. The museum collection includes an 1810 tavern, an 1850 dogtrot house, a one-room schoolhouse, a grist mill and more, with the 1850s Ordeman House serving as the nucleus for the historic site. There is no food available here but you are encouraged to bring a picnic lunch and relax in Old Alabama Town's Kiwanis Park or take advantage of some of the nearby restaurants.

When you visit, docents in clothes from the era tell the stories of how people lived in the 19th century. Owned by the Landmarks Foundation, the mission of Old Alabama Town is to educate and to restore historic properties that are at-risk for demolition. More than 60,000 people visit the museum annually.

Visit www.oldalabamatown.comfor more information.

Sculpture on the grounds of The National Memorial for Peace and Justice

HANK WILLIAMS MUSEUM

While exploring downtown Montgomery, you'll also want to tour the Hank Williams Museum (118 Commerce St.; 334-262-3600), where you'll find the 1952 baby-blue Cadillac that the singer passed away in on Jan. 1, 1953, rare videos, photographs and more. Each New Year's Day, hundreds of Hank fans brave the wintry elements and gather at Oakwood Cemetery Annex (1304 Upper Wetumpka Road; 334-240-4630) to pay tribute to the man who sang his way into the hearts of millions.

The historic cemetery, where the country singer/songwriter is buried, features some of the most elaborate monuments and headstones in the state. It dates back to the early 1800s and is also the burial site for many of Alabama's forefathers. Nearby is a section of the cemetery with the graves of approximately 75 French soldiers from World War II.

GETTING THERE

Getting to Hank's grave is a bit tricky, particularly if you are from out of town. Heading down East Jefferson Street from downtown Montgomery, you'll want to veer to the left past the Police Department to get on Upper Wetumpka Road. Go to the entrance past St. Margaret's Cemetery to the Oakwood Annex, where you will see a granite Hank

Marchers cross the Edmund Pettus Bridge.

Hank Williams' blue Cadillac convertible is one of many artifacts at the Hank Williams Museum.

Williams marker on the left pointing the way to go. As you enter, begin looking for the tall monument on your left featuring a white, stone-carved cowboy hat. This spot marks the singer's gravesite. Hank's wife Audrey is buried beside him and his mother nearby. The country music legend gave his last performance in Montgomery three days before his death.

The downtown Hank Williams Museum

WHERE TO STAY

Montgomery offers about 70 hotel facilities, three of which are in the heart of downtown: Embassy Suites, Hampton Inn & Suites, and the Renaissance Montgomery Hotel & Spa at the Convention Center (201 Tallapoosa St.; 334-481-5000). The Renaissance, situated near Maxwell Air Force Base – the site of aviation history – is a combination of regal architecture and modern amenities, including a rooftop pool. It also features an 1,800-seat performing arts center, a grand exhibit hall, a European spa and two restaurants. For alternative downtown lodging, three historic bed and breakfast establishments are in close proximity: the Hillcrest Manor, the Lattice Inn and Red Bluff Cottage.

WHERE TO EAT

Entertainment and dining in downtown Montgomery centers on The Alley, where you'll find places such as Dreamland (12 West Jefferson St; 334-273-7427), Wintzell's Oyster House (105 Commerce St.; 334-262-4257), Central (129 Coosa St.; 334- 517-1155), Sa Za (138 Commerce St; 334-495-7292) and Jalapeños in the Alley (130 Commerce St.; 334-262-4939).

For a complete list of Montgomery's dining and lodging options, go to www.visitingmontgomery.com.

VISIT THE ANIMALS AT THE ZOO

The Montgomery Zoo and Mann Wildlife Center on the north side of the city, is home to about 750 animals representing 140 species. The zoo (2301 Coliseum Parkway, 334-625-4900) was founded in the 1920s. With improvements and additions through the years, it is now a premiere zoological facility.

A few visitor favorite activities include the petting zoo, lion training session, parakeet cove and giraffe encounter. Train rides are available for $3 per person, two or under are free.

In 2003, the Mann Wildlife Learning Museum opened its doors. Animals from arrow trophy hunter George Mann are on display. The collection represents one of the most complete presentations of North American wildlife.

Before you go, enjoy a meal at the Overlook Café or refreshments at the playground kiosk. Don't forget to stop by the gift shop, which does not require the admission charge.

The zoo is open year-round, seven days a week, except for Thanksgiving and Christmas Day and New Year's Day. But, the facility is open on the evening of December 25 for the Christmas Night for Christmas Lights Festival. Joint admission to the zoo and learning museum is priced from $17 (adults) to $13 (children 3-12) to free for children two or younger.

SELMA TO MONTGOMERY:
CROSSING A BRIDGE INTO HISTORY

by Marilyn Jones Stamps

The Edmund Pettus Bridge, spanning the Alabama River in Selma, has become one of the most iconic symbols of the modern struggle for civil and voting rights in America. It is also a focal point for the 54-mile route now memorialized as the Selma to Montgomery National Historic Trail.

Along the Trail, beginning in Selma, you are invited to go back in time nearly 50 years and become an eyewitness to history. Visit an interpretive center and a voting rights museum to hear the stories behind the historic 1965 voting rights marches. Cross the famous Edmund Pettus Bridge, following in the path of foot soldiers along U.S. Hwy. 80 to a place called "Tent City" in Lowndes County. From there, continue to Montgomery, stopping at the City of St. Jude, the Rosa Parks Museum and other sites before arriving at the Alabama State Capitol. Stand at the base of the Capitol steps where Dr. Martin Luther King Jr. rallied a crowd of more 25,000 with his "How Long ... Not Long" speech on March 25, 1965 and laid the demands of black Alabamians at the doorstep of Gov. George C. Wallace, the most powerful political figure in state government at the time.

When planning your visit to the Trail, allow sufficient time to stop and see the sites, cross the bridge, and learn more about the century-long struggle for civil and voting rights that ultimately led to the passage of the landmark Civil Rights Act of 1964 and the Voting Rights Act of 1965.

To begin your tour, start at the Selma Interpretive Center. Strategically located at the foot of the Edmund Pettus Bridge, the center serves as an introduction to the National Historic Trail that also includes an interpretive site in Lowndes County, near White Hall, and a planned site on the campus of Alabama State University in Montgomery. The center features brochures, videos, exhibits and a small bookstore for you to explore.

Historic Edmund Pettus Bridge, Selma

EXPLORE THE HISTORY OF THE MARCHES

On March 7, 1965, during the first of three events now collectively called the Selma to Montgomery marches, some 600 protestors, including men, women and children, set out on a march from Selma to Montgomery. Just after crossing the Pettus Bridge, they were trampled, brutally assaulted with billy clubs, and tear-gassed by heavily-armed state troopers and deputies, all with photographers and journalists looking on.

The marchers were protesting for voting rights in Dallas County and marching to commemorate the death of Jimmie Lee Jackson, a 26-year-old army veteran, Baptist church deacon and civil rights activists, who had been shot three weeks earlier by a state trooper while trying to protect his mother and grandfather at a demonstration in nearby Marion.

During the first attempted Selma to Montgomery march, which has become historically known as "Bloody Sunday," ABC television interrupted a Nazi war crimes documentary to show footage of the violence taking place on the outskirts of Selma as marchers crossed the Pettus Bridge. Within 48 hours, demonstrations in support of the marchers were

Don't Miss This

THE BRIDGE CROSSING JUBILEE

Held the first full weekend of March, the annual Bridge Crossing Jubilee (334-418-0800), hosted by the National Voting Rights Museum, is a commemoration of the anniversary of "Bloody Sunday" and the Selma to Montgomery marches, as well as a celebration of the right to vote. Activities include a pageant, a dance, women and youth conferences, a parade, the Jubilee, interfaith service and the National Voting Rights Hall of Fame induction. The Jubilee weekend draws visitors each year from all walks of life and provides an unparalleled opportunity to foster knowledge and understanding of the ongoing struggle to eliminate discrimination.

taking place in 80 cities around the country.

The second march, called the "Ministers' March," galvanized thousands of religious leaders, including Dr. Martin Luther King Jr. and others who had been called to Selma to assist with the demonstrations. This march occurred on March 9, 1965 on what is referred to as "Turnaround Tuesday." It resulted in 2,500 protesters turning around after crossing the Pettus Bridge. Jim MacDonell, one of the participating ministers, described the event as "ominous."

"We walked up one side of the bridge, over the top of the bridge and down the other side. As we came down the highway, we looked across the highway, and there as far as we could see were flashing lights and police cars and helmeted troopers carrying shotguns blocking the way," MacDonell said.

NATIONAL VOTING RIGHTS MUSEUM AND INSTITUTE

From the Interpretive Center, you are encouraged to walk across the famous Edmund Pettus Bridge to the National Voting Rights Museum and Institute (6 U.S. Hwy. 80E; 334-526-4340), where you will learn more about the marches and the unfair treatment of blacks in Dallas County in terms of voting and civil rights.

The main gallery of the museum features the Footprints Hall of Fame with footprints of voting rights marchers forming a continuous theme throughout the facility. Standing in front of the museum's "whites only" water fountain exhibit, try and imagine what it must have been like to be forbidden by law from enjoying a sip of water from the fountain because of the color of your skin. Other exhibits include a voting booth and a jail cell. There are eight other galleries in the museum, including the Church Gallery, Legal Gallery and the Obama Gallery.

Several outside murals painted on garage shop doors show a triumphant end to the struggle for the right to vote in America. One of the murals depicts President Barack

Obama with a caption that reads "Hands that picked cotton picked a president." Mr. Obama's inauguration as America's first black president on January 20, 2009 was a defining moment in the long race for civil rights, both in the U.S. and around the world.

While touring Selma, you'll want to also visit the Ancient Africa, Enslavement, and Civil War Museum, 334-526-4000. A sister facility to the National Voting Rights Museum, this is the only museum in the country offering a sensory reenactment of the history of enslavement in America through side-by-side exhibits and virtual interactive exchanges.

MARTIN LUTHER KING JR. STREET HISTORIC WALKING TOUR

From the Voting Rights Museum, go back across the bridge and take the Martin Luther King Jr. Street Historic Walking Tour (800-45-Selma). The tour highlights 20 memorials, churches and wayside exhibits detailing the history of the Voting Rights Movement in Selma. A must-visit is Brown Chapel A.M.E. Church (410 Martin Luther King St.; 334-874-7897). It was the site of early mass meetings during the 1960s voting rights campaign and the staging point for voter registration marches to the Dallas County Courthouse.

The "Bloody Sunday" march originated from the steps of Brown Chapel after a First Sunday communion service. Marchers were forced back to the church from the foot of the Pettus Bridge after many had been beaten, sprayed with tear gas and run down by deputies on horseback. Horses were ridden up the steps of the church as participants tried to seek sanctuary inside. A monument to Dr. Martin Luther King Jr. was dedicated in front of the church in 1979.

Directly across the street is the housing complex known as the George Washington Carver Homes. Many participants in the march lived here and civil rights workers from out of town lodged here.

Selma's Brown Chapel AME Church

Down from Brown Chapel is First Baptist Church, which took the early lead in the civil rights struggles in Dallas County. Members of the congregation allowed the Student Nonviolent Coordinating Committee to use the facility as its first organizational base and rallying point when it arrived in Selma in 1963.

Before ending your walking tour, be sure to visit the Old Depot Museum (4 Martin Luther King Jr. St.; 334-874-2197).

It features a fine collection of artifacts and memorabilia depicting life in Selma and Dallas County from 1820 to the present, including a component on African American history and culture.

LOWNDES COUNTY INTERPRETIVE CENTER

From Selma, travel along Hwy. 80 to the Lowndes County Interpretive Center, located near the site of "Tent City" approximately midway between Selma and Montgomery. Tents were set up at the site after many families who registered to vote were evicted from the land they worked as tenant farmers as a result. Tent City housed up to 20 families in two years until they were able to get back on their feet and find employment.

Timothy Mays, a former Student Non-violent Coordinating Committee worker in Lowndes County, assisted Tent City inhabitants with meals and other needs. Mays became famous to the world on March 7, 1965 during "Bloody Sunday," when he set out along with other marchers during the first attempt to march to Montgomery. A state trooper clubbed and knocked down Mays, who was carrying an American flag. Mays didn't drop the flag but held onto it as a symbol of the injustice he and others had endured for the cause of freedom.

Inside the Interpretive Center, you can view a 30-minute historic video. Wander through the displays that include the flag carried by Mays and touch and feel the interactive exhibits.

Before departing, be sure and purchase a piece of history at the gift shop. You can select from books, posters and memorabilia relating to the marches, including a video documentary of events.

OTHER SITES ALONG THE TRAIL

Continue along U.S. Hwy. 80 to Montgomery, stopping along the way to visit Trail markers, such as the one that marks the spot where Viola Liuzzo, a white woman from Michigan, was killed. Luizzo was one of the people transporting marchers from Montgomery to Selma after the rally at the State Capitol on March 25, 1965. Accompanied by a young African-American man, she had returned to Selma, dropped off her passengers and was returning to Montgomery to pick up more marchers when she was spotted by the Ku Klux Klan. Liuzzo was pursued at high speed until she was shot and killed.

Heading toward Montgomery from Selma, the marker is approximately five minutes past the Interpretive Center on the right, just before County Road 97. Look for the sign pointing to Wright Chapel.

The Saint James Hotel built in 1837, is a Hilton property.

The church is no longer there, but this is a good place for you to park if you want to get out and take a photograph of the marker.

CITY OF ST. JUDE AND DOWNTOWN ATTRACTIONS

The third and final Selma to Montgomery march began March 16. Protected by 2,000 soldiers of the U.S. Army, 1,900 members of the Alabama National Guard under federal command, and many FBI agents and federal marshals, the marchers arrived in Montgomery on March 24 and finally at the Alabama State Capitol on March 25, 1965.

When you enter Montgomery, continue to follow the Trail signs throughout the city to historic sites such as the City of St. Jude, just off I-65 on West Fairview Avenue. Voting rights marchers camped here and held a "Stars for Freedom" rally on the St. Jude campus before their arrival at the Capitol.

In downtown Montgomery, you'll want to visit the Rosa Parks Museum & Library and Children's Wing (252 Montgomery St.; 334-241-8615), located on the site where Parks was arrested in 1955 for refusing to give up her seat to white passengers on a city bus.

A block away is the Freedom Rides Museum at the historic Montgomery Greyhound Bus Station (201 S. Court St.; 334-414-8647), and at the top of Dexter Avenue is the Alabama State Capitol (600

Dexter Ave.; 334-242-3935), where the final and successful Selma to Montgomery march ended.

Just west of the Capitol is Dexter Avenue King Memorial Baptist Church (454 Dexter Ave.; 334-263-3970), the only church where Dr. Martin Luther King Jr. served as pastor. A block behind the church is the Civil Rights Memorial Center (400 Washington Ave.; 334-956-8439) which honors the 40 martyrs who died during the civil rights struggles between 1954 and 1968.

At Alabama State University, a short drive away, the National Center for the Study of Civil Rights and African American Culture (915 S. Jackson St.; 334-229-4876) documents the Civil Rights Movement and Montgomery's role in it. Also on the campus is the former home of civil rights pioneer Ralph David Abernathy.

Another important march took place on March 7, 2015, the 50th anniversary of Bloody Sunday. President Barack Obama delivered a speech at the Edmund Pettus Bridge and then, along with other U.S. political figures such as former President George W. Bush and Civil Rights Movement activists such as Amelia Boynton Robinson, led the annual march across the bridge.

About 40,000 people gathered at the bridge that day to commemorate the original march and reignite efforts to improve U.S. current civil rights.

MONROEVILLE:
THE "TO KILL A MOCKINGBIRD" EXPERIENCE

You've read the book or maybe you've seen the movie with Gregory Peck. Now experience *To Kill a Mockingbird* and lots more firsthand on a visit to Monroeville.

As the home of Nelle Harper Lee and her neighbor and childhood friend Truman Capote, Mark Childress – the acclaimed author of the novel *Crazy in Alabama* – and other distinguished writers, Monroeville is considered the "Literary Capital of Alabama."

Each spring, in addition to performances of *To Kill a Mockingbird*, Monroeville hosts the Alabama Writers Symposium. All events are divided between the campus of Alabama Coastal Community College in Monroeville, at the Monroeville Community House, and at the Monroe County Museum. This literary festival brings together some of the state's most distinguished writers and scholars for a weekend of lectures, readings and discussion, with the highlight of the symposium being the presentation the Harper Lee Award for Alabama's Distinguished Writer of the Year.

THE OLD COURTHOUSE MUSEUM

Your visit to Monroeville should begin on the courthouse square with a tour of the Old Courthouse Museum (31 N. Alabama Ave., Monroeville; 251-575-7433). Through photos and exhibits, you will discover personal stories about Harper Lee, known to her friends as Nelle, and others surrounding her Pulitzer Prize-winning novel, *To Kill A Mockingbird*, as well as her other novel, *Go Set A Watchman*, which was published in 2015. You will also get a glimpse into the life of Truman Capote, the famed author of the 1966 book *In Cold Blood*. Capote spent much of his childhood in Monroeville and was not only

Lee's neighbor, but the two also became close friends. Photographs of Capote and Lee can be seen in the second-floor exhibit.

To Kill a Mockingbird, which has been performed in Monroeville for more than 25 years, will take you back in time.

Visit the gift shop where you will find unique items related to Lee's novel as well as crafts and other items from the local area, such as stone-ground grits from Rikard's Mill in nearby Beatrice. While in the historic courthouse, walk up the steps to see the courtroom made world famous by the novel and movie. Feel free to move throughout the courtroom. Walk up to the balcony area to imagine scenes from the famous trial.

The old Monroeville Courthouse annually hosts performances of To Kill A Mockingbird.

See the witness chair, judge's bench and tables used by the prosecutor and defense attorney during the trial. Throughout her childhood, Harper Lee, herself, often sat in the balcony as she watched her father practice law in the very same courtroom.

Set in the 1930s in the fictional town of Maycomb, Ala., the novel tells the story of a black man named Tom Robinson who is accused of attacking a white woman and goes to trial during a time when racial discrimination was legal and culturally accepted in the South. It is also a coming-of-age story of a young girl named Scout and the imaginations of her brother Jem and her childhood friend, Dill. Locals say that the character of Dill is based upon Truman Capote.

While watching the all-local cast perform, you will develop a fondness for Robinson as well as his lawyer Atticus Finch, the father of Scout and Jem. And, you will meet characters like Arthur "Boo" Radley, a recluse and one of the novel's "mockingbirds," described by critics as "a good person injured by the evil of mankind."

The first act of the two-act play takes place at the amphitheatre on the lawn of the Courthouse Museum. Act II takes place inside the historic courtroom. Once inside the courtroom, you will see the trial unfold as Finch makes a passionate plea in Robinson's

Don't Miss This

THE ANNUAL PERFORMANCES OF *TO KILL A MOCKINGBIRD*

Plan your visit to Monroeville to coincide with the annual performances of To Kill a Mockingbird *(251-743-3386; ToKillAMockingBird.com), from mid-April through mid-May. This play, which has been performed here for more than 25 years, will take you back in time.*

Monroe County Courthouse Gift Shop

defense. The members of the jury are always selected from the audience, so you might get a shot at sitting on the jury during the second act.

A prerequisite for your visit to Monroeville is to purchase your tickets early. This is a very popular event and tickets sell fast. In addition to the main performances, which feature a VIP reception on certain nights, special performances are held for various groups, including young audiences. Group tickets (10 or more) and tickets for museum members go on sale in January. General public ticket sales begin the first of March. To purchase tickets by phone, call 251-743-3386, or purchase them online at ToKillAMockingBird.com.

WALK MONROEVILLE

On your way into Monroeville, stop by the Monroeville and Monroe County Chamber of Commerce (86 N Alabama Ave; 251-743-2879) and pick up a walking-tour guide. (You can also download the guide at VisitMonroevilleAL.com.) This 30-stop tour takes you through the center of downtown, highlighting Monroeville's Courthouse Square, which is part of its National Register Historic District. You'll see such sites as the "Celebration of Reading" bronze sculpture on the Courthouse square, a nod to the town's title of Alabama's Literary Capital, and the Truman Capote Historical Marker located on

the site of the original Faulk house, owned by Truman Capote's cousin, Jennie Faulk. The marker is virtually all that is left of Truman Capote's Monroeville childhood. Furthermore, you'll see the beautiful Queen Anne–style Hybart/Hendrix/Lewis/Brewton Home, built between 1906 and 1920, and the Pineville Road Cemetery, a combination of three cemeteries that date back to 1846.

MORE TO SEE AND DO IN MONROEVILLE

Those who like to shop will find charming Monroeville quite agreeable. The Bird's Nest gift shop, located inside the Old Courthouse Museum, has a sweet selectin of home goods, clothing, children's items, and jewelry. Be sure to make your way to the Art Room Gifts and Framery (58 N. Alabama Ave.; 251-743-2190) where you can purchase unique gifts, such as splatterware, skin-care products, candles, pottery, and season items. Roots Clothing Company (11 West Claiborne St.; (251-743-3199) offers upscale men's and women's clothing on the square. Bonehead Boots (118 Mildred St.; 251-867-4800) offers clothing, accessories, and, of course, foot ware. At Cobbwebs (879 S Alabama Ave; 251-575-5053), you'll find vintage goods as well as candles, coffee, pottery, and more. For those who love antiquing, Backroads Antiques (8 East Claiborne St.; 251-575-4725) will be a delightful find.

End your tour in downtown Monroeville with a stop at the Katherine Lee Rose Garden & War Memorial Gazebo. Located at Monroe County's new courthouse (65 N. Alabama Ave.; 251-743-2879), the garden features more than 90 different roses maintained by the garden club. The gazebo is used for weddings and other functions.

While in the Monroeville area, you may also want to visit Rikard's Mill Historical Park (4116 Highway 265 N; Beatrice; 251-789-2781) in Beatrice. The mill site is a nod to the folk traditions of grist-milling, blacksmithing and cane syrup making.

Settled among pine trees alongside Flat Creek, the park reopens each spring during the same time frame as the *To Kill a Mockingbird* performances, making it an excellent enhancement to your road trip experience. For more information on things to do and see in Monroeville, visit VisitMonroevilleAL.com or talk to the Chamber of Commerce (86 N Alabama Ave; 251-743-2879).

WHERE TO EAT

All the walking around downtown will make you hungry. Stop at the Court House Café (27 W. Claiborne St.; 251-743-3663) to refuel with sandwiches, burgers, friend pickles, and more. Close by is The Prop and Gavel (42 E. Claiborne St.; 251-575-7767), where you'll find chicken and dumplings, fish and chips, and other Southern staples. Venture to David's Catfish House (145 Hwy. 84 E; 251-575-3460) to eat your fill of shrimp, crab, fish, and more. Their catfish and cheese grits ha been named one of the 100 Dishes to Eat in Alabama Before You Die. For a sweet ending to your meal, Sweet Tooth Bakery and Deli (5 W. Claiborne St.; 251-575-7040) and Mel's Dairy Dream (216 S. Alabama St.; 251-743-2483) are calling your name.

For a complete list of area restaurants, visit www.monroecountyal.com.

WHERE TO STAY

Monroeville has several affordable hotels available for overnight lodging. Country Inn and Suites (120 Hwy. 21 S.; 251-743-3333), Mockingbird Suites (4389 S. Alabama Ave.; 251-743-3297), and Best Western Inn (4419 S. Alabama Ave.; 251-575-9999) are all located just minutes from downtown. Bed and breakfast options, such as The Loft (1594 Mexboro Road, Frisco City) in the Mexia community and the Mary Elizabeth Stallworth House in Beatrice (1197 Main Street), are short drives away.

For a complete list of area accommodations, visit www.monroecountyal.com.

ROSA PARKS, PAUL "BEAR" BRYANT AND JESSE OWENS:
A CENTENNIAL ADVENTURE

by Marilyn Jones Stamps

Rosa Parks Museum exhibit of Montgomery bus from civil rights era

What do Rosa Parks, Paul "Bear" Bryant and Jesse Owens have in common? Besides the fact that each of them has a museum named in their honor, all three of these famous Alabamians were born in 1913, and each played a role in integration.

EXPERIENCE THE STORY OF ROSA PARKS FROM TUSKEGEE TO MONTGOMERY

Rosa Parks, the daughter of a carpenter and a schoolteacher and the oldest of two children, was born in Tuskegee as Rosa Louise McCauley on Feb. 4, 1913, to James and Leona Edwards McCauley.

When you visit Parks' birthplace, you'll drive down a street named in her honor and tour a downtown museum that showcases her place in Macon County history. The centerpiece of the Tuskegee Human and Civil Rights Multicultural Center (104 S. Elm St.; 334-724-0800), founded by attorney Fred Gray who represented Parks during the Civil Rights Movement, is an exhibition of im-

portant chapters in the civil rights struggle that are often overlooked – from the story of Rosa Parks' birth to that of Samuel Younge Jr., a civil rights worker shot in cold blood in 1966 by a gas station attendant who was later found "not guilty" of his murder by an all-white jury.

Rosa moved with her family to Abbeville when she was two years old, and later to Montgomery. She did not attend public school until she was 11. It was while attending elementary school in rural Montgomery County – where school buses took white students to their school and black students walked to theirs – that she received one of her first introductions to segregation in America.

"I'd see the bus pass every day. But to me, that was a way of life; we had no choice but to accept what was the custom.

The bus was among the first ways I realized there was a black world and a white world," Parks once recalled.

Heavily influenced by the Jim Crow laws of the South, Rosa Parks became deeply concerned about freedom and justice for all people. In 1932, shortly after marrying Raymond Parks at age 19, she joined the civil rights organization known as the NAACP and went to work immediately helping to raise money for the now-famous Scottsboro Boys. She fought for justice in whatever way she could until she became the catalyst for local civil rights efforts being led by a young

minister named Martin Luther King Jr. from Atlanta.

From the seat of a Montgomery bus on Dec. 1, 1955, the 42-year-old seamstress jump-started the 381-day Montgomery Bus Boycott when she was arrested for refusing to give up her seat to white passengers. When King heard that Parks had been arrested, he organized a meeting at Dexter Avenue Baptist Church where he was pastor, and the core of the Civil Rights Movement was formed. Parks' courageous act of civil disobedience brought nationwide attention to the problem of segregation and racial discrimination in the South and spurred people from all walks of life to action.

To understand the whole of the Rosa Parks story and the Civil Rights Movement, history buffs and visitors alike should step back to the Civil War of the 1860s, which was essentially a fight over slavery, to learn about Jefferson Davis and the Confederatacy he so staunchly defended. One of the most outstanding statesmen during the first 60 years of the 19th century, Davis sacrificed everything to defend the South's position, particularly the rights of the states regarding slave ownership.

As you explore the place where both Jefferson Davis and Rosa Parks made history a century apart, you'll discover irony in the fact that the Rosa Parks Museum stands on the corner of the same street where the former

George Washington Carver Museum at Tuskegee

Don't Miss This

THE ROSA PARKS MUSEUM

The Rosa Parks Museum & Library and Children's Wing (252 Montgomery St.; 334-241-8615) is one of Montgomery's most popular attractions. It exposes important elements in the struggle for civil rights and racial equality in America and offers insight into other aspects of African-American history, including the Underground Railroad. Following a historical timeline, you'll see photos of Parks' arrest, newspaper clippings, interactive exhibits and a replica of the bus on which she was riding. You'll also learn about the court case that ended bus segregation in Alabama in 1956 and efforts that eventually led to the signing of the landmark Civil Rights Act by President Lyndon Johnson in 1964 and the Voting Rights Act the following year.

1927 Jefferson Davis Hotel now serves as a housing complex for seniors and the disabled. A mere six blocks away is the Alabama State Capitol (600 Dexter Ave.; 334-242-3935) where Davis took the office as president of the Confederacy in 1861 and where the Selma to Montgomery March (in which Rosa Parks participated) ended in 1965.

Adjacent to the Capitol is the First White House of the Confederacy (644 Washington Ave.; 334-242-1861), where Davis and his family lived from February to May 1861, while the capital was in Montgomery. Nearby are several civil rights attractions.

Rosa Parks moved to Detroit in 1957 where she continued her humanitarian efforts. She lived there until her death on Oct. 24, 2005. Her body was flown to Montgomery and taken in a horse-drawn hearse to the St. Paul African Methodist Episcopal Church. The following evening, her casket was transported to

Washington, D.C., by a bus similar to the one in which she had made her historic protest and was permitted to lie in state in the rotunda of the U.S. Capitol. This allowance made her the only woman and second African-American in history to receive such an honor.

PAUL "BEAR" BRYANT AND THE INTEGRATION OF COLLEGE FOOTBALL

From Montgomery, travel Interstate 65 north toward Birmingham and take I-20/59 for your trip to Tuscaloosa, where the legendary Paul "Bear" Bryant made history in the sports arena in more ways than one. Born Sept. 11, 1913, to William Monroe and Ida Kilgore Bryant, Paul William Bryant was raised poor in Cleveland County, Arkansas. He was the 11th of 12 children born to the couple; three others had died in infancy. His father was disabled much of his life, forcing Bryant and his siblings to work on the family farm.

Although he is best remembered as the longtime winning head coach of the University of Alabama football team, Bryant achieved many accolades prior to Crimson Tide stardom. Standing a little over six feet tall, he was a successful player on his high school

Paul W. Bryant Museum

football team in Fordyce, Ark., where he earned his nickname for supposedly wrestling a bear for $1. He attended college at the University of Alabama in the 1930s and also played football there.

Between graduating college and returning to Tuscaloosa to become head coach, Bryant completed a brief stint in the Navy in the 1940s and held several athletic positions in the late 40s and 50s.

These included serving as head coach at the University of Kentucky for eight seasons and as head coach at Texas A&M University. It was at Texas that he continued a quest he had begun earlier, which was to integrate the game of football. "We'll be the last football team in the Southwest Conference to integrate," Bryant was told by a Texas A&M official. "Well," Bryant replied, "then that's where we're going to finish in football."

Ironically, years before he took over the Alabama football team in 1958, Bryant was accused of racism for refusing to recruit black players. His response to that was the prevailing social climate would not let him do this. When asked why he came to Alabama, he replied, "Momma called. And when Momma calls, you just have to come runnin.'"

It was following the Crimson Tide's 1970 season opener against the University of Southern California team led by a black fullback named Sam Cunningham that Bryant took the ball running and convinced the administration at Alabama to allow him to recruit black players. After Cunningham rushed for 150 yards and three touchdowns in a 42-21 victory against the Tide, Bryant recruited Wilbur Jackson as Alabama's first black scholarship player. However, he could not play because he was a freshman. John Mitchell (a junior college transfer) was the first to play against Southern Cal in 1971. By 1973, one-third of the team's starters were black.

"Bear" Bryant was by far the most successful football coach of his era. During his 25-year tenure at the University of Alabama, he amassed six national championships and 13 conference championships.

When he retired in 1982, he held the record for most wins (323) as head coach in collegiate football history. Alabama's legendary and beloved coach died on January 26, 1983. One month later, he was posthumously awarded the Presidential Medal of Freedom by President Ronald Reagan.

When you arrive in Tuscaloosa, take Exit 71 and follow the signs to the campus. Park in the rear of the Paul W. Bryant Museum (300 Paul W. Bryant Drive; 205-348-4668) for a tour. Once inside, you'll walk the Hall of Honor to see the large bust of Coach Bryant surrounded by photos of each of his teams.

Various exhibits chronicle the history and tradition of Crimson Tide football from 1892 to present day. Visitors can get a glimpse inside Coach Bryant's office, see the Waterford crystal replica of his famous houndstooth hat and experience Crimson Tide moments from the broadcast booth. The museum is open seven days a week except for major holidays.

OAKVILLE, BIRTHPLACE OF AN OLYMPIC CHAMPION

Born one day after "Bear" Bryant on Sept. 12, 1913, in Oakville, near Moulton in Lawrence County, James Cleveland "Jesse" Owens was the youngest of 10 children. He was nine years old when he migrated northward with his parents Cleveland Owens and Mary Emma Fitzgerald to Ohio, taking his strong Southern accent with him. When his new teacher asked his name, he said "J.C.," but she thought he said "Jesse." The name took, and he was known as Jesse Owens for the rest of his life. Early in his life, Owens realized that he had a passion for running. He first came to national attention when he was in high school in Cleveland. When it came time to go to college, Owens was reluctant to enter because he knew he was needed to help take care of his family. After much consideration, he was recruited by Ohio State University. Although he experienced racism there, it strengthened his resolve to succeed. In 1935, while at Ohio State, he broke or equaled four world track

records in one day, setting a new long-jump record that would stand for 25 years. Owens would also experience racism overseas when he competed as a member of the 1936 U.S. Olympic team in Berlin. The black members of the squad faced the challenges not only of competition but also of Hitler's boasts of Aryan supremacy. Not knowing the word "defeat," Owens surprised Hitler (as well as many others) and won a total of four gold medals during the Olympic Games that year. As a stunned Hitler angrily left the stadium, German athletes embraced Owens as spectators chanted his name.

The gold medalist returned to America to a hero's welcome. However, discrimination at home made it hard for Owens to find suitable work. To earn money, he took exhibition jobs that pitted his athletic prowess against race horses and cars. He later held a number of paid and unpaid positions, including heading his own public relations firm in Chicago and lecturing and mentoring youth throughout much of his life. "Although I wasn't invited to shake hands with Hitler, I wasn't invited to the White House to shake hands with the President, either," Owens recalled later.

It would take 40 years for Owens to be officially recognized by the U.S. government

Images and history of Alabama's Jesse Owens at Oakville museum

for his extraordinary achievements. He was presented the Presidential Medal of Freedom by President Gerald Ford in 1976 and the Living Legend Award by President Jimmy Carter in 1979. Owens died March 31, 1980 of lung cancer. Ten years after his death, he was posthumously awarded the Congressional Gold Medal by President George Bush.

The man who rose from humble beginnings as the son of a sharecropper and the grandson of a slave in Lawrence County, Alabama became recognized as one of the most important sports figures of the 20th century. He is fondly remembered at a park and museum near Moulton in North Alabama. Through interactive exhibits, a rare film and family memorabilia, the Jesse Owens Memorial Park and Museum (7019 County Road 203, Danville; 256-974-3636) tells the story of Owens' personal triumphs as a world-class athlete and record holder that were the prelude to a career devoted to helping others.

ABOUT TUSKEGEE, MONTGOMERY, TUSCALOOSA AND OAKVILLE

Tuskegee (about 35 miles east of Montgomery) is home to historic Tuskegee University and boasts a proud heritage in its connection to people like Booker T. Washington, George Washington Carver, Rosa Parks, the Tuskegee Airmen and Lionel Richie. Montgomery is Alabama's capital city and it holds the distinction of being the birthplace of both the Civil War and the Civil Rights Movement. Located in West Alabama on the Black Warrior River, Tuscaloosa was the seat of state government from 1826-1846. Here, where the name Paul "Bear" Bryant is spoken with reverence, you'll find a proud tradition being preserved by the championship Crimson Tide football team. Oakville, near Moulton in Lawrence County, is the birthplace of Olympic gold medalist Jesse Owens and site of the state's largest Woodland ceremonial Indian mound.

ALABAMA'S HISTORIC STATE CAPITALS TOUR

by Lee Sentell

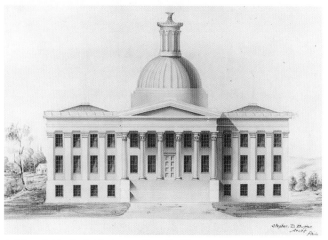

Artist's rendering of early Montgomery Capitol building.

Because of its connections to both the Civil War and the Civil Rights Movement, the Alabama State Capitol building in Montgomery is one of only a few Capitol buildings listed as a National Historic Landmark. Montgomery is also the only place in the U.S. where a foreign government was created: the Confederate States of America in 1861.

Neither the Capitol building nor the city it resides in, however, is the first to serve as the seat of government for Alabama. Before Montgomery became the capital in 1846, four other places held the honor: St. Stephens, Huntsville, Cahawba and Tuscaloosa.

WHERE TO BEGIN

Since Montgomery (334-261-1100) is the site of the current State Capitol (600 Dexter Ave.; 334-242-3935) and one of the most historic cities in the country, it is only fitting that Alabama's Historic State Capitals Tour begins here. After all, the white, Greek Revival domed building overlooking Dexter Avenue is where the Alabama Legislature met for more than a century from 1851 until 1985. It is also where Jefferson Davis was installed as president of the Confederacy in 1861 and where important chapters in the Civil Rights Movement,

led by a young preacher named Dr. Martin Luther King Jr., were written in the 1960s.

The current Capitol is Alabama's fourth purpose-built Capitol building, with the first at Cahawba (also spelled Cahaba), the second at Tuscaloosa and the last two in Montgomery. The first building in Montgomery, located where the current Capitol stands, burned after only two years. The latter one was completed in 1851, with additional wings added over the course of the following 140 years.

In 1985, when the Alabama Legislature moved to the Statehouse across the street, a renovation of the state Capitol was begun. It reopened in 1994 to welcome visitors from around the world. Upon reopening, the governor and numerous state offices moved back into the Capitol, but the Legislature remained at the Statehouse.

INSIDE THE CAPITOL

Two cantilevered staircases that connect three floors dominate the foyer. Portraits of former governors, beginning with William Wyatt Bibb, line the halls. The office of the governor is to the left in the north wing. Offices for the secretary of state and state treasurer are in the south wing.

FIRST FLOOR

The original governor's suite (1851-1912) is on the first floor. Fragments of *trompe l'oeil* ("fool the eye") painting that dates from the

1870s surround an old door opening on the right. Across the hall, the outer office of the 1851 secretary of state's suite is a museum space with antiques of the 1880s, as is the larger, inner office. Down the hall is the current governor's suite, which isn't open for tours. The room has changed little since Gov. Emmet O'Neal of Florence moved into the office in 1912. Portraits of recent governors are in the rotunda. Look up toward the dome to see eight murals painted in 1927 that depict periods of Alabama history.

SECOND FLOOR

Walk up the winding stairs to the original House and Senate chambers to see where Southern delegates gathered and debated secession and states' rights following the election of Abraham Lincoln in 1860. On Feb. 4, 1861, delegates wrote a constitution and formed the Confederate States of America, electing former U.S. Secretary of War Jefferson Davis of Mississippi president on Feb. 9. Within two months, Davis's government telegraphed a message to Confederate soldiers in South Carolina to fire on Fort Sumter, effectively starting the War Between the States.

THE HISTORIC CAPITOL STEPS

The steps of the Capitol are symbolic of two important chapters in state history: the Civil War and the Civil Rights Movement. A century after Jefferson Davis took the oath of office as president of the Confederacy, congregations in African-American churches, under the leadership of Dr. Martin Luther King Jr., were conducting peaceful protests to outlaw segregation in public facilities, restaurants, stores, transportation and schools.

It was at the foot of the Capitol steps, at the end of the Selma to Montgomery march (March 16-25, 1965), that King delivered his "How Long, Not Long" speech. Before a crowd of more than 25,000, he laid the demands of African-American Alabamians at the doorstep of Gov. George C. Wallace, proclaiming, "The end we seek is a society at peace with itself, a society that can live with its conscience. And that will be a day not of the white man, not of the black man. That will be the day of man as man." Although at least two people were killed in response to King's remarks, on Aug. 6 President Lyndon Johnson signed the Voting Rights Act of 1965.

Note: Tours of the Capitol are offered Monday through Saturday. Groups must schedule their visits in advance and enter the building through the rear entrance at all times. Individuals must also enter and exit from the rear if visiting on Saturdays.

VISIT NEARBY STATE BUILDINGS AND OTHER HISTORIC SITES

While in Montgomery, a visit to notable state buildings and other historic sites near the Capitol is a must. Adjacent to the Capitol is the First White House of the Confederacy (644 Washington Ave.; 334-242-1861), which was the executive residence of President Jefferson Davis and his family from February to May 1861.

The only church where Dr. Martin Luther King Jr. served as pastor, the Dexter Avenue King Memorial Baptist Church, is located a block from the Capitol. It offers regular tours and features a mural in the basement showing

King's legendary journey from Montgomery as the leader of the Civil Rights Movement to his death in Memphis, Tenn., on April 4, 1968.

EARLY ALABAMA CAPITALS

After visiting Montgomery, head south toward the port city of Mobile. Located 67 miles north of Mobile and bordering the west bank of Washington County's Tombigbee River is St. Stephens (251-246-6790). It was the designated temporary seat of government of the Alabama Territory from 1817-1819. Beginning in the 1790s to its decline in the 1820s, it was the site of a Spanish fort, an American fort and a trading post.

Visitor Center and Museum at St. Stephens

Today, the 200-acre Old St. Stephens Historical Park represents one of Alabama's most important archaeological sites. It not only documents the history of the once-vibrant capital town but gives insight into the people who inhabited the area for centuries.

Old St. Stephens is also a wonderful recreational destination featuring an abundance of outdoor activities, from fishing and camping to hiking, biking and bird watching. Nature lovers can take a refreshing walk through the forest, enjoying the view of dogwoods and butterflies and the sounds of migratory birds

and other animals as they go along. The park is open daily, year-round.

While in St. Stephens, a must-stop is the 1854 St. Stephens Courthouse, which is now open to the public as a visitor center and museum. The museum displays portraits of early residents and exhibits a large dugout canoe made by prehistoric Native Americans, a collection of ancient fossils from local limestone deposits and artifacts from the historic town. A gift shop offers books and other items for sale. Individuals can tour the beautifully restored courthouse and museum without appointment on Thursday from 10 a.m. to 2 p.m. Call the park to schedule visits at other times.

HUNTSVILLE: THE PATH TO STATEHOOD AND SPACE EXPLORATION

At the north end of the state is Huntsville (Huntsville/Madison County Convention & Visitors Bureau; 256-551-2230), site of Alabama's statehood and home of space exploration in America. Huntsville was the largest town in the Alabama Territory in 1819. It was here that 44 delegates gathered and wrote the first constitution granting Alabama statehood on Dec. 14, 1819.

The reconstructed Constitution Hall Park (109 Gates Ave. SE; 256-564-8100), featuring costumed tour guides, is a part of the EarlyWorks Family of Museums that also

Don't Miss This

THE MUSEUM OF ALABAMA

Alabama celebrated 200 years of statehood in 2019. However, the Alabama Department of Archives and History (624 Washington Ave.; 334-242-4435), next door to the First White House of the Confederacy, displays tools, pottery and dioramas that document more than 14,000 years of human habitation in Alabama. Located inside the Archives, the Museum of Alabama showcases the state's evolution through roughly a half-million items, including Native American, pioneer and military artifacts. Archaeological fragments, uniforms, household goods and weapons from wars fought by Alabamians fill the stately museum.

include the Historic Huntsville Depot and the EarlyWorks Children's History Museum. Collectively, the downtown museums represent the state's largest hands-on history museum complex. You can climb aboard a 46-foot river keelboat, explore an 1860s-era depot or visit the cabinet shop where delegates stood to sign the Alabama Constitution.

No trip to Huntsville would be complete without a visit to the U.S. Space & Rocket Center. Called "a national treasure resource" by the Smithsonian Institution, the center contains more than 1,500 artifacts documenting America's achievements in space exploration, from putting man on the moon to development of the space shuttle program. Children and adults alike are sure to get "lost in space" as the center is home to Space Camp and Aviation Challenge and features the Spacedome Theater, Rocket Park, an Education Training Center and more. The Mars Grill provides a great place to relax and grab a bite to eat without leaving the site.

CAHAWBA: SITE OF ALABAMA'S FIRST PERMANENT CAPITAL

Located near Selma, Cahawba (9518 Cahaba Rd., Orrville; 334-872-8058) was the state capital from 1820-1826. It was once a thriving antebellum river town but became a ghost town shortly after the Civil War, when the site had to be abandoned because of flooding and other problems.

Today, Cahawba is an important archaeological site and a place of picturesque ruins. While standing on Arch Street in Old Cahawba Archaeological Park, perhaps you can make out the fact that the concourse was originally a ditch surrounded by a palisade with a Native American mound in the center – at the site where Governor Bibb wanted to put the Capitol building. At the bluff overlooking the Alabama River, see if you can identify the foundations of Cahaba Federal Prison. It's in the same location that Bibb wanted to construct a permanent Statehouse.

Constitution Hall Park complex in Huntsville

Columns still standing at Cahawba

Crocheron Columns is all that's left of the mansion where Confederate Gen. Nathan Bedford Forrest and Union Gen. James Wilson discussed an exchange of prisoners captured during the Battle of Selma.

While at Cahawba, be sure to stop by the welcome center and museum at the southwest corner of Capitol and Ash. Inside, you can get brochures and other information and

view artifacts, photographs and treasures that reveal what life at Cahawba was like during its heyday and discover how to interpret the landscape of the site today. The park is open daily from 9 a.m. to 5 p.m. Special ghost tours are held each October.

VISIT CAPITOL PARK IN TUSCALOOSA

A growing Tuscaloosa (Tuscaloosa Tourism Department; 205-391-9200), situated on the banks of the Black Warrior River, was chosen as the capital in 1825 as a replacement for Cahawba. It served as the seat of state government from 1826 until 1846. When the capital was moved to Montgomery, the former Capitol building became the home of the Alabama Central Female College, which burned in 1923.

The only visible reminder of the old Capitol building is the stone foundation and two small columns located in Capitol Park (205-391-9200) at the intersection of University Boulevard and 28th Avenue. Today, the historic city is noted as the home of the University of Alabama and its trophy-winning Crimson Tide football team.

WHERE TO STAY, WHERE TO EAT

Visitors looking for lodging and dining options should contact the respective cities for detailed information or request an Alabama Vacation Guide at www.alabama.travel or by calling Alabama Tourism Department; 334-242-4169.

Remaining ruins at site of the Tuscaloosa capital

PIKE COUNTY:
ART, PIONEERS, PEANUT BUTTER AND MORE
by Jennifer Kornegay

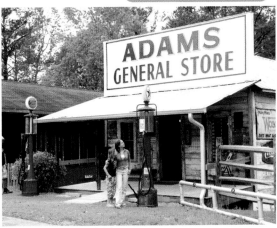

Troy's Pioneer Museum of Alabama

There's a lot to love about Pike County, which is just southeast of Alabama's capital city and includes the cities of Troy and Brundidge. Discover an emerging arts scene, the pioneering spirit of the past, a top-ranked university, antiques, an annual peanut butter party and more.

START AT THE SQUARE

At the center of downtown Troy sits a pretty little park; its grass, live oaks and flower beds mark the center of the town square. One corner is anchored by Byrd Drug Company (81 N. Court Square; 334-556-0100), which has been serving the Pike County area for decades. Byrd's old-fashioned soda fountain is still running, turning out sandwiches and ice cream treats that keep locals and visitors alike coming back year after year. Stroll around the square to find Pink Parlor (77 N. Court Square; 334-566-5525), a cute boutique; Troy Antiques (66 W. Court Square; 334-566-2601), packed with yesterday's furniture, china and more; Cotton Creek (50 E. Court Square; 334-566-1454), full of fashionable gentlemen's clothing; Glow (70 W. Court Square; 334-770-4569), offering flirty accessories, makeup and more; and First Impressions (62 Court Square; 334-566-2707), which has clothing, jewelry, and gifts. Unwind after all your shopping at Sips on the Square (60 S. Court Square; 334-770-0176), a relaxing wine bar.

TAKE IN THE TROJAN PRIDE

Troy University's lovely campus is right in the middle of town, and its presence adds a shot of energy to the city's small-town atmosphere. In 2018, *The Princeton Review* named Troy among the best colleges and universities in the Southeastern United States for the 14th straight year. Visitors are welcome to walk around the campus and check out all the university offers.

WALK BACK IN TIME

If you've ever wondered what life was like before modern technology took hold, a visit to the Pioneer Museum of Alabama (248 Hwy. 231 N.; 334-566-3597) is a must. With historic structures and 18,000 artifacts on 40 acres, the museum brings to life Alabama's rich history – from prehistoric times up to the 18th and 19th centuries – through exhibits and demonstrations, with a focus on our state's rural heritage.

The museum was founded in 1971 with this mission: "that others may learn from the past." Today, it is fulfilling its original vision with displays of farm equipment from days gone by, textile arts such as quilting and weaving, southeastern Native American arrowheads and spear tips, Civil War and WWI artifacts, an 1800s steam locomotive, a copper turpentine still, a sugar cane processing mill, a horse-drawn jail, a gristmill, 19th

century church and more.

On Saturdays and other scheduled times, you'll be treated to "hands-on history" in the four primitive log cabins on the property. You'll see interactive folk-life activities including churning butter, blacksmithing, checking the henhouse for fresh eggs, cooking cornbread and even spinning raw cotton. Before you leave, take a good look around the Hearth & Homestead Giftstore and pick up some local honey and homemade preserves or a hand-embroidered kitchen towel made by local artisans. The gift store's locally made natural soy candles capture signature Southern fragrances like magnolia and hydrangea.

HISTORY ON EXHIBIT

The past meets present at the Johnson Center for the Arts in Troy (300 E. Walnut St.; 334-670-2287). This 1911 building with its imposing brick columns was once the city's post office. It's now a spacious, airy gallery featuring rotating exhibits that showcase works from one of Alabama's most famous folk artists, Mose Tolliver or "Mose T," as well as art by local students, contemporary pottery pieces and Southern landscapes. Be sure to head down to the basement gallery at

TROYFEST

TroyFest celebrates fine arts as well as crafts in April each year. The weekend-long show draws more than 10,000 people to downtown to experience art, food, entertainment and activities for all ages. Another annual event occurs each December, when Troy's Director of Public Relations and Tourism Shelia Jackson sings a different tune in promotion of her city, putting on a popular holiday variety show called "Shelia Jackson & Company" as part of the Troy Arts Council's Christmas events.

the center where amid exposed brick walls and wood-beamed ceilings state-of-the-art lighting and gallery design give artwork a spot to truly shine. The center's annex features arts education activities, including art classes and performing arts practice sessions. Other cultural opportunities are abundant in Troy as well, thanks to the Troy Arts Council, which, in partnership with Troy University, routinely brings world-class musicians to the city. The Vienna Boys Choir and the Polish Symphony Orchestra have performed in recent years.

GO ON A TREASURE HUNT

Only eight miles from Troy is little Brundidge, which calls itself Alabama's Antique City and is a good place to begin a search for something old. Main Street boasts several antiques shops; Brundidge Florist (104 S. Main St.; 334-735-2009) is a good bet for carnival glass, china, stemware and other small antiques. Just down the road from downtown, weathered gas station and cola signs welcome you to City Antiques (108 E. Troy St.; 334-735-5164), home of "the sign man" and hundreds of vintage place-markers that earned the owner his nickname. Feel free to wander around the collection of rustic buildings and peruse the options for furniture and other antique items, but the signs advertising everything from oil and cigarettes to flour and fertilizer are the main attractions here.

On your way to Brundidge from Troy, make a stop at Adams Nut Shack and Glass

Studio (12144 Hwy. 231 S.; 334-735-2143). Homemade nut brittles are salty sweet, the homemade "half-day" suckers are just sweet and the leaded glass sun catchers in fanciful shapes make a great take-away to remember your trip.

A NIGHT AT THE THEATER

In the fall and again in spring, a dedicated group of Brundidge citizens dons costumes and takes the stage in the shell of a burned-out brick building downtown that was once City Hall. There's sawdust on the floor and laughter in the air as the audience enjoys a home-style dinner and then watches "Come Home, It's Suppertime," Alabama's official folklife play performed in the We Piddle Around Theater (102 N. Main St.; 334-344-9417). The play portrays age-old stories about hard times and good times, tales you've probably heard from your grandparents. The entire venture is a project of the Brundidge Historical Society. We Piddle Around Theater also hosts the annual Pike Piddlers Storytelling Festival held the last weekend in January, an event that brings nationally renowned storytellers to the area to spin their yarns for packed houses. The Saturday night session is held in Troy at the Trojan Center Theater.

GO NUTS AT THE PEANUT BUTTER FEST

Each October, the entire city of Brundidge gets a little nutty during the annual Peanut Butter Festival. This free harvest and heritage festival was started more than two decades ago to honor and celebrate the role peanut butter processing has played in Brundidge's past and present. The Johnston Peanut Butter Mill began operations in Brundidge in 1928, and city leaders believe it was the first company to make

peanut butter commercially in the Southeast. At the height of its production in the 1930s, it was putting out 2 million jars of peanut butter a year. A second mill, the Louis-Anne Peanut Butter Company, was also at full production during this time.

Peanut butter was made continually in Brundidge until the 1960s. Today, anywhere from 5,000 to 7,000 people each year congregate downtown to indulge in all kinds of peanut butter treats as well as participate in some interesting peanut butter projects. There's a 5K Peanut Butter Run, live entertainment, games, a George Washington Carver presentation, a peanut butter recipe contest, the Nutter Butter Parade, a street dance and, of course, plenty of peanut butter sandwiches on hand for sampling.

WHERE TO EAT

In Troy, enjoy classic Southern comforts like fried okra, field peas, macaroni and cheese, fried chicken and other meat-and-three staples at Sisters (13153 Hwy. 231; 334-566-0064), owned and operated by sisters Pat Rogers and Geraldine Umbehagen. Finish on a sweet note with banana pudding. Full of 'nana flavor and 'nilla wafers, it's good enough to have earned a spot on the "100 dishes to eat in Alabama before you die" list. Sante Fe Cattle Company (1270 Hwy. 231 S.; 334-807-8484) will fill you up with their delicious steaks, grilled shrimp, and baked potatoes. This small-town Alabama establishment serves Texas-size portions. Don't miss the barbecue, ribs, baked beans, and potato salad and Hook's BBQ (103 Hwy. 231; 334-808-8008).

WHERE TO STAY

The Hampton Inn (103 Troy Plaza Loop; 334-807-5900) and Best Western Inn (100 Hunter's Mountain Pkwy; 334-566-1585) are comfortable hotels to stay in that place you close to downtown Troy. For other accommodation recommendations, contact the City of Troy Office of Public Relations and Tourism at 334-670-2283.

Performers in Brundidge's official state folklife play "Come Home, It's Suppertime."

SELMA:
CIVIL WAR HISTORY IN THE RE-MAKING
by Marilyn Jones Stamps

Sturdivant Hall is one of Selma's fine old homes of the 1800s.

The 1820s town of Selma, situated on the banks of the Alabama River in west-central Alabama, is a place where the past reaches out to you like the branches of the town's moss-draped trees. And part of that past is Selma's role in the War Between the States (1861-1865).

During the war, Selma produced a variety of munitions and weapons for the Confederate armed forces as well as warships that included the CSS *Tennessee* and the CSS *Tuscaloosa*. The town also boasted a large workforce and was connected to other key points in the Confederacy by rail, which enhanced Selma's importance.

This road trip will take you into the heart of Alabama's Black Belt, where you can learn more about Selma's role in the Civil War. You can also stroll through a burial ground where some notable Civil War soldiers are buried, and see the remnants of the mighty CSS *Tennessee*.

BACKGROUND TO THE BATTLE

Selma's location on the navigable Alabama River, far inland from the coast, and its close proximity to furnaces in central Alabama put it in a strategic position for serving the Southern effort through much of the war. This also made the town a prime target for Union raids during the latter part of the war.

On March 30, 1865, Union Gen. James H. Wilson sent Brig. Gen. John T. Croxton's brigade to destroy all Confederate property at Tuscaloosa, approximately an hour and a half from Selma. After capturing a Confederate courier, whose messages from defender Nathan Bedford Forrest described the strength and disposition of his forces, Wilson

sent another brigade to destroy the bridge across the Cahaba River at Centreville. This hindered Forrest from obtaining reinforcement, and ultimately began a running fight that did not end until after the fall of Selma on April 2, 1865. On that fateful day, the Union rounded up hundreds of prisoners, including Gen. Forrest. However, Confederate and Union soldiers continued to fight in every direction, all the way down to the Alabama River near the mouth of Valley Creek (where the present-day Battle of Selma Reenactment is held).

In the dark of night, Union soldiers looted the city while many businesses and private residences were burned. After spending the next week destroying the arsenal and naval foundry, they left Selma and headed to Montgomery and on to Columbus and Macon, Ga., and ultimately to the end of the war.

By the time Selma's Civil War saga had ended, Wilson had captured 2,700 Confederate prisoners and the city of Selma, with only 46 of his men killed and 300 wounded. Although Forrest and a few of his comrades escaped, the most feared Southern commander and "the man that had never lost a battle" at last had been beaten.

The old Selma Depot is a museum of artifacts.

Be sure to visit the Bienville Monument, at the intersection of Lauderdale St. and Water Ave., which was erected in 1932 by the National Society of Colonial Dames of America in honor of John Baptiste Le Moyne Sieur De Bienville. Selma, once called Écor Bienville, was originally named for this French explorer to the area. At Heritage Village, across the street form Sturdivant Hall and at the corner of Mabry St. and McLeod Ave., you can tour a law office, doctor's office, servants' quarters, and a pigeon house, all from the 1800s. Don't miss the 1912 Jackson Home Historical site (1416 Lapsley Ave.; 404-792-0666), where world leaders resided while planning the Selma to Montgomery March in late 1964 until April of 1965. Tour the home and view artifacts of the American Voting Rights Movement. The Selma Art Guild Gallery (508 Selma Ave.; 334-874-9017) offers a chance to view the work of local artists inside a turn-of-the-century cottage. The gallery is open Friday through Saturday from noon to 4 p.m. For a place to swim, hike, fish, and camp, visit Paul M. Grist State Park (1546 Grist Road; 334-872-5246). The park is open daily from 7 a.m. until sunset, and admission is charged.

OTHER SITES IN HISTORIC SELMA

To learn more about the history of Selma and all there is to see and do in the area, stop at the Selma Chamber of Commerce and Tourism Information (912 Selma Ave.; 800-457-3562). Their hours are M-F 8:30 a.m. to 4:30 p.m. You can pick up brochures on each

of Selma's museums and select from five self-guided tours. The Selma Welcome Center is open Monday through Friday, 10 a.m.-4 p.m., and on Saturday, 11 a.m.–3 p.m.

Visit the Old Depot Museum (4 Martin Luther King Jr. St.; 334-874-2197). This interpretive history museum, located in the old L&N Railroad Depot at the foot of historic Water Avenue, features a fine collection of artifacts and memorabilia depicting life in Selma and Dallas County from 1820 to the present. The museum is open Monday through Friday, 10 a.m.–4 p.m.

The 1840s building housing the Vaughan-Smitherman Museum (109 Union St.; 334-874-2174) allows visitors to view a wonderful collection of Civil War memorabilia and antiques. Over the years, the building has served as a school, a Confederate hospital, the Freedman's Bureau Hospital (Selma's first African-American hospital), the Dallas County Courthouse, a military school and the Vaughan Memorial Hospital. Now as a museum, it depicts Selma's history from its founding until the 1960s. The museum is open Tuesday through Saturday, 9 a.m.–4 p.m.

Old Live Oak Cemetery (110 W. Dallas Avenue; 334-874-2160) serves as the resting place for more than 8,000 people, including two of the most famous Confederates of the Civil War: William J. Hardee, and Capt. Catesby Ap Roger Jones. Hardee was corp commander of the Army of Tennessee, former commandant of West Point and author of Rifle and Light Infantry Tactics. His funeral was reported to be the largest ever held in Selma.

Jones commanded the CSS *Virginia* (the *Merrimack*) in its battle with the USS *Monitor* at Hampton Roads, Va., the world's first modern naval battle. Jones also commanded the Confederate naval ordnance works that built the Brooke rifle for the CSS *Tennessee.*

Among other notables buried at Old Live Oak are Elodie Todd Dawson, staunch Confederate supporter and sister-in-law to Abraham Lincoln; Frances John Hobbs, well-known suffragist who sewed the most valuable treasures from her jeweler husband's shop into her petticoats, saving them from Union Army looters; Selma's founder, William Rufus King, who was elected vice president of the United States; and Edmund Winston Pettus, a Confederate general for whom Selma's historic bridge is named.

Old Depot Museum

THE HISTORIC ST. JAMES HOTEL

Make your reservations for the weekend at the historic St. James Hotel (1200 Water Ave.; 334-872-3234). Built in 1837 and known originally as the Brantley Hotel, this classic structure has overlooked the scenic Alabama River in Selma for more than 150 years.

During the Civil War, the hotel was occupied by Union troops, but while the occupying army burned much of the city, the St. James and other structures on Water Avenue were spared. Following the war, Benjamin Sterling Turner, the first African-American ever elected to the United States Congress, operated the hotel.

In 1892, the St. James fell upon hard times

and ceased operations. During its period of vacancy, ghosts, including those of Jesse James and his girlfriend Lucinda, are said to have taken up residence here. In later years, the community galvanized to save its beloved landmark, prompting the restoration of the antebellum gem in 1997. Today, the St. James showcases a blend of classic and contemporary sophistication.

SELMA'S FAMED IRONCLAD WARSHIP

Before departing the area, be sure to stop by the Selma City Hall (222 Broad Street). On the lawn, you'll see one of the nation's unique military artifacts – the stern pivot gun of the famed CSS *Tennessee.* Manufactured in Selma and weighing 15,300 pounds and with a range of 4.5 miles, the Tennessee gained undying fame in the South when it tackled an entire Union fleet during the Battle of Mobile Bay on August 5, 1864.

WHERE TO STAY

Lodging accommodations in Selma include Hampton Inn (2200 W. Highland Ave.; 334-876-9995) and Holiday Inn Express Hotel and Suites (2000 Lincoln Way; 334-874-1000). For local charm, look for the McCleod cottage on Airbnb.com. The cottage is located in Selma's Old Town district, across the street from the Sturdivant Hall, and in a neighborhood with pre-Civil War era houses. Or check for Airbnb openings in the Woolworth Lofts, in the renovated 110-year-old Woolworth Building in the historic district.

WHERE TO EAT

Tally Ho (509 Magnum Ave.; 334-872-1390) has been a popular destination for Oyster Royale, seafood gumbo, and chicken parmesan as well as quality service for 60 years. With exposed beams and log walls, the atmosphere is decidedly English pub meets log cabin. For a cup of coffee and light lunch fare, visit The Coffee Shoppe (308 Broad St.; 334-878-2739)."

GEE'S BEND:
PASTIMES TO PATCHWORK
by Erin Bass and Marilyn Jones Stamps

Perhaps you've read about the women from Gee's Bend in rural Wilcox County, who have been piecing together some of the world's most beautiful patchwork quilts and passing their skills down for generations. The Gee's Bend Pastimes to Patchwork Tour will take you to the hidden treasures of Alabama's Black Belt region and to the little hamlet at the bend in the Alabama River where the story of the Gee's Bend Quilters began.

THE GEE'S BEND QUILTERS

Surrounded on three sides by water and located in a bend of the Alabama River, Gee's Bend is accessible by ferry from Camden and County Road 29 from Alberta. This area, located in the Black Belt region of Alabama, was founded by the wealthy Gee family of North Carolina in the early 1800s, and the land sold to Mark Pettway in 1845. Joseph Gee brought several slaves with him to Alabama that he later sold with his land. After the Civil War, the freed slaves took the name Pettway and founded their own all-black, isolated community.

About a century later in the mid-1960s, the Freedom Quilting Bee , a quilting collective made up of women of Alberta and Gee's Bend, was founded as an offshoot of the Civil Rights Movement to foster community development by selling crafts. At that time, residents of the area also began taking the ferry across the river to Camden, which was only about seven miles away by water, to try and register to vote. Ferry service was eliminated in 1962 to halt this effort, and service did not resume for 44 years. Lack of a ferry and the subsequent hour's drive to Camden contributed to Gee's Bend remaining isolated and untouched by the outside world.

The story goes that art collector William Arnett, founder and chief curator of the Atlanta-based company, Tinwood, came

across a photograph of one of the quilts while working on a history of African-American vernacular art. He set out to find the quilt and its maker, and arrived in Gee's Bend.

The following year, the Gee's Bend Quilters Collective was founded. There are several good photo books on Gee's Bend, including those under the Tinwood label that can be ordered through online booksellers.

Gee's Bend quilts at Camden's Black Belt Treasures

Despite the isolation of the area, the Collective managed to capture the attention of fashion designers in New York and inspired a nationwide revival of interest in patchwork quilting. In 1997, in recognition of quilting as a unique art form, the Alabama Legislature voted to name the Pine Burr Quilt as the official state quilt of Alabama. The Pine Burr quilt pattern, boasting an intricate, three-dimensional design, has deep roots in the African-American community, particularly among the women of Gee's Bend. Lorretta Pettway Bennett, who created a Pine Burr quilt that she later donated to the state archives, learned how to make the quilt pattern from her mother Quinnie Pettway, a Gee's Bend quilter.

In 2002, the Museum of Fine Arts in Houston, Texas, presented an exhibition of 70 quilts from Gee's Bend that propelled the handcraft activity and the quilters to new heights in the world of art.

With an advance reservation, an organized tour group can request singing as a part of the quilting tour package and also arrange to have a sit-down meal at the Quilt Collective or at the Ferry Terminal. Feel free to engage quilters like Tinnie Pettway in a conversation about the history of the area and how the Gee's Bend Pettways got their name. Tinnie will also gladly share poems from her book

of personal remembrances about growing up in Gee's Bend. To plan a visit to Gee's Bend or the greater Wilcox County area, contact the Black Belt Treasures Cultural Arts Center (209 Claiborne Street, Camden; 334-682-9878). This non-profit organization exists to highlight and promote the wealth of artistic talent and heritage crafts in Alabama's Black Belt region. It represents more than 450 artists, such as painters, sculptors, potters, basketweavers, quilters, and woodworkers and offers a variety of community programs, including visual arts classes, a book club, an art gallery, and school outreach through their Teaching Artists program. Located next door to Gee's Bend, the organization also functions as a travel agency for its legendary neighbor, booking and leading on-site tours. Before visiting Gee's Bend, you may want to watch *The Quiltmakers of Gee's Bend* PBS documentary to familiarize yourself with the artisan community.

OTHER TREASURES OF THE BLACK BELT

After spending the day with the quilters in Gee's Bend, head to Camden. If you plan to depart the area via the ferry, be sure to check departure times. If you opt to drive by way of Alberta, plan to leave Gee's Bend before dark as there are no street lights and some of the roads may hit a dead end without warning. The Gee's Bend Ferry runs seven days a week from 6:40 a.m. to 5:00 p.m. Prices range from $2-$10 depending on vehicle type.

Leaving Gee's Bend by ferry will give you an opportunity to enjoy a portion of the Alabama Scenic River Trail that runs through southwest Alabama. The trail begins near the Alabama/Georgia line near Cedar Bluff and winds its way down to Mobile. It represents the nation's longest one-state river trail system.

While in Camden, peek into history at local attractions like the Dale Masonic Lodge, Wilcox Female Institute and the Wilcox County Courthouse, all in the National Register Wilcox County Historic District. The area follows an irregular pattern along Broad Street, which makes for an interesting walking tour of downtown Camden. The Alabama Bass Trail runs through nearby Roland Cooper State Park (285 Deer Run Drive; 334-682-4838) and offers a nine-hole golf course, campground, boat rental, and picnic area. Some of the attractions are open by appointment only, so contact the Wilcox Area Chamber of Commerce (334-682-4929) prior to your visit.

WHEN TO VISIT

A good time to visit Gee's Bend is during annual events like the May Day Festival and

performances of the Gee's Bend Play. Held at the beginning of May each year in a big open area not far from the old Boykin Mercantile Store and the post office, the festival includes quilting, along with other crafts, food, a parade, music and the maypole dance. The play, based on the true story of the women of Gee's Bend and their quilts and written by Elyzabeth Gregory Wilder, normally takes

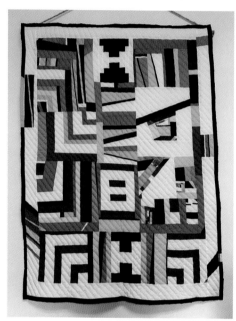

place in September and stars an all-local cast, several of them Pettways.

Another great time to visit is in the last days of April when the Hog Wild for Art Festival takes place in downtown Camden. This event

is hosted by the Black Belt Treasures Cultural Arts Center (334-682-9878) and the Wilcox Area Chamber of Commerce (334-682-4929) and includes an annual barbecue cook-off, arts and crafts vendors, live entertainment, kids activities, and food.

WHERE TO STAY

Currently, there are no hotels in Gee's Bend. Roland Cooper State Park in Camden is the closest place to stay and does have five two-bedroom cabins that start around $90 a night, four "tiny house" cabins that have one to two bedrooms and can be rented by the day, week or month, and 47 campsites. Camden has the Southern Inn Motel & Restaurant (40 Camden Bypass; 334-682-4148) and American Inn (39 Camden Bypass; 334-682-4555). For historical atmosphere and loads of charm, choose to say at the Liberty Hall Bed and Breakfast (627 Highway 221; 334-412-3513), a 1950s Greek revival plantation home. Liberty Hall is available to overnight guests by reservation only and is also open for tours by reservation only for $7.00 per person.

WHERE TO EAT

For those wanting a quick bite to eat, Keitsha's (13181 County Road 29; 334-573-2007) is the only restaurant in Gee's Bend, serving sandwiches, salads and chicken fingers.

Don't Miss This

THE GEE'S BEND QUILT MURAL TRAIL

Ferry service was restored in West Alabama in 2006, which reconnected the communities of Camden and Gee's Bend, and a Quilt Mural Trail was erected in 2008. The Gee's Bend Quilt Mural Trail begins at the Freedom Quilting Bee in Alberta with Patty Ann Williams' "Medallion with Checkerboard Center" quilt. Next, keep an eye out for "Blocks and Strips" by Annie Mae Young, then "Pig in a Pen" by Minnie Sue Coleman.

Follow the trail to the ferry, the Quilters Collective and an old school. Although they are now world famous, the women of Gee's Bend still hone and teach their craft daily at the Quilters Collective at the Boykin Nutrition Center (14570 County Road 29, Boykin; 334-573-2606), and their little wood frame houses dot the rural community. For those "Housetop" pattern fans, there are two on the trail: Lottie Mooney's "Housetop – Four Blocks," or "Half-Log Cabin," and Mary Lee Bendolph's "Housetop" variation. Altogether, there are 10 murals on the trail located at or near the homes of many of the original quilters

like Bendolph, who was the subject of a 1999 Pulitzer Prize-winning Los Angeles Times article.

Anyone is welcome to visit the Quilt Collective, purchase a quilt and even sew a square or two. The quilters meet at the center on certain days but they do not have regular hours, so be sure and call ahead when planning your trip. They will gladly meet you at the center and will even give you tips on making your own quilt. In addition to the Collective, quilting by local women can be seen most days at the Gee's Bend Ferry Terminal and Welcome center.

ABBEVILLE:
YATTA ABBA AND YELLA FELLA
by Marilyn Jones Stamps

Abbeville, a small town tucked away in the southeastern corner of Alabama since 1823, was shrinking into obscurity. Thanks in part to the commitment and passion of a man you have seen on television many times, it is being revitalized. Jimmy Rane, the big guy wearing the bright yellow hat and cowboy boots in TV commercials, known as the "Yella Fella," headed up a posse of business leaders dedicated to saving their hometown. The changes they've made are quite striking.

As other merchants and citizens worked to restore Abbeville's small-town charm, Rane focused his attention on turning an old Standard Oil Filling Station into office space for his company, Great Southern Wood Preserving, Inc. He also made a 1950s-style restaurant named Huggin' Molly's a local mainstay and gave many downtown buildings a facelift.

Each April, and at various other times during the year, you can follow the antics of the Yella Fella. You can also meet a "hugging ghost," see the former home of a civil rights pioneer, and discover the history and heritage of the place Native Americans called "Yatta Abba," meaning "a grove of dogwood trees."

FILL 'ER UP (OR NOT) AT THE OLD STANDARD OIL FILLING STATION

Probably one of the first sites you'll reach is the Old Standard Oil Filling Station on Washington Street. You can't get gas here nor can you tour the interior of the building. It houses some of the Yella Fella's company offices. You can, however, pull in and view the exterior, filling up on a slice of Americana when you do.

Downtown Abbeville is where you will see much of the handiwork of Rane. He has lovingly restored many of the storefronts and office buildings, including the facade of the Archie Theater where he used to watch western movies on Saturday afternoons. As the founder and CEO of the world's leading producer of pressure-treated lumber products, Rane never minds slipping into his whimsical Yella Fella cowboy character to promote the history of Abbeville and bring vivid memories to life for a new generation of residents and visitors.

In addition to enjoying a variety of activities, you're invited to take a trip through time at the Pioneer Cemetery located behind First Baptist Church at 100 Columbia Rd. Re-enactors stationed at the cemetery will entertain you with stories of the area's early settlers, prominent families and others. You'll meet brigadier gen-

Abbeville's most famous citizen, Jimmy Rane, is easily recognized by his company's treated wood commercials.

ABOUT ABBEVILLE

Abbeville is the county seat of Henry County. It is located in southeastern Alabama in the Wiregrass region and, according to local history, was known as Yatta Abba by the Creek inhabitants. Abbie Creek runs through the town. Future Alabama governor William Calvin Oates established a law practice in the town in 1859.

During the Civil War, he raised a company of Abbeville men that fought at Little Round Top in the Battle of Gettysburg. Today, Abbeville is called "the City of Dogwoods" because they still bloom along Abbie Creek and are abundant in many other parts of the city.

erals and war veterans, and even learn about Abbeville's own Cinderella. A burial plot at the cemetery bears the name of one Cinderella Phoebe Hutto Epsy. Of course, it's not a memorial to the Cinderella from the fairytale, but the mere thought of having perhaps the only burial site dedicated to a Cinderella gives Abbeville boasting rights.

The stories from the grave are endless. One marker bears the names of seven children all in one grave. Another tells of a local citizen who lived to be 110 years old, and yet another remembers Abbeville's real Huggin' Molly.

Visitors are invited to take a guided tour to see historic homes and churches in the area or walk along lamp-lit sidewalks, where classics from the Big Band era flow from local storefronts and beckon you to explore even more of beautiful and historic Abbeville. On your journey, you'll discover retail establishments offering great discounts and diverse shopping opportunities, such as Town Square Shoppes and Dogwood Abbey's. You'll also get to meet wonderful people who value friendships and family traditions and are always willing to give you a glimpse of life in their hometown.

If you have the time, consider adding Dothan or Eufaula to your Yatta Abba Yella Fella tour experience. You just might see the Yella Fella anywhere, as he is well known throughout the Wiregrass region of Alabama and each of these cities is only about a 30-minute drive from Abbeville.

UNIQUE DINING

While in Abbeville, be sure to visit Huggin' Molly's Restaurant (129 Kirkland St.; 334-585-7000;). Legend has it that the town was once inhabited by a friendly ghost named Molly. She was supposedly seven feet tall and "as big around as a bale of cotton." As told by the Yella Fella, Molly would walk the city streets at night and if she saw you, she'd chase you down, scream in your ear and give you a huge hug – hence, the name.

You can't always count on a big hug from Molly, but what locals and visitors have come to count on is getting a cherry Coke, some Molly's Fingers and a heaping helping of home fries at the restaurant named in her

Huggin' Molly's offers up the nostalgia of an old soda fountain, great food and a folklore tale of Abbeville's most famous hugger.

lurking about, and if it's left up to Jimmy Rane, you might even spot the Yella Fella dining at the table next to you. Huggin' Molly's is open daily for lunch and for dinner Thursday through Saturday.

MORE TO EXPLORE IN ABBEVILLE

Before leaving Abbeville, be sure to pull to the side of the road to read and photograph the historic marker (one mile west of U.S.

Abbeville shortly after she was born on Feb. 4, 1913. In 1915, she and her mother moved to Pine Level. She married Raymond Parks in 1932. In 1943, she joined her husband as a member of the NAACP. Parks championed her first cause for civil rights when she returned to Abbeville and Henry County in 1944 to investigate the alleged rape and abduction at gunpoint of a young African-American woman by seven white men.

Today, a small rundown wooden house with a battered tin roof in the middle of Abbeville farmland is all that remains of the place that cradled Parks as a baby. The roadside marker, however, serves as a testament to the genteel woman who was not afraid to fight the giants of racism and prejudice in the South. In taking on the case of injustice in Abbeville, Parks was already in the process of launching a movement that would ultimately change the world.

Don't Miss This

EXPERIENCE A YATTA ABBA WEEKEND

Abbeville is enjoyable anytime of the year. However, Yatta Abba weekend in late April provides an even greater reason to visit. During this special spring event, you can spend time with area artists and craftsmen, hear live music in various venues, take a driving or walking tour of historic homes and churches (held as part of the Yatta Abba experience and the statewide Saturday Walking Tours), see a parade of antique vehicles and sample food provided by local restaurants, all while strolling through the beautiful and historic area nicknamed "the City of Dogwoods."

honor. An old-timey soda fountain beckons guests to sit, sip and enjoy. On any given day, you could probably feel the spirit of Molly

GETTING THERE

Abbeville is approximately two hours (89 miles) from Alabama's capital city of Montgomery. From Montgomery, take U.S. 231 South through Troy. In Brundidge, turn left on AL Hwy. 10 and continue to Abbeville.

Hwy. 431 on AL Hwy. 10;) near the farmstead where Rosa Parks lived as child. While many people tend to connect Montgomery with the 42-year-old seamstress who made history as the "Mother of the Civil Rights Movement in America," few realize that the little girl born Rosa Louise McCauley in Tuskegee spent a short part of her childhood in Henry County.

Parks moved with her family to her grandparents' 260-acre farm on the outskirts of

WHERE TO STAY

For overnight accommodations, the GuestHouse Abbeville (1237 U.S. Hwy. 431 S.; 334-585-5060;) provides reasonable accommodations for those wishing to experience everything there is to see and do in the local area. For other options, Eufaula boasts beautiful Lakepoint Resort State Park Lodge, several hotels and the Baker Street Bed and Breakfast (343 N Eufaula Ave.; 334-695-6870). Many hotel accommodations are located in Dothan, about 30 miles away.

TUSKEGEE:
LIONEL RICHIE'S HOMETOWN
by Marilyn Jones Stamps

On this road trip, you can experience centuries of history —
from the time Native Americans occupied the area to settlement by
European Americans and the many contributions of African-
Americans at the Tuskegee History Center discover a treasure-trove of
souvenirs and local history on the downtown square, learn about the
importance of Tuskegee University and the Tuskegee Airmen, and take
a walk through nature inside the Tuskegee National Forest. Whatever
your interest, there are reasons aplenty to visit historic Tuskegee.

A RICH HISTORY

Formed from land once claimed by the Creek tribe, the Alabama
Legislature created Macon County on Dec. 18, 1832, naming it for
Nathaniel Macon, a Revolutionary War soldier and long-serving political leader from North Carolina. The town of Tuskegee was founded
and laid out in 1833 by Gen. Thomas S. Woodward, who fought in the
Creek wars under Gen. Andrew Jackson. Woodward selected Tuskegee
as the county seat and also built the first home in the town. Tuskegee
was officially incorporated in 1843. Since that time, it has been the site of
major achievements by African-Americans in fields ranging from education, science and aviation to art, literature, music and civil rights.

WHERE TO BEGIN

A good place to begin your tour is at the Tuskegee History Center
(104 S. Elm St.; 334-724-0800). In addition to providing visitors with
information on things to see and do in the area, this walk-through-
time museum, founded by noted civil rights lawyer Fred Gray, offers a
historical overview of Tuskegee and Macon County. Exhibits showcase
Macon County's Native and European heritage as well as highlight
Tuskegee's role in the Civil Rights Movement, the impact of the infamous Tuskegee Syphilis Study and the contributions of local citizens
to state and national history.

As you enter the museum, you will get a brief introduction to the
work of contemporary artist and sculptor Ronald Scott McDowell,
whose distinctive figures of a Native American, European American
and an African-American grace the entryway. The California native
spent a considerable amount of time in Tuskegee and has documented
many of its legends through his artwork. A gift shop to the right of the
entrance showcases some of his work as well as features items by local
artisans, including caps, T-shirts, books and jewelry.

Strolling through the museum's interactive exhibits, you'll find
yourself in awe over the amount of civil rights history associated with

Famed statue of Tuskegee's Booker T. Washington lifting the veil of ignorance

Don't Miss This

THE VEIL OF IGNORANCE MONUMENT

After touring the Carver Museum, walk down the sidewalk and
cross the street to see the monument depicting Booker T. Washington lifting the veil of ignorance from the African-American race.
Continue down Booker T. Washington Boulevard to see the historic
gravesites of both Washington and Carver and the historic Tuskegee
Chapel next door with its "singing windows." The Tuskegee Chapel
has been described as one of the most remarkable structures designed for any college in the United States and abroad.

After leaving the chapel, return to your car and exit the Kellogg Center parking deck, turning left onto Booker T. Washington
Boulevard. Continue through the main gates and turn left onto
West Montgomery Road for a tour of The Oaks. Inside the house
museum, you'll learn about Washington's philosophy on education
and self-help and view the surroundings that characterized
his family life.

Tuskegee. Meet civil rights activists Rosa Parks who was born in Tuskegee as Rosa Louise McCauley on Feb. 4, 1913. Discover the exploits of the Tuskegee Airmen who overcame segregation and stereotypical barriers as fighter pilots during World War II, and consider the Tuskegee Syphilis Study, an experiment conducted by the U.S. government and Tuskegee Institute from 1932 to 1972 on black males in and around Tuskegee without their consent. The experiment ended only after a media exposé prompted a national outcry.

Following the museum's timeline, you'll learn about landmark civil rights cases such as Gomillion v. Lightfoot (1958) and Lee v. Macon County (1963), which guaranteed voting rights and equal education for blacks. Both of these cases took place in Tuskegee. And you will hear the tragic story of Tuskegee native Samuel Younge Jr. (1944-1966), who was the first African-American student activist killed during the Civil Rights Movement. His shooting death at a Macon County service station became a rallying point for opponents of racial inequality during the late 1960s.

Civil rights installations at the center are highlighted by a mobile phone tour that is certain to enhance your visit. At the end of the tour, you will have an opportunity to tell your own story and leave it as a recorded legacy for future generations. Hours are seasonal, so be sure to call ahead when planning your visit.

A HISTORIC DOWNTOWN COURTHOUSE AND SQUARE

Another good reason to visit Tuskegee is the historic downtown area. While driving or walking downtown, it's impossible to miss the Macon County Courthouse and the Historic Courthouse Square featuring the monument of a Confederate soldier standing gallantly in the midst of it. The first courthouse, a log cabin, was built in 1833 and located in the

center of the square. The current courthouse (the third one built) was begun in 1905 and completed in 1906.

Sporting a Richardsonian Romanesque-style design with a brick façade and granite trim, this handsome facility is the only courthouse in Alabama that has gargoyles at each corner of its clock tower. It was placed on the National Register of Historic Places on Nov. 17, 1978, and still serves as the seat of government for Macon County.

EDUCATIONAL EXCELLENCE AND THE TUSKEGEE INSTITUTE NATIONAL HISTORIC SITE

From the downtown square, head to Tuskegee University, an institution many consider the heart and soul of African-American education in America. To get there from the square, take Martin Luther King Jr. Hwy. (Old U.S. Highway 80) to Fonville Street and turn right. Continue on Fonville until it dead ends. Turn left onto West Montgomery Road (locals call it Old Montgomery Road) and follow it to the stoplight. Turn right into the main gates of the campus onto Booker T. Washington Boulevard.

Tuskegee Normal School for Colored Teachers, later called Tuskegee Institute and now Tuskegee University, was founded in 1881 for the expansion of higher education for African-Americans following the Civil War. In that year, 25-year-old Booker T. Washington of Hampton, Va., came to Tuskegee to assist with development of the school. Washington arrived in Alabama and started building Tuskegee Institute, both in reputation and literally brick by brick from the confines of a small church and a little shack. He recruited, among others, George

Washington Carver, a research scientist, botanist and inventor whose innovations in agriculture expanded Tuskegee's standing throughout the country.

Since its founding, Tuskegee University has been at the center of excellence in a variety of fields, from science, agriculture and aviation to literature, sports and music. Two of America's foremost writers – Ralph Ellison and Albert Murray – were products of Tuskegee. The first African-American fighter pilots were trained at Tuskegee University's Moton Field in 1940. In addition, the nation's first African-American four-star general and one of the original Tuskegee Airmen, Daniel "Chappie" James, was a 1942 graduate of the university, as were nationally syndicated radio talk show host Tom Joyner, who graduated in 1970, and Lionel Richie, who graduated in 1974. The Tuskegee University Golden Tigers have also earned the school honors. The university boasts America's "winningest" football team among historically black colleges and universities.

The historic campus is a good place to end

First-time visitors to the Tuskegee History Center might be surprised when they arrive and are welcomed by historical greeters who are dressed as noted Alabamians such as Zora Neale Hurston (author of Their Eyes Were Watching God*), who was born in nearby Notasulga in 1891; Mrs. Booker T. Washington; or jazz musician Teddy Wilson, who studied piano and violin at Tuskegee Institute. Wilson changed the color of music when he joined the Benny Goodman Trio in 1935 and became the first black musician to perform publicly with a previously all-white jazz group. Note: The greeters are not always available, but they can be pre-arranged for groups.*

the day as it is part of the Tuskegee Institute National Historic Site (334-727-3200). Operated by the National Park Service, the site also includes the George Washington Carver Museum and former university President Booker T. Washington's historic home, known as The Oaks. Next to the Carver Museum, you'll find the beautiful Kellogg Hotel & Conference Center (334-727-3000)

The museum at the Tuskegee Airmen National Historic Site takes you back to the 1940s.

where you can enjoy breakfast, lunch and dinner at Dorothy's Restaurant and great overnight lodging.

For your campus and museum tour, you'll want to go past the front of the hotel and look for the entrance that leads to the hotel's parking deck. From the top floor of the parking deck, walk through the breezeway that faces the back of the Carver Museum. Inside the museum, exhibits showcase the history of Tuskegee Institute as well as Carver's empirical research with the peanut, the sweet potato, soybeans and other crops.

A VISIT TO THE TUSKEGEE AIRMEN NATIONAL HISTORIC SITE

Get up early the next morning and head to the Tuskegee Airmen National Historic Site, which provides another excellent reason for a visit. The museum in Hangar #1 is open open Monday through Saturday and consists of and consists of two main visitor areas. The orientation room includes a four-minute video that introduces you to the Tuskegee

Airmen, the struggles of those who overcame adversity to become decorated fighter pilots during World War II.

The museum area houses two World War II-era training aircraft and takes you on a journey back to the 1940s through a recreation of some of the sights and sounds of Moton Field during its heyday. Individual and group tours are welcomed; however, groups of 10 or more are asked to call 334-724-0922 one to two weeks in advance of their planned visit to make a reservation.

A scenic overlook is available at the site for picnicking and relaxing. From there you can enjoy a great view of the historic core where original buildings from the 1940s bear witness to a bygone era. More than 20 wayside exhibits are also strategically placed throughout the site to allow you to take a leisurely stroll through Tuskegee Airmen history while collecting tidbits of trivia.

ABOUT TUSKEGEE

Tuskegee, named for a tribal town of the Creeks, is the county seat of Macon County and has a population of about 10,000. Tuskegee and Tuskegee University have been important sites in various stages of African-American history, from science and aeronautics to medicine, literature, sports and music. The names Booker T. Washington, George Washington Carver, Rosa Parks, the Tuskegee Airmen, Fred Gray and Lionel Richie and the Commodores, are all associated with this historic town.

THE TUSKEGEE NATIONAL FOREST

Offering camping, hiking, horseback riding and scenic nature walks, the Tuskegee National Forest (Tuskegee Ranger District: 125 National Forest Rd. 949; 334-727-2652) is a must-stop for any visitor. Included in the forest is the scenic Bartram Trail, which was the first trail in Alabama to be designated a National Recreation Trail. It runs through the forest for about 8.5 miles, passing through various types of forest and wildlife habitat.

When R&B and pop singer/songwriter/producer Lionel Richie named his album "Tuskegee" after his hometown, it cemented the idea that no matter where you go in the world, you can always come home. Visitors to Tuskegee, located in Macon County in east-central Alabama, will discover a myriad of reasons why Richie is proud to call the small town where he grew up "home."

DOTHAN:
HEART OF ALABAMA'S WIREGRASS
by Marilyn Jones Stamps

Dothan is an ideal place for a fun and affordable family vacation. Symbols of a bygone era await your visit at a 135-acre park on the outskirts of town. Art and history can be found in giant colorful murals painted on downtown buildings, and numerous shopping and dining options await your travel downtown and along historic Ross Clark Circle. Known as the "Peanut Capital of the World," Dothan is home to the National Peanut Festival each fall and pays homage to its agricultural heritage through a series of whimsical and "nutty" statues scattered around town. There is also a monument downtown dedicated to Dr. George Washington Carver.

variety of farm animals, such as sheep, mules, cows, chickens, goats and pigs. It also features a collection of historic structures, including

GETTING THERE

Dothan, located on U.S. Hwy. 231 S. in Houston County in Southeast Alabama, is within a two-hour drive of the state capital in Montgomery and a short drive from Troy, Brundidge, Ozark, Enterprise and Fort Rucker.

Landmark Park on the outskirts of Dothan is Alabama's Official Museum of Agriculture.

EXPLORE LANDMARK PARK

Begin your tour of Dothan at Landmark Park (430 Landmark Dr.; 334-794-3452). The 135-acre park was built to preserve the natural and cultural heritage of southeast Alabama's Wiregrass region. The 1890s living history farm allows visitors to observe a

an old farmhouse, a smokehouse, a cane mill and syrup shed.

During your visit, you can drift back in time and experience the simple pleasures of a bygone era. Relax in a Victorian gazebo. Enjoy a refreshing drink at the soda fountain in the old-fashioned drugstore. Sift through

the wares of a country store or stroll through a one-room schoolhouse. You can also experience the solitude of a turn-of-the-century church, take a nature walk through the woods on an elevated boardwalk, explore the night skies inside the Digitarium Planetarium or visit the interpretive center to see wildlife exhibits.

In addition to showcasing period attractions, Landmark Park plays host to several special activities throughout the year, ranging from folklife festivals, antique car shows and traveling exhibits to demonstrations and hands-on activities for kids, concerts and workshops. In March, you can get up close and personal with the animals during Spring Farm Day. The Wiregrass Heritage Festival in October lets you learn how peanuts were harvested in the region more than a half-century ago. And during Victorian Christmas, you can enjoy the sights, sounds and smells of an old-fashioned holiday gathering, complete with hot chocolate, handmade decorations, music, crafts and a seasonal message delivered by a circuit-riding preacher on horseback.

Dothan's Visitor Information Center

ABOUT DOTHAN

In the late 1700s and 1800s, horse and ox-drawn covered wagons creaked across the South as pioneer families searched for places to start a new life. Those pioneers would stop at a spring known as Poplar Head, in what is now Dothan. From its humble beginnings, Dothan established itself as an agricultural stronghold.

It has become known as the "Peanut Capital of Alabama" and hosts the National Peanut Festival each fall. Dothan's downtown area is noted for its historic murals and Ross Clark Circle has become a popular retail hub for visitors from Alabama, Georgia and Florida.

WIREGRASS MUSEUM OF ART AND MURAL CITY ART FEST

During your visit, you can drift back in time and experience the simple pleasures of a bygone era.

After touring the murals, don't miss the opportunity to enjoy other downtown attractions. The Wiregrass Museum of Art (126 Museum Ave.; 334-794-3871) showcases six galleries featuring changing exhibits of visual and decorative arts. A good time to visit the museum is the first Saturday in May when the Mural City Art Fest takes place. During this spring event, artists, musicians and dancers gather on the grounds and entertain visitors throughout the festival. Children can enjoy crafts, games and other activities while the adults mingle with vendors and search for the perfect piece of artwork to take home.

Visitors are drawn to this and a number of other murals adorning downtown Dothan buildings.

CARVER MUSEUM, A HARDWARE STORE AND MORE

Located within walking distance of downtown shops and restaurants is the G.W. Carver Interpretive Museum (305 N. Foster St.; 334-712-0933). The museum commemorates the life and legacy of Dr. George Washington Carver and provides a comprehensive look into the historical influences of African-Americans in science, space exploration, the military and other areas. Hailed as an agricultural genius, Dr. Carver developed more than 300 uses for the peanut, more than 100 for the sweet potato, and many others for the soybean – including soybean plastic for car parts. Also downtown you'll find the former Porter Hardware store, which was the

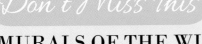

MURALS OF THE WIREGRASS

From Landmark Park, head to the heart of Dothan, now known as "Alabama's Mural City." The Murals of the Wiregrass, an ongoing outdoor art project, features 22 murals painted on downtown buildings by nationally and internationally acclaimed artists. Depicting the history of the Wiregrass, the murals range in subject matter from "DeSoto's Journey Throughout the Wiregrass Region" and "Salute to the Peanut Industry" to "Fort Rucker" and "Wiregrass Music."

Captured in the murals are renderings of country and pop singer/songwriter Bobby Goldsboro who grew up in Dothan in the 1940s and football player-turned Hollywood actor Johnny Mack Brown, who was born in Dothan in 1904, played football for the University of Alabama and went on to have a string of hits on the silver screen in country and Western films. Guided tours are available by calling the Wiregrass Museum of Art at 334-794-3871.

G.W. Carver Interpretive Museum

G.W. Carver Interpretive Museum

WHERE TO EAT, WHERE TO STAY

In Dothan's downtown area, stop by the Basketcase Café (228 S. Oates St.; 334-671-1117) for an outstanding lunch. While it is noted for its homemade soups, guests will tell you that every item on the menu is absolutely delicious.

For overnight lodging, Dothan offers more than 30 outstanding accommodations for every budget. For more information on dining, lodging and shopping in the area, go to www.VisitDothanAL.com.

oldest continually operating hardware store in Alabama until it closed in 2014. Though Porter Hardware no longer operates as a retail store, the site has now reopened as a museum that can be toured Tuesday through Friday from 10 a.m. to 5 p.m (136 E. Main St.; 334-699-8118). Admission is free. For antique lovers, Dothan also boasts several shopping venues downtown and along Ross Clark Circle. Each offers a plethora of treasure-hunting experiences to spice up your road trip.

A MUST-STOP: WORLD'S SMALLEST CITY BLOCK

First-time visitors to Dothan might find maneuvering around the city to be a bit challenging, especially with the downtown area somewhat removed from the main thoroughfare known as Ross Clark Circle. Visitors with a sense of humor, however, might delight in discovering the World's Smallest City Block. From downtown, where U.S. Highways 84 and 431/231 intersect, drive east three blocks along Main Street to Museum Avenue. Turn left and drive north one block to the intersection of North College Street, North Appletree Street and East Troy Street). This triangular piece of land, recorded in the Guinness Book of World Records as the "World's Smallest City Block," features a stop sign,

yield sign, street signs and even a monument denoting the block's claim to fame.

State Route 210, also known as Ross Clark Circle, or simply "The Circle" to locals, is a much longer stretch of highway overlaid by U.S. Highways 84, 431/231. The divided four-lane highway encircling Dothan is highly developed and heavily used both by those who live and work in the area and by motorists who use it as a bypass of the city. With a number of antique shops, quaint boutiques and eclectic restaurants lining the thoroughfare, Ross Clark Circle has become a popular retail hub for visitors from Alabama, Georgia and Florida.

Wiregrass Festival Of Murals tribute to Sherman Rose

"PEANUTS AROUND TOWN"

While exploring Dothan, you'll quickly discover it's a town that loves peanuts. In fact, the folks here love peanuts so much that they've created a citywide art project centered on the little goobers. Peanuts Around Town, a novel and nutty public art exhibit sponsored by Dothan Downtown Redevelopment Authority (334-793-3097) in coordination with local businesses and organizations, enables the citizens of Dothan to celebrate the peanut and the agricultural heritage of the Wiregrass all year long. The project consists of more than 70 peanut sculptures (with others constantly in the works), thematically decorated by local artists. Visitors to the city are encouraged to take the challenge to find all the peanut sculptures, some of which are located in front of local businesses and restaurants, inside museums, in green spaces, on street corners and in parks.

Among the popular statues on the tour are: "The Peanut Man," which honors Dothan's own peanut peddler, Byron "Cotton" Traywick who sold boiled peanuts from a stand on Main Street for more than 25 years. Printed on the barrel of the statue placed in his memory on the corner of Ross Clark Circle and West Main Street is one of Traywick's favorite sayings to his patrons, "Have a good day and let the Lord ride with ya." Another favorite is the "hunk of burning love" statue of Elvis Presley that greets tourists at the Dothan Visitors Center. Employees there say the King of Rock 'n' Roll is perhaps the most popular of the peanut characters, as he cost about $2,500 and was known to be taken without permission several times before he was given a permanent home inside the visitor center.

Another nut statue is of a gentleman standing downtown on the corner of North Foster and Main Street. Sporting a gray suit and wide-brimmed hat, he hails travelers to come explore downtown businesses, such as the Poplar Head Farmers Market, which opens each summer. Maps detailing all the sculpture locations are available through the Dothan

Approximately half of the peanuts grown in the United States are grown within a 100-mile radius of Dothan, AL, which makes the area a natural destination for the nation's largest peanut festival.

Downtown Redevelopment Authority and at the Dothan Visitors Center.

CELEBRATE THE NATIONAL PEANUT FESTIVAL

The National Peanut Festival (5622 U.S. Hwy. 231 S.; 334-793-4323) is held each fall at the fairgrounds on U.S. Highway 231 S. just three miles south of the Ross Clark Circle to honor peanut growers and to celebrate the harvest season. Numerous fun-filled family events are a part of the festivities, including amusement rides, animal acts, agricultural displays, live music concerts, beauty pageants, arts and crafts displays, contests, food, a parade and, of course, tons of peanuts. The National Peanut Festival dates to 1938 and has grown from a three-day local event to a celebrated agricultural fair encompassing 10 days of activities for people from throughout the region.

MORE TO SEE AND DO IN DOTHAN

When visiting Dothan, you'll find plenty of entertainment for both children and adults. Options include the Dothan Area Botanical Gardens (5130 Headland Ave. off U.S. Highway 431 N.; 334-793-3224), consisting of 50 acres of cultivated gardens, nature trails and undeveloped, wooded landscape.

Adventureland Theme Park (3738 W. Main St.; 334-739-9100) is a family entertainment center featuring two jungle golf courses, go-karts, bumper boats, batting cages and an arcade.

Fun Zone Skate Center (465 Westgate Pkwy.; 334-678-7529) houses an indoor skating rink, a laser tag arena, a softplay gym, arcade, pizza shop, gyro chair, jump-shot court, and climbing wall..

Water World (401 Recreation Rd.; 334-615-3750), a seasonal attraction which opens each May, offers a giant wave pool, a 400-foot triple-flume water slide, a kiddie pool and the Great White Water Slide.

Not far from Dothan and well worth the 30-minute drive is the U.S. Army Aviation Museum (Bldg. 60000, Novosel St.; 334-598-2508) in Fort Rucker. The museum offers the largest collection of Army helicopters, airplanes and unmanned aircraft in the county. It features historic military artifacts, photos, video kiosks and films and an extensive archives and gift shop.

FAMOUS ALABAMIANS HOMETOWN HEROES

by Marilyn Jones Stamps

Each room of Hank Williams' boyhood home in Georgiana is filled with memorabilia.

The Famous Alabamians Hometown Heroes Road Trip will take you to towns and museums in South Alabama associated with legendary figures and others who were either born in the state or lived here.

MOBILE: HANK AARON'S HOMETOWN

Traveling I–65 south from Montgomery or I–10 from Mississippi or Florida, begin your tour in Mobile where a stadium and museum honor one of Alabama's most famous native sons, Henry "Hank" Aaron. Located at the home stadium of the Mobile Bay Bears, the Hank Aaron Childhood Home and Museum (755 Bolling Brothers Blvd.; 251–479–2327) includes seven rooms and hundreds of artifacts relating to the athlete.

Aaron ascended the ranks of the Negro Leagues to become a major league baseball icon. He played 23 years as an outfielder for the Milwaukee/Atlanta Braves, during which time he set many of baseball's most illustrious records. Aaron was inducted into the Baseball Hall of Fame in 1982.

Five miles from the stadium is the home of Confederate Rear Adm. and Brig. Gen. Raphael Semmes who left an enduring legacy as captain of the CSS Alabama, the most famous of the Confederate commerce raiders. The nearby History Museum of Mobile (111 South Royal St.; 251–208–7569) is a good place to stop to learn of the history and heritage of the area. After a day of touring, check into The Battle House Renaissance Hotel & Spa (26 N. Royal St.; 251–338–2000) where the AAA-rated, Four-Diamond hotel offers Mobile's only Four-Diamond restaurant, with a bar honoring Joe Cain, another hometown

hero. Mardi Gras originated in the New World here in 1703 when Mobile was a French colony. It continues with more than two weeks of parades and balls, beads, candy and Moon Pies. The Sunday before Fat Tuesday is observed as Joe Cain Day. Cain, who took to the streets in a one-float parade on Shrove Tuesday in 1866 and returned the following year accompanied by some off-key musicians, is credited with resurrecting Mardi Gras in Mobile after it was banned by Union troops following the Civil War.

GEORGIANA AND MONTGOMERY: WHERE HANK LEARNED GUITAR

From Mobile, take I–65 north and continue 104 miles to Exit 114 in Georgiana. Just two miles off the interstate is the Hank Williams Boyhood Home & Museum. The best time to visit is during the Hank Williams Music Festival in June. Born Sept. 17, 1923 on a farm in Mount Olive, Ala., Williams moved with his family to Georgiana in the late 1930s when his father was admitted into a veteran's hospital. While visiting, you'll see the surroundings that shaped the singer's life and learn about a black street singer named Rufus "Tee-Tot" Payne, who taught Hank how to play the guitar.

Continue up I–65 and take Exit 172 to downtown Montgomery. Park your car on Commerce Street where another museum also honors the legend of country music.

Containing photos and more than 17 pieces of clothing, boots, ties, rare videos, albums and furniture, the Hank Williams Museum (118 Commerce St.; 334–262–3600) boasts the most complete collection of memorabilia relating to the singer in the country, including the 1952 baby blue Cadillac in which he made his final journey.

ROSA PARKS: THE MOTHER OF THE MOVEMENT

Three blocks away from the Hank Williams Museum is a museum that pays tribute to Rosa Parks, who was born Rosa Louise McCauley in nearby Tuskegee on Feb. 4, 1913. Located on the site where she was arrested Dec. 1, 1955 for refusing to give her seat to white passengers on a city bus, the Rosa Parks Museum & Library and Children's Wing (252 Montgomery St.; 334–241–8615) chronicles the history of the Civil Rights Movement and the 381-day Montgomery Bus Boycott. During your visit, you'll see historical photos of Parks' arrest, newspaper clippings, interactive exhibits and a replica of the bus on which she was riding.

MONTGOMERY: HOME TO DAVIS AND KING

Six blocks away on Dexter Avenue, you'll find the Alabama State Capitol, with a history that's intertwined with both the Civil War and the Civil Rights Movement. Adjacent to the Capitol and facing Washington Avenue is the First White House of the Confederacy, where President Jefferson Davis and his family lived when Montgomery was the capital.

Down the street is the red-brick Dexter Avenue King Memorial Baptist Church (454 Dexter Ave.; 334–263–3970) where Martin Luther King Jr. preached his message of hope and brotherhood and rose to prominence as the leader of the Civil Rights Movement. In 1964, at age 35, he became the youngest man to receive the Nobel Peace Prize.

MEET THE HEROES OF HISTORIC TUSKEGEE

From Montgomery, travel about 35 miles east on I–85 to Tuskegee, where you'll visit museums dedicated to heroes like Booker T. Washington, George Washington Carver and the Tuskegee Airmen. To get to Tuskegee University (formerly Tuskegee Institute), take Exit 32 and turn right onto Pleasant Springs Drive. Travel about two miles and turn left onto Franklin Road and continue for 3.8 miles to where Franklin Road ends at a traffic light at West Montgomery Road. If you look across the street while stopped at the light, you'll see the private residence where singer/songwriter Lionel Richie grew up. At this stoplight, turn left onto West Montgomery Road. Turn left at the following stoplight and continue through Lincoln Gates onto Booker T. Washington Boulevard. This is the main entrance into the campus. Veering to your right, you will see the Kellogg Hotel & Conference Center (334-727-3000). Go past the front of the hotel and look for the entrance that leads to the hotel's parking deck. Park on the top level of the deck for easy access to campus and the Tuskegee Institute National Historic Site (334-727-3200), which includes the George Washington Carver Museum and The Oaks, where President Booker T. Washington and his family lived during the formative years of Tuskegee Institute.

From the top floor of the parking deck, walk

Hank Williams lived in Montgomery off and on from 1937 through 1952. Although he only lived to be 29, he sang his way into the hearts of millions with such songs as "Your Cheatin' Heart," "Hey Good Lookin'" and "I'm So Lonesome I Could Cry." Williams is buried at Montgomery's Oakwood Cemetery Annex next to his ex-wife, Audrey.

through the breezeway that faces the back of the George Washington Carver Museum. Go inside the museum to see exhibits that showcase the scientist's empirical research with the peanut, the sweet potato, soybeans and other crops.

After touring the Carver Museum, exit through the front door and turn right. Walk down and cross the street to see the monument depicting Booker T. Washington lifting the veil of ignorance from the black race. If you continue, you will see the historic Tuskegee Chapel. Next to the chapel are the gravesites of both Washington and Carver.

Return to your car and exit the Kellogg Center parking deck to the left. From the short driveway, turn left onto Booker T. Washington Boulevard. Continue to Lincoln Gates and turn left onto West Montgomery Road for a visit to The Oaks. Past Inside the house museum, you'll learn about Washington's philosophy and view the surroundings that characterized his family life. Visitors should call ahead for a tour schedule (334-727-3200).

Leaving The Oaks, turn right onto West Montgomery Road. Continue downtown to Elm Street for a visit to the Tuskegee Human & Civil Rights Multicultural Center.

THE HEROIC TUSKEGEE AIRMEN

Next, prepare to soar with the "Red Tails" at the Tuskegee Airmen National Historic

Site (1616 Chappie James Ave.; 334-724-0922), also managed by the National Park Service. To get there from the Multicultural Center, turn left onto Elm Street. At the traffic light, turn right onto Martin Luther King Highway (Highway 80). Just on the outskirts of town, you'll see Chappie James Avenue and signs directing you to the Airmen Site.

The 99th Pursuit Squadron established on March 19, 1941 and the 332nd Fighter Group, now known as the Tuskegee Airmen, had already made history. Tasked with the mission of proving its young men were fit for military service and on par with whites as

Visitor at exhibit honoring civil rights heroes

fighter pilots during World War II, Tuskegee trained 994 pilots and sent approximately 450 overseas. Their lasting legacy was integration of the U.S. military in 1948.

Don't Miss This

HUMAN & CIVIL RIGHTS MULTICULTURAL CENTER

A walk-through-time museum, the Tuskegee History Center(104 S. Elm St.; 334–724–0800), provides an overview of the Tuskegee and Macon County area from the period when Native Americans lived here to today. Exhibits showcase the role of Tuskegee in the Civil Rights Movement, the impact of the Tuskegee Syphilis Study and the people who have helped to shape local, state and national history.

Bird watching at Gulf State Park

The coastal city of Mobile, steeped in 300 years of international history, is shaded by ancient live oaks dripping with Spanish moss and bordered with azalea bushes as big as cars.

Fought over by the French, Spanish and British, the city retains many elements from its past occupations, yet is every bit a genteel, hospitable Southern belle. Mobile is the gateway to the legendary Bellingrath Gardens, home to the USS Alabama battleship, and its story is grandly told at the Museum of Mobile. The Battle House Hotel is the city's *grand dame*.

The heritage, culture and lifestyle separate it from the rest of the state. Mobilians feel more of a kinship to New Orleans and Pensacola than to Montgomery and Birmingham.

The beautiful sparkling white beaches along the Gulf of Mexico are the number one destination for people visiting Alabama. The 32 miles of beach stretching from Fort Morgan at the western tip to the Flora-Bama at the Florida line lure sun lovers to parks, restaurants, shops, condos and charter boat fishing.

Although the gulf's coastline hugs eastern Texas, Louisiana and Mississippi, the westernmost white beaches are in Alabama, specifically Dauphin Island at the tip of Mobile County, and Gulf Shores and Orange Beach in Baldwin County.

The center of beach activity is at the southern end of Alabama Highway 59. Fort Morgan, 22 miles west, anchors the western end of the island and guarded the entrance to Mobile Bay during the Civil War. To the east are Gulf State Park and then Orange Beach, where condo towers faces the beach.

MOBILE:
A ROMANTIC GETAWAY
by Lee Sentell

If you're considering a romantic getaway, put Mobile at the top of your list. This beautiful city alongside Mobile Bay is an original French settlement more than 300 years old, with spreading live oaks that create shady canopies over the downtown and the wrought iron balconies on historic mansions.

Residents don't really consider their city as part of Alabama, but rather as part of the Gulf Coast that stretches from New Orleans to Pensacola and Savannah. Because of the city's fascinating history, you'll find a number of museums and dramatic architecture that encourage strolls along broad sidewalks. The proximity to the Gulf of Mexico puts fresh seafood on most menus.

As you'll discover when you visit, everything about Mobile is steeped in history, so a Cliff's Notes about the origin of Mobile's Mardi Gras is in order. Although some forms of religious celebrations leading up to Lent began in the 18th century, Michael Krafft led a rowdy bunch of friends on New Year's morning in 1830 that evolved into an annual celebration with parades that lasted until the Civil War. The city was occupied by Union troops after the war and the celebrations ceased. On Shrove Tuesday in 1866, town market clerk Joe Cain dressed up like a Chickasaw Indian and drove a charcoal wagon through the streets while singing. His merry portrayal of Chief Slacabamorinico was a political statement aimed at the Union army troops because the Chickasaws had never been defeated in battle. Cain returned the following Shrove Tuesday with a band of off-key musicians, whose antics eventually caught the fancy of Mobile society who organized and refined the event. By 1872, Carnival had its first monarch, King Felix, and the formal balls and parades were staged by the leading social clubs.

Joe Cain died in 1904 and his epitaph in

the Church Street Graveyard (251-208-7411) reads, "Here lies old Joe Cain, the heart and soul of Mardi Gras." Each year, the Sunday before Mardi Gras is celebrated here as Joe Cain Day, when numerous "Cain widows" lead mourners to his grave. You can pay homage to Joe Cain daily by having a drink in the bar named for him at the Battle House hotel.

Joe Cain's residence still stands in the historic district that surrounds Oakleigh Mansion (300 Oakleigh Pl.; 251-432-1281), a lovely raised cottage-style home built in 1833. Visit the Oakleigh house museum to see an important portrait collection, including a portrait of socialite Octavia Walton that Thomas Sully painted in his Philadelphia studio in 1833. Cain's home, a private residence, is at 906 Augusta.

Michael Krafft is not forgotten either. Modern-day Mardi Gras revelers head for Magnolia Cemetery (1202 Virginia St.; 251-432-8672) to pay their respects and scatter plastic trinkets on his grave. His obelisk marker with symbols of the Cowbellion Society is at the southeast corner of square 6. (To reach the historic cemetery, turn south off Government Street to Ann and go a mile to the entrance on your left.)

WHERE TO STAY

Mobile offers 7,500 rooms with lodging options to fit every budget. Located just steps from Mobile's entertainment district and downtown attractions is the Battle House Renaissance Hotel and Spa (26 N. Royal St.; 251-338-2000) which has been a favorite of celebrities, sports legends, a president and a king since 1852. Completely restored to its original grandeur, this AAA-rated, four-diamond hotel offers The Trellis Room, Mobile's

Mobile's Bragg-Mitchell Mansion

only four-diamond restaurant; a magnificent ballroom; and a 10,000 sq.-ft. spa. The Renaissance Mobile Riverview Plaza Hotel (64 S. Water St.; 251-438-4000) is perfect for conventions, stylish social gatherings or weekend escapes. Enjoy dining in the Harbor Room or listening to live music in Fathoms Lounge. A luxury hotel with 170 guest rooms, the Admiral Semmes Hotel (251 Government St.; 251-432-8000) opened in 1940 and has hosted stars like Bob Hope and Elvis Presley.

EXPLORE HISTORIC SITES

After checking into your hotel, head for the recreated 1735 Fort of Colonial Mobile (150 S. Royal St.; 251-802-3092), known in Mobile simply as Fort Condé that is the official welcome center. The foundations were uncovered during construction of an I-10 interchange and the French fort was rebuilt during the U.S. Bicentennial in 1976. Costumed guards give tours and explain the history of the city.

Enjoy the romance of the Battle House Hotel.

A few steps away from Fort Condé is a museum that will help you understand Mobile. City government moved from the 1857 City Hall into the modern building nearby and made room for the History Museum of Mobile (111 S. Royal St.; 251-208-7569) in time for Mobile's tricentennial in 2003. Some of the notable exhibits found in the museum include a 700-year-old canoe, a model of the Confederate submarine H. L. Hunley, a large terra cotta statue of a French peasant raising the torch of freedom, and tributes to hometown heroes Admiral Raphael Semmes, captain of the famed CSS Alabama; baseball legend Hank Aaron, and Joe Cain, the Mardi Gras booster.

The museum that many visitors remember from their trip is the Mobile Carnival Museum (355 Government St.; 251-432-3324), or what most people call "the Mardi Gras museum." The main difference is Mardi Gras is only one day (Fat Tuesday) whereas carnival is the social season of galas and parades that leads up to the day before Lent starts. This is a showcase of glittering, handmade coronation costumes that denote the social status of the most important families dating back to Old Mobile. Fur-lined trains and crowns that date back to the 1860s fill gallery after gallery.

Bellingrath Gardens and Home (12401 Bellingrath Gardens Rd.; 251-973-2217), located 20 miles southwest of Mobile off I-10, was the creation of Walter and Bessie Bellingrath, local philanthropists who opened their gardens to the public year-round beginning in 1934. As described by Mr. Bellingrath, "The Gardens are like a beautiful woman with a different gown for each week of the year." With the blooming of the camellias in winter, the azaleas in spring, roses in the summer, chrysanthemums in autumn and the fabulous Magic Christmas in Lights during the holiday season, the 65-acre estate is a parade of beauty throughout the year.

In addition to strolling through the gardens, you can tour the elegant home, explore the gift shop and dine in the Magnolia Café.

Don't Miss This

FOOTBALL AND MARDI GRAS

The period from New Year's Eve to the beginning of Lent is the best time to visit, because the semi-tropical climate coaxes camellias and azaleas to bloom while the rest of the Deep South is still chilly. Plus, there are football games, parades and parties in significant numbers. The National Football League practically takes over the city's hotels in January during the week leading up to the Senior Bowl (Ladd-Peebles Stadium; 251-432-4109), a showcase game where college all-stars try to impress NFL scouts.

Mobile is the original home of Mardi Gras (251-208-2000) in the New World, from a celebration in 1703 (Saint Louis Day on Aug. 25) that evolved in 1840 to today's parades by krewes or social clubs. Two prominent Mobile businessmen who moved to New Orleans in that era took the concept of parades and balls to the Crescent City.

Unlike the bawdy Bourbon Street festivities, Mobile's two weeks of parades are much more family friendly, suitable for all ages. Revelers on the parade floats throw plastic beads, but also Moon Pies, the marshmallow snacks baked in Chattanooga. That explains the giant Moon Pie on the corner of one of the tallest office buildings that is "counted down" at midnight on New Year's Eve as locals and tourists cheer.

For family-friendly viewing of Mobile Mardi Gras parades, stand on Church Street near Fort Condé. Royal Street is also a good area near many downtown hotels and restaurants, as well as Bienville Square. For a more "adult" experience, you can catch a parade near its end at Dauphin and Washington streets, which provide easy access to local bars.

STEPPING OUT IN MOBILE

Mobile offers a variety of culinary options stretching from one end of the city to the other. Located near Battleship Memorial Park, on the Causeway between the Eastern Shore and Mobile, is the Original Oyster House (3733 Battleship Pkwy.; 251-626-2188) which first opened its doors in Gulf Shores in 1983. The Causeway location opened in 1985. Among other restaurants, you will find Ed's Seafood Shed, (3382 Battleship Pkwy.; 251-625-1947), home of "Yo Mamma's Platter."

In downtown Mobile is the Spot of Tea (310 Dauphin St.; 251-433-9009). This famous spot in Cathedral Square is an excellent choice for breakfast, lunch or dinner. The Eggs Cathedral and strawberry lemonade are two items you should definitely try. The Nobel South (203 Dauphin St.; 251-6824) offers fresh, local farm-to-table fare. Panini Petes (102 Dauphin St.; 251-405-0031) is a local favorite for breakfast and lunch. You must try their beignets that are served with lemon wedges, an iconic Mobile twist on the Crescent City classic.

Wintzell's Oyster House (605 Dauphin St.; 251-432-4605) is also a downtown Mobile landmark. Located on historic Dauphin Street, the small Alabama chain has been serving fresh seafood here since 1938. Though known for its oysters – fried, stewed or nude – they also serve shrimp, fish, crab, crawfish and gator tails for die-hard seafood lovers.

If you are worried about what to do when many of the local restaurants have shut down for the day, don't fret. You can keep the party going at night with a visit to hot spots like hot spots like local dive bar Hayley's (278 Dauphin St.; 251-433-4970) and Veet's Bar and Grill (66 S. Royal St.; 251-694-3090). They open early, stay open late and offer great appetizers, drinks and wonderful after-hours entertainment.

For a list of additional lodging and dining options and other things to see and do in the Mobile area, visit www.mobilebay.org.

ALABAMA'S GULF COAST:
WHERE KIDS DRIVE THE FUN HOME
by Annette Thompson

Youngsters splash seaward into the clear emerald and blue waters of the Alabama coast.

Some of the best family memories are made on a beach vacation. Ditching your regular routine and setting out for Alabama's 32 miles of sandy seashore welcomes a bit of magic into your lives. The special times aren't simply limited to the beaches though.

The entire coastal region – the wetlands, rivers, and bays – is a rich playground full of a variety of adventures.

Youngsters will not only like to play in the surf, but they also will soak up the culture of the coast. So plan your trip with a healthy mix of downtime combined with several outings to explore the watery ecosystem and the region's role in American history. And don't leave out a few squeal-producing activities.

SURF'S UP!

Until your teens or tots sink their toes in the sand, you haven't really arrived at the beach. So make haste down AL Highway 59 (Gulf Shores Parkway) to land's edge where you can slather on the sunscreen and catch a wave. All of the major resorts in Gulf Shores and Orange Beach maintain beach services with lounge chairs and umbrellas (typically about $25 per day), and some even rent kayaks or catamarans (typically about $50 an hour).

ABOUT ALABAMA'S GULF COAST

The Alabama Gulf Coast region, sporting 32 miles of white-sand beaches, is the state's most popular tourist destination. In addition to the bountiful recreational activities that can be found in Gulf Shores and Orange Beach, visitors come here to explore the history and culture in places such as Mobile and Dauphin Island.

Look beyond the high-rises to discover less-crowded strands, where you'll feel as if the entire beach belongs to your family. At these tranquil spots, you'll need to bring your own blankets, chairs and umbrellas for comfort (don't forget a cooler with cold drinks, snacks and wet cloths to wash hands and faces). One of the best sites along AL Highway 182 is Gulf State Park (20115 AL Highway 135; 251–948–7275). The 3.5 miles of sugary sands separate Gulf Shores and Orange Beach. The park features the second-longest fishing pier (1,540 feet) anywhere along the Gulf of Mexico. (Kids younger than 16 don't need fishing licenses, but adults do. They can be purchased right on the pier.)

When renovations were made to Gulf State Park, it wasn't just to add a new conference center, but to make it one of the most innovative environmental sites in the country. The 6,150-acre Gulf State Park in Gulf Shores features restored sand dunes, expanded walking and biking trails, new interpretive centers, a learning campus and a new lodge and conference center. The Lodge at Gulf State Park, a Hilton Hotel, opened in November 2018 and has 350 rooms including 20 suites. It offers guests access to 28 miles of educational hiking and biking trails, a nature center, outdoor classrooms, an interpretive center, tennis, kayaking, guided nature walks, a butterfly garden, a forest and beach pavilions.

Perhaps most importantly, it is designed to be one of the country's cutting-edge environmental sites. The Interpretive Center at Gulf State Park is in the process of obtaining a Living Building Challenge environmental designation currently afforded to only 16 buildings in the world. The park's Eagle Cottages are undergoing an evaluation to become the first lodge in the Southeast and one of only seven in the country to be designated a National Geographic Unique Lodge of the World.

After substantial rains or high tides push extra water onto the shore, small ponds develop along Alabama's beaches. Families with toddlers especially love these seaside lakes, which can remain for days at a time. It's Mother Nature's way of creating little kiddie pools. While there's no guarantee you'll encounter one, when you do, it's a special bonus. Parents can watch older kids ride boogie boards in the Gulf's gentle waves and splash around with their youngest kiddos in the warm shallow waters – all just a few feet apart.

CROSS OVER THE BAY

When you're ready for a break from the beach, make tracks for Mobile Bay. As the fourth-largest estuary in the U.S., the bay is home to dolphins and seabirds as well as two 19th-century forts.

The entire bay encompasses 413 square miles, with six different rivers feeding into it. Plus, a really cool auto ferry crosses its southern tip. Pack up the kids for a full day of ecological and historical adventure.

Drive out Fort Morgan Road (AL Highway 180). As the peninsula narrows, the bay laps against the north shore of the road, and the Gulf on the south. At road's end (just over 20 miles), spend a morning climbing over the 1834 star-shaped fortifications at Fort Morgan (110 Highway 180 W.; 251-540-5257). Exhibits describe the events of the War of 1812 as well as the Civil War. Barrel-vaulted ceilings carry echoes between masonry walls that whisper of centuries past.

Be ready for your imaginative youngsters to shout out the phrase "Damn the torpedoes. Full steam ahead!" made famous by Adm. David Farragut in the Battle of Mobile Bay during the Civil War. The bay was heavily fortified with sunken mines (called torpedoes then). Farragut led the Union boats past Fort Morgan, Fort Gaines and the bay's mine-

Sea life from the Alabama gulf and bays are a highlight for young visitors.

riddled waters to end the Confederate hold on the coast.

Afterward, drive your vehicle (or walk) onto the Mobile Bay Ferry (1008 Alabama Ave.; 251-861-3000) to putter across the mouth of the bay "($32 round trip for one car with driver, plus an additional $5 per passenger; children under 6 free). The ferry is an adventure in itself. Dolphins frolic in the ferry's wake as it crisscrosses the three miles to Dauphin Island. Huge tankers use the ship channel to make their way in and out of the bay. On clear days, take along some binoculars to spy the historic Sand Island Lighthouse a couple of miles south. Built in 1873, the 125-foot lighthouse and its island have been ravaged by time and hurricanes.

Upon arrival, visit The Estuarium (101 Bienville Blvd.; 251-861-7500). Run by Sea Lab, a university-level research facility, the aquarium is a hands-on touch-the-horseshoe-crab kind of place geared toward families. Exhibits explain the local ecosystems, from barrier islands (Dauphin Island is a classic example) and river deltas to living marshes and the universe of the Gulf. You'll learn about salt marshes, sponges, oil production and even Gulf weather.

Afterward, wander into Fort Gaines, (251-861-6992) which was built to protect the western entrance to the Mobile Bay. Completed during the Civil War, Fort Gaines also played host to soldiers on U-boat watch

during World War II. Today, Farragut's anchor is on display where living-history actors enact the fort's legends.

SCOOPING UP THE BAY, ONE NET AT A TIME

Drop by Dauphin Island's Ship and Shore store (401 Lemoyne Drive; 251-861-2262) to pick up an inexpensive net, cooler, bait and some hand wipes. Then make your way to one of the bay access points on either Dauphin Island or Fort Morgan Road. Wade into the knee-deep water to throw the net out to catch small fish, or scoop up crabs with a pole net. Another way to catch crabs is to tie a piece of bacon or a chicken neck on the end of a string and toss it into the water. Use your

Don't Miss This

GULF COAST EXPLOREUM

Add an extra day to your bayside travels and scoot the 30 miles north into Mobile to the Gulf Coast Exploreum (65 Government St.; 251-208-6893). This huge science museum features an IMAX theater, hands-on science exhibits (laser harps, optics galleries, digital DJ), the iHealthy Lab that tests human health and physical limits, and a dramatic play area for young scientists.

Sand Island Lighthouse has stood in Mobile Bay since 1873.

scoop net to pick the snappy creature up.

Afterward, drive under the bay through a tunnel (via I–10) to the Battleship USS ALABAMA. The 680-foot behemoth served in both the Atlantic and Pacific arenas during World War II. Families may explore the brigs, walk the decks and man the gun turrets. Students can even arrange to spend the night on the iron beauty. The park also includes the 311-foot USS Drum submarine plus a massive hangar with more than 25 war planes, ranging from the World War II-era through the Cold War.

All this exploring will work up an appetite, so take the kids over to Felix's Fish Camp Grill (1530 Battleship Parkway; 251–626–6710). Set on the edge of the bay, Felix's feels like a big old screened-in porch with ceiling fans, wooden tables and a kitchen cooking up tasty seafood dishes. It's a great place to watch the sunset.

TAKE A WALK ON THE WILD SIDE

Let your offspring discover their animal nature at a duo of wild parks. Alligator Alley (19950 Highway 71; 866–994–2867), just north of Summerdale, is home to some really big gators. These gators like people, too. Without owner Wes Moore to save them, game officials would probably have destroyed the big lizards. Instead, Wes created an alligator sanctuary for the goliaths who've lost their fear of humans. You don't need to fear either – you will walk on a nice raised boardwalk through the piney wood forest and marsh where the gators roam. Wes tells about gator nature and, of course, he welcomes you to watch during feeding times. To get to Alligator Alley, take AL Highway 59 north through Summerdale about 19 miles. Turn right on Couch Plant Road, and take the first left onto County Road 71. Alligator Alley is on the right.

The region is home to a zoo that wants you to touch the animals. The Alabama Gulf Coast Zoo (1204 Gulf Shores Parkway; 251–968–5731) has many young creatures among their 500-plus wild residents. They

have an interaction program that lets you hold a kangaroo, pet a lemur or a sloth and tamandua. (Make reservations in advance for the tiger interaction.) Don't leave your camera behind this time.

ENJOY FAMILY-FRIENDLY EVENINGS

Get a bird's-eye perspective of Orange Beach's Intracoastal Waterway at The Wharf (23101 Canal Rd. , Orange Beach; 251–224–1000), home to one of the Southeast's tallest. It soars 120 feet above the amphitheater and boutiques that line the development. Afterward, check out the waterfront eateries. The best view is at The Villaggio Grille (4790 Main St; 251-224-6510), a fine dining Italian-inspired restaurant and bar. Mom and Dad may want to sip a cool drink at The Boat Bar outside, but the kids will relish icy Dippin' Dots. To get to The Wharf from Gulf Shores, take AL Highway 59 S., turn left on AL Highway 182 E. (Perdido Beach Blvd.) and continue to Orange Beach. Turn left on AL Highway 161 (Orange Beach Blvd.) and follow it until it ends at AL Highway 180 (Canal Road). Take a left on Canal Road. The Wharf will be on your right just before the turn for the Beach Expressway toll bridge. For more information about The Wharf, visit www.alwharf.com.

Gulf Shores also revs up the nighttime with adventures at Waterville U.S.A. (906 Gulf Shores Pkwy.; 251–948–2106). In the

warm summer months, the water park stays open till 10 at night, making the slides and themed rides even more fun – without the worry about sunburn. Or, if you have some young golfers, take them around the 36 holes at Pirate's Island Adventure Golf (3201 Gulf Shores Parkway; 251–968–4653) with Jean Lafitte and Blackbeard.

WHERE TO EAT

Everyone feels uber cool at The Hangout (101 E. Beach Blvd.; 251–948–3030), the centerpiece of Gulf Shores beachfront gatherings. Huge juicy burgers and fresh shrimp lead the menu in the open-air dining room that sidles up to the beach. And when the kids aren't eating, they can build sand castles or play in the bubbles from the bubble machine.

WHERE TO STAY

Kids are happy anywhere along the Gulf, but two properties cater to them best. If you want to stay away from the crowds, go to The Beach Club (925 Beach Club Trail; 866–348–9112) on Fort Morgan Road. Condos, cottages, multiple restaurants, plus a spa, and more than 40,000 square feet of pools and a lazy river make this a top resort.

On the edge of Orange Beach, the Caribe Resort (28103 Perdido Beach Blvd.; 888–607–7020) features more condo accommodations where your family can spread out. You'll appreciate the multiple pools, spa, boat rentals and even parasailing.

The Hangout in Gulf Shores

OUTDOOR BEACH ADVENTURE:
GULF SHORES/ORANGE BEACH

For those who love fast-paced activities and the great outdoors, Gulf Shores and Orange Beach provide the ideal vacation destination. This road trip takes you to Alabama's beautiful Gulf Coast region for fishing, parasailing, hot air balloon rides, scuba diving and exciting dolphin cruises. Down along the Alabama coast, where 32 miles of sugar white-sand beaches offer fun 365 days of the year, you'll discover adventure at every turn — on land, by sea and in the air.

ADVENTURE ON THE WATER

There's nothing like reeling in a big catch. So if the thrill of the open waters lures you, charter a boat and head out for a day of deep-sea fishing to catch red snapper, marlin and other saltwater fish. Dozens of outfitters in the area offer inshore and offshore fishing excursions from daily to weekly charters and most welcome groups and families. For a list of available charters and cruises, visit the Gulf Shores/Orange Beach website.

If you prefer fishing from dry land, cast a line from the shore or off the second largest pier on the Gulf of Mexico at Gulf State Park (251-967-3474). The pier is 1,540 feet long, 20 feet wide and boasts 2,448 feet of fishing space. Restrooms and a snack bar are located on the pier. There is also a great bait and tackle shop, where you can load up on fishing lures, nets and snacks. And don't forget your fishing license, as you'll need one to fish in Alabama.

WORTH THE DRIVE

If you're on the coast in July be sure to check out the Deep Sea Fishing Rodeo on Dauphin Island. It's the oldest and largest multispecies fishing tournament in the world. The fishing rodeo began in 1929 and attracts some 3,000 anglers and more than 75,000 spectators. From Gulf Shores, you can get there via the Fort Morgan Ferry or Scenic Highway 98, which is part of the National Scenic Byway.

If sailing is more your idea of adventure, plan a trip with Orange Beach Sailing Charters (Hudson Marina, 4575 S. Wilson Blvd., Orange Beach; 251-981-7245). They offers all-day, overnight, and one-hour sails in addition to their two- and 4-hour and sunset sails. Take your camera along because you're likely to see dolphins, sea gulls, sea turtles, jellyfish and other wildlife. They also offer a sunset cruise for a more relaxing adventure.

On the back bays of Orange Beach, you can get up close and personal with bottle-nosed dolphins. All you have to do is hop aboard a catamaran cruise vessel with The Fun Boat Dolphin Cruises (27075 Marina Road, Gulf Shores; 251-971-1893). Sailaway Charters (24231 Gulf Bay Road, Gulf Shores; 251-974-5055) and Surf's Up Dolphin Cruises (28101 Perdido Beach Blvd., Orange Beach; 251-965-7873) will also provide intimate dolphin excursions.

UNDERWATER ADVENTURE

Let the fun continue underwater on a diving adventure. Several outfitters are available including Gary's Gulf Divers (27844 Canal Road, Orange Beach; 251-716-0151) who are equipped to handle all of your gear and boat needs for scuba diving. You can dive to spots along the coast to see sunken Navy ships and old bridges that resemble Roman ruins. The dives along Perdido Pass offer great opportunities for photographs and spear fishing.

The Down Under Dive Shop (1129 Gulf Shores Pkwy., Gulf Shores; 251-968-3483), another local outfitter, specializes in guided snorkeling trips and scuba charters. Check the website for schedules and pricing.

You'll want to keep your head above water as you jet along the coast on a WaveRunner or Jet Ski. Wahoo Watersports (26214 Garrett Lane, Orange Beach; (251-981-1998) offers personal watercraft rentals and pontoon boating daily from 9 a.m. to 6 p.m., and Happy Harbor Watersports (251-981-6111) features a large variety of vessels to provide many

ALABAMA FISHING LICENSE INFORMATION
State law requires an Alabama fishing license for residents and nonresidents to fish in any public waters of the state, whether fresh or salt.

hours of fun on the water. You can choose from personal watercraft, pontoon boats, runabouts and kayaks.

ADVENTURE IN THE AIR

Looking to get off the ground for more adventure? Take it up a notch by parasailing 800 feet above the shores of the Gulf of Mexico. You will enjoy spectacular views of turquoise waters and white-sand beaches as you glide through the breeze while being pulled along by a power boat. There are several outfitters in the area that offer fun high above the beautiful Gulf waters. Pleasure Island Parasail, which offers two Gulf Shores locations: 137 East Gulf Place; 251-946-9000 and 605 West Beach Blvd.; 251-923-9636. They offer Jet Ski rentals, beach chair rentals, and parasailing. o Chute em Up Parasail is located at Happy Harbor Marina in Orange Beach (27212 Marina Road; 251-303-8524) and also offers dolphin cruises and watersports. and Chute for the Skye Parasail is located on Safe Harbor Drive in Orange Beach (251-979-2475).

SAIL WITH THE PIRATES OR TAKE OFF IN A HOT AIR BALLOON

Come back down to earth and set sail with Orange Beach pirates when you take the Pirate Cruise (4575 S. Wilson Blvd., Orange Beach; 251-981-4127). Take your young pirates aboard for swashbuckling fun that includes water gun battles, singalongs, treasure hunts and contests. The two-hour cruise will take you on a fun-filled adventure around Terry Cove in Orange Beach.

Be sure to take a camera along for many great photo opportunities.

Next, experience the scenic vistas of Alabama's beautiful coast from a unique vantage point when you climb aboard a hot air balloon with Taking Off Hot Air Balloon Company (14770 Oak St., Magnolia Springs; 251-970-3598). You'll soar 1,500 to 2,000 feet over the Gulf Coast. Flights are either early morning or late evening when the winds are light. The pilot can carry two to three passengers. A typical flight lasts one hour.

FUN ON LAND

After a day of outdoor adventure, you'll want to visit the Flora-Bama (17401 Perdido Key Drive, 251-980-5118). A roadside icon since the 1970s, this lounge, package store and oyster bar sits on the Alabama/Florida line and is considered one of the last great American roadhouses. Nightly entertainment includes live bands offering country, rock, blues and beach music. An especially good time to visit the Flora-Bama is during the last week of April when thousands gather for the annual Interstate Mullet Toss. In this nationally recognized beach party, beach-goers throw dead fish back and forth across the state line.

For added fun, plan a visit to historic Fort Morgan (51 Highway 180 W.; 251-540-5257) located at the mouth of Mobile Bay in Gulf Shores. Tour the remains of the brick Civil War fort that was pivotal in the Battle of Mobile Bay where Rear Adm. David Farragut coined the phrase, "Damn the Torpedoes, Full Speed Ahead." Guides will take you through the fort as you walk in the footsteps of Confederate soldiers. You'll hear stories and learn the history of the fight to protect Mobile Bay from Union troops. A living-history program is conducted weekly during the summers, and candelight tours are held every Tuesday at 6:00 in June and July. In August, you can watch a living-history reenactment of the Battle of Mobile Bay. Guided tours of the fort are offered on Tuesdays and Thursday in

Don't Miss This

THE BLUE MARLIN GRAND CHAMPIONSHIP

Your fishing adventure continues at The Wharf Marina in Orange Beach with the Blue Marlin Grand Championship Billfish Tournament. You can enjoy a week of music events, parties and weigh-ins during "Billfish Week" in July as well as the Miss Billfish Contest and a concert at the amphitheater.

GULF COAST HOT AIR BALLOON FESTIVAL

Held every Father's Day weekend in June in Foley, the Gulf Coast Hot Air Balloon Festival features nearly 50 hot air balloons that float through the skies, providing spectacular balloon glows in the evenings.

March, April and May.

OWA, a 520-acre family-friendly tourist destination just seven miles from Alabama's popular Gulf Coast beaches, opened in 2017. The 21-ride, themed amusement park complex built by the Poarch Band of Creek Indians features the second longest roller coaster in the nation, thrill rides, midway games, kids rides, a 150-room Marriott TownePlace Suites hotel and a wide selection of restaurant and shopping opportunities. OWA has already announced plans to add an indoor waterpark, a new hotel and more restaurants and shops

Parasailing offers a bird's-eye view of the Gulf.

EASTERN SHORE:
GIRLFRIENDS BAY GETAWAY

Experience a girlfriends getaway on Alabama's Eastern Shore where the charming small town of Fairhope offers boutiques, bistros, art and the top-rated Marriott spa in the world just down the road. As you cruise along Scenic Highway 98 to Fairhope, you'll drive under canopies of oak trees draped with Spanish moss. The picturesque views are breathtaking and the beautiful buildings include the modern Daphne City Hall, built in 2008 and inspired by Italian architecture. A statue of Daphne sits atop a water fountain surrounded by palm trees.

the breathtaking beauty of Fairhope at the Fairhope Pier and Park on the bay located at the west end of Fairhope Avenue). The park is half a mile from downtown and has a fantastic display of flowers. The pier is a quarter-mile long with restrooms and a covered area. It's a great place to watch birds and spectacular sunsets over Mobile Bay.

Your getaway starts as you exit I-10 onto Hwy. 98 in Spanish Fort (Exit 35) and take the scenic route through Daphne and Fairhope. After exiting I-10, drive approximately 1.7 miles and turn right onto Scenic

resort by *Travel Leisure* magazine. The Grand is a luxurious resort offering 405 guest rooms right on Mobile Bay. Plenty of activities will keep you busy like relaxing on the white sand beach, bicycling, golfing, playing tennis on one of 10 courts, kayaking or relaxing at two pools where a poolside bar offers food and drinks. The hotel has bicycles for rent, so you can bike along the boardwalk or Scenic Hwy. 98 to take in the sights.

PAMPER YOURSELF: SPA AT THE GRAND

Get ready for a weekend of pampering at the Spa at the Grand Hotel, one of the highest-rated Marriott spas in the world. It offers 20,000 square feet of total bliss.

Fairhope is built for walkers and shopper, with boutiques and artsy shops of every description lining the sidewalks.

The waterfront village of Fairhope on Mobile Bay includes residences of writers Winston Groom and Fannie Flagg and the gallery of artist, Nall, who lives in Fairhope when not in France. The downtown streets are lined with flowers and dress shops, antique stores, cafes, B&B's, a bookstore and shops where you'll find that unique gift to take home. It has been named "Best Small Southern Town" by *Southern Living* and a Top 25 Place to Retire by *CNN Money. Coastal Living* magazine wrote, "this charming village nestles on the eastern shore of Mobile Bay like an idealized, movie-set small town."

Get away, relax and unwind as you take in

Nobody knows when a Jubilee will happen, but some locals say it has to do with tides and the pull of the moon. Fish, crabs, shrimp, eel and other sea creatures are washed ashore due to low oxygen levels in the water. Locals and lucky visitors run to the shores with buckets to scoop up the bounty. Friends, family and neighbors call out to alert each other to the phenomenon by yelling, "Jubilee!"

Hwy. 98 (just past the Publix shopping center). Downtown Fairhope is approximately 9.8 miles.

Drive along Scenic 98 under the live oaks draped with Spanish moss from Daphne and Fairhope to the Grand Hotel in Point Clear. Make a quick stop in Daphne at the beautiful city hall and take a picture of the statue of Daphne. A historic marker in front provides a brief history of the city. Stop at the pier in Fairhope to relax and watch the birds flying gracefully over the bay. It's also a great spot to watch the sun set.

Spend your getaway in a room at the Four-Diamond Grand Hotel Marriott Resort in Point Clear (1 Grand Blvd., Point Clear, 251-928-9201), a bedroom community next to Fairhope. This hotel, once referred to as the "queen of Southern resorts," was named a top

Indulge in the luxury of aromatherapy, a Swiss or custom massage, shiatsu, body treatment, facial and manicure/pedicure. Relax in a quiet room where you can enjoy the soothing sounds of a bubbling hot tub and tranquil music. Step into the hot tub, soak in a therapy bath, unwind in the steam room and sauna or take a dip in the indoor pool.

The pampering continues with makeup applications and hair styling in the salon. Buy a Spa Trail card for $50 and receive a gift card and discounts on services, food and your hotel room.

The Grand Hotel includes this luxurious spa.

DINE IN AT THE GRAND

You must experience a meal in the main dining room at the Grand to take in the breathtaking views of Mobile Bay. While enjoying the mouth-watering cuisine, you can watch the sun set over the water as pelicans fly across the rippled surface. For breakfast, try the crab scramble, a culinary delight listed in "100 Dishes To Eat in Alabama Before You Die."

STORYBOOK CHARM OF FAIRHOPE

Stroll the waterfront village of Fairhope and you'll discover its storybook charm along the flower-lined streets. Find a bargain in one of the dozens of trendy boutique shops and art galleries filled with designer clothes, art galleries, souvenirs, antiques and more. There are a number of restaurants, a hotel and B&Bs, as well. The city is also known for its beautiful flowers throughout the year.

You may want to make your first stop at the Fairhope Museum of History (24 N. Section St., Fairhope; 251-929-1471) to learn about this small town from its early beginnings. The museum features changing exhibits and is also the place to get information on Fairhope's history such as the origin of its utopian single tax. Visitors can also see the old town jail, toys, Native American artifacts and other displays. The museum is open Tuesday through Saturday, 9 a.m.-5 p.m.

Next door to the museum is the Fairhope Welcome Center (20 N. Section St.; 251-928-5095). It's a great place to pick up bro-

FAIRHOPE ARTS & CRAFTS FESTIVAL

On the third weekend in March, more than 200 artists bring their works from across the U.S. to show and sell at the Fairhope Arts & Crafts Festival, a prestigious, juried art show. The three-day weekend also includes live entertainment and has been chosen as a top-10 event by the Alabama Tourism Department and the Southeast Tourism Society.

chures, coupons and a layout of the shops. They also have public restrooms.

Take home a work of art from the Eastern Shore Art Center (401 Oak St., Fairhope; 251-928-2228). You can purchase works by local painters, sculptors and woodworkers. The center also holds workshops for adults and children.

You'll find books by Winston Groom, Fannie Flagg, Rick Bragg and more Alabama authors at the quaint bookstore on the corner in downtown Fairhope, Page & Palette (32 S. Section St.; 251-928-5295). Enjoy a cup of coffee or a latte at the Latte Da coffee shop while you're there.

WHERE TO EAT

Take a break from shopping and stop for lunch at Panini Pete's (42½ S. Section St.; 251-929-0122) in the French Quarter section of downtown. Try the muffuletta and taste why many celebrity chefs have stopped in. Or try the hot beignets for breakfast. The restaurant has been featured on Guy Fieri's Diners, Drive-ins and Dives on the Food Network. It's open for breakfast and lunch until 2:30 p.m. Monday through Saturday and also offers brunch on Sundays from 9:30 a.m. to 2:30 pm..

After your shopping adventure in Fairhope, head out for another shopping excursion at the Eastern Shore Centre in Spanish Fort (30500 State Hwy. 181, Malbis, Exit 38; 251-625-0060). The retail center features specialty stores, a movie theater and a variety of dining options. Stroll through delightfully landscaped

Point Clear's Grand Hotel is the epitome of gracious Southern hospitality.

streets and stop to enjoy an open-air musical performance or the dancing fountain at the community courtyard.

WHERE TO STAY

Emma's Bay House (201 Mobile St.; 251-990-0187) is located on Mobile Bay and overlooks the Fairhope Municipal Pier. It's only a few blocks from the heart of downtown Fairhope and its many charming boutiques.

Located on the water but within easy walking distance of the downtown area sits the Bay Breeze Guest House (742 S. Mobile St.; 866-928-8976).

The only hotel in downtown Fairhope is the Hampton Inn & Suites (23 N. Section St.; 251-928-0956) which blends beautifully into the surrounding architecture of the town. Step outside the hotel and you are ready to shop. It's across the street from the Fairhope Welcome Center.

For a complete listing of area lodging facilities, visit the Eastern Shore Chamber of Commerce.

GETTING THERE

The Eastern Shore consists of the towns of Spanish Fort, Daphne, Fairhope and Point Clear and is located on the east side of Mobile Bay. To get there from downtown Mobile, take I-10 across the bay bridge to the first exit (Exit 35). Take a right onto Hwy. 98 and make sure to turn right on the Scenic 98 route about one mile from I-10. The scenic route will take you through Daphne, Fairhope and Point Clear. You'll drive along streets lined with aged oak trees draped with Spanish moss.

FORT MIMS:
CREEK WAR BICENTENNIAL
by Edith Parten

Creeks and settlers battle in Fort Mims massacre reenactment.

For nearly a century, prior to the start of the War of 1812, whites and Creeks had lived side by side with good trade relations, intermarriage, and reliable treaties. There was almost full cooperation between the two groups, but this would soon change. In the fall of 1811, believing that whites were encroaching upon their land, the great Shawnee Chief Tecumseh traveled to Alabama to rally all Creeks to war against the whites and mixed-breed families in the region. He gave a speech at Tuckabatchee, near Tallassee, on the banks of the Tallapoosa River, challenging them to regain their former glory and retain their Indian culture and lifestyles.

By June 8, 1812, when the U.S. declared war on Great Britain and so started the War of 1812, the Creeks had become significantly divided among themselves. Most Upper Creeks, called Red Sticks because of their bright-red war clubs, wanted to resist white encroachment while most Lower Creeks, more accustomed to whites, were inclined

toward peace. As principal Red Stick leaders William Weatherford, Menawa and others violently clashed with the other chiefs of the Creek Nation, their dispute became a part of the War of 1812 and eventually led to the Creek War of 1813–14.

On this Bicentennial Road Trip, you are invited to follow the progression of the Creek Indian War from Burnt Corn and Fort Mims to Atmore, where many Creek descendants now live in sovereignty. As an added option, continue to Tallapoosa County, near Dadeville, where Andrew Jackson and his large army

ABOUT TENSAW AND ATMORE

Tensaw, home of historic Fort Mims, is an unincorporated community in Baldwin County about 16 miles from Stockton.

Atmore, headquarters for the federally-recognized Poarch Band of Creek Indians, is located in Escambia County about an hour's drive from Mobile.

Horseshoe Bend in Tallapoosa County is claimed by the cities of Alexander City, Dadeville (the county seat) and Daviston, all within a 20-mile radius of the park.

defeated the Red Sticks during the Battle of Horseshoe Bend and effectively brought the Creek War to a close with the signing of the Treaty of Fort Jackson five months later.

BATTLE OF BURNT CORN – THE FIGHT THAT STARTED IT ALL

On July 27, 1813, after learning that the British in Pensacola had armed the Indians to fight against them, local militia staged a surprise attack on the encamped Red Sticks in the first battle of the Creek War – the Battle of Burnt Corn, on Burnt Corn Creek. The Indians had left the Alabama River valley and were returning from Pensacola with supplies and ammunition when they were attacked. The militia moved in quickly and drove the Red Sticks into nearby brush before looting their camp.

The Red Sticks, not to be outdone, quickly regrouped and mounted an aggressive counterattack. After the Battle of Burnt Corn, with the Red Sticks more intent than ever on "regaining their former glory," word spread like wildfire that war was imminent.

MASSACRE AT FORT MIMS

On August 30, 1813, one month after the Battle of Burnt Corn, warring Red Sticks, led by William Weatherford, attacked the small stockade by the name of Fort Mims in Baldwin County. They killed nearly all of the 400 or more people who sought refuge at the fort – including families who were of Creek/European mixed blood as well as the militiamen who were ill prepared to protect them – before burning most of the fort to the ground. The battle raged for five hours.

Accounts differ on exactly how many people were killed during the fight – but only around 50 of the people in the fort were

Fort Mims reenactment musicians

site is owned by the Alabama Historical Commission but is operated by the Fort Mims Restoration Association, which hosts an annual commemorative event the last weekend in August. Fort Mims is open daily from daylight to dark (1813 Fort Mims Road, Stockton; 251-533-9024).

FORT MIMS LIVING HISTORY WEEKEND

Before leaving the area, visit the burial ground of William Weatherford in the nearby Little River community. The gravesite is about a 10-mile drive north on Highway 59. To get there, turn west on Dixie Landing Road, travel about 2.3 miles and then take a left on T.J. Earle Road. Drive one mile to Red Eagle Road on the right. At the end of the road you will find the stone grave marker of Weatherford beneath beautiful moss-laden oak trees.

He is buried next to his mother, Sehoy, who was also a prominent Creek Indian.

2013 marked the 200th anniversary of the attack at Fort Mims, as well as the beginning of the Creek War in Alabama. The best time to visit is in August during the annual Fort Mims Re-enactment and Living History Weekend (251-937-5665 or 251-533-9024).

known to have escaped. Pickett's *History of Alabama*, records that nearly one-half of the Indian force also died that fateful day. Other accounts, such as Gregory Waselkov's *A Conquering Spirit* (2006), put the numbers at 350 dead at the fort and many killed and wounded on the Indian side.

Today, the five-acre site is surrounded by a rail fence and has native plants, six historical markers, a picnic pavilion and a backdrop of the reconstructed wooden walls.

A block-house, similar to structures built in the early 1800s, is located at the southwest corner of the fort wall. Interpretive signs throughout the area tell the story of the attack and lists family names of those killed as well as the survivors so visitors can see if they are descendants.

A recorded five-minute narrative about Fort Mims is available at the west end of the pavilion with the push of a button. The

Don't Miss This

In Atmore, find David's Catfish House (1504 S Main St.; 251-368-3063) for some of the best catfish in the South. You'll find more than catfish there, too. The shrimp, crab claws and oysters are purchased from Alabama's seafood capital, Bayou La Batre. The batters, breadings and mixes are made from scratch each day. David's Catfish House is open Tuesday through Saturday 11 a.m. to 9 p.m.

Volunteers dress in period clothing to re-enact the Battle of Burnt Corn followed by the Battle of Fort Mims. You can witness living history as well as enjoy period music, arts, crafts, covered wagons, tomahawk throwing, blacksmithing, concessions, dancing and 1800s cooking demonstrations.

The fort, which was hurriedly constructed as a log stockade in 1813 around the home of Samuel Mims, consisted of 17 buildings including the Mims home. Mims, settling in the 1790s in what was then the Mississippi Territory, had become wealthy taking passengers and all their belongings across the Alabama River on his ferry at the terminus of the Federal Road that crossed Alabama and Georgia.

Fort Mims reenactment

ATMORE AND THE POARCH BAND OF CREEK INDIANS

About 20 minutes northeast of Fort Mims in Atmore, descendants of a segment of the original Creek Nation, the Poarch Band of Creek Indians, have lived together for nearly 200 years. This group represents the only federally recognized tribe in the state of Alabama, operating as a sovereign nation with its own system of government. The tribe owns the nearby Wind Creek Casino & Hotel (303 Poarch Road; 866-946-3360), just off I-65, where you can enjoy entertainment, a spa treatment, overnight lodging and your choice of four restaurants.

It also plays host to the annual Thanksgiving Day Pow Wow, which features dance and drum contests, various tournaments, food and the crowning of the Indian princesses.

For more information, visit the Atmore Area Chamber of Commerce website or call 251-368-3305.

WHERE TO EAT

On your way to Atmore, the Stagecoach Cafe (52860 AL Highway 59; 251–580–0608) in Stockton is a good place to stop any day of the week, but especially on Sundays when the restaurant is serving its shrimp and grits and Miss Cathy is singing and playing the piano.

TRAVEL TIP:

To prepare for your visit to Fort Mims, be sure to bring chairs, bug repellent, comfortable shoes and light clothing as the summer heat and humidity can be intense. "Cool Zones" can be found during the Living History weekend with tents and fans to dissipate the summer heat. The site is in a wooded area near Boatyard Lake and the Alabama River.

GETTING THERE

Note that Fort Mims has a Stockton address, but the actual site is closer to Tensaw, about 4 miles away. To get to Fort Mims, take Exit 34 (Highway 59) from I-65 and travel 3.5 miles west to Stockton. Continue on Highway 59 for 12 miles, turn left onto Boatyard Road (County Road 80) and follow it approximately three miles to Fort Mims Road. You will see a historical marker at the intersection. Turn right onto Fort Mims Road and continue around the curve through a camping-style neighborhood. The site will be on the right. Note: There are portable restroom facilities at Fort Mims.

DAUPHIN ISLAND:
YOUR ISLAND GETAWAY

Dauphin Island is the perfect destination for a relaxing getaway. A natural environment surrounded by the beautiful turquoise waters of the Gulf of Mexico, this small barrier island is set apart by white-sand beaches, walking trails, bountiful wildlife and lots of history. In fact, the entire island is a designated bird sanctuary and has been named one of the nation's "birdiest coastal communities."

As you drive across the 3-mile-long high-rise bridge from the mainland to the island, you'll discover panoramic landscapes, boats of all sizes and a unique small-town charm. The island is so low-key there are no traffic lights anywhere, making it easy to navigate. The road connecting the island to the mainland (Highway 193) ends in a "T" at the water tower with the island's main road, Bienville Boulevard, stretching from historic Fort Gaines on the east end to the scenic and pristine beaches on the west end.

Stop at the Dauphin Island Welcome Center (1018 Bienville Blvd.; 521-861-2150) for a brief introduction to the area and for brochures, information, restrooms and free wi-fi.

BIRD MIGRATIONS ACROSS THE ISLAND

Dauphin Island has been named one of the top four places in North America to view bird migrations in the spring. Self-guided tours through the Audubon Bird Sanctuary (109 Bienville Blvd.; 251-861-3607) and Shell Mound Park should be included in your visit. Located on the island's eastern end, both sites are easily accessible and have plenty to offer for bird watchers and other outdoor enthusiasts.

The 137-acre bird sanctuary covers a diverse landscape of maritime forests, marshes, sand dunes, a lake, swamp and beach and is the first landfall for many neotropical migratory birds after their long northerly flight across the Gulf from Central and South America. The sanctuary has three miles of trails, which together have been designated a National Recreation Trail. From here, an amazing 420 species have been reported on the island.

The 11-acre Shell Mound Park dates back to A.D. 900-1500. Early Native Americans are believed to have visited the island during the winter in search of oysters and fish. So many oysters were consumed at the site over the centuries that massive mounds of shells eventually formed. Giant, moss-draped live oak trees adorn both parks in their pure, natural setting. Botanists have estimated some at approximately 800 years old, meaning many of these massive oaks were already mature by the time the Spaniards first visited the shores of Dauphin Island in 1519.

Hands-on exhibit at the Dauphin Island Estuarium

The Bird Sanctuary and Shell Mound Park are two renowned "hot-spots" for observing neotropical migratory birds. The two sites attract birders from around the world each spring and fall and have become a "must see" stop on the Alabama Coastal Birding Trail. Tip: As with most outdoor excursions along the Gulf Coast, bring bug spray during the summer months to keep mosquitoes at bay.

Don't Miss This

THE ESTUARIUM

Dauphin Island Estuarium and Sea Lab (101 Bienville Blvd.; 251-861-7500), a marine science research lab and education center, showcases marine life native to local waters. The hands-on area of the Estuarium contains preserved fish, eels, sharks and stingrays and provides a great opportunity for kids to learn about sea life. You'll also see live baby alligators, octopus, turtles, seahorses, glowing jellyfish and so much more. An outdoor exhibit displays stingrays and baby sharks from around Mobile Bay.

Dauphin Island is a 14-mile-long barrier island located three miles south of the mouth of Mobile Bay in the Gulf of Mexico. To get to the island, one must cross a 3-mile-long high-rise bridge that opened in 1982 after the original was destroyed by Hurricane Frederic in 1979. A ferry from the Eastern side of Mobile Bay offers an entry point for vehicles and passengers. The eastern six miles of the island are inhabited while the western eight miles are undeveloped. Dauphin Island is home to approximately 1,200 permanent residents, but that number dramatically increases during vacation and holiday times. The entire island has been designated a bird sanctuary, and thousands of visitors come each year to experience the annual migrations. The island and its beaches are pet friendly, but please observe the local leash laws.

GETTING THERE

Shell Mound Park is located on North Iberville Street. To reach the park, arrive on the island via Highway 193, turn left on Bienville Boulevard, proceed two blocks, and then turn left on North Iberville. The park is free to visit. An estimated 25,000 people, comprising student tours, snowbirds and birding groups, visit the mounds each year. Call Alabama Marine Resources Division (251-861-2882) for more info.

The Audubon Bird Sanctuary is located on the eastern end of the island near the ferry terminal. When traveling from Highway 193, take a left at the stop sign and continue straight until you see signs on the right side of the street approximately one mile east. If you reach the ferry terminal, you've gone too far.

OTHER ISLAND PARKS

East End Park, next to Fort Gaines on the extreme eastern shore of the island, includes a small pier, free boat launches at Billy Goat Hole, picnic tables and great views of Mobile Bay. Fishing is popular from the pier.

The Dauphin Island Beach and Pier – an 850-foot structure with benches, picnic tables and a concession stand – serves as easy access to the main Dauphin Island public beach. Shifts in the shoal system and previous storm activity have altered this natural landscape, rendering an expansion of the beach and a

temporary fusion of Little Sand Island with the Dauphin Island Public Beach.

Aloe Bay Landing Park, a small waterfront park in the industrial section of the island, offers calm waters from which to launch a canoe or kayak. It's also a great place to watch the fishing and shrimp boats arrive with the day's catch, or to enjoy a simple picnic and the sunset.

Bayou Heron Park is a small waterfront park popular with bird watchers. It has a small pier, picnic tables and benches.

Magnolia Park, between the ferry landing and Fort Gaines on the eastern side of the island, is a very small park that is only accessible by foot traffic. A porch swing hanging from a beautiful magnolia tree provides an opportunity to relax in the shade.

OTHER AREA ATTRACTIONS

For a small community, Dauphin Island offers visitors access to a variety of area attractions that will keep the family busy. West End Beach has acres of beautiful sand beaches with lifeguards, showers and air-conditioned facilities as well as a water-slide for kids of all ages. Vendors provide chairs, umbrellas, boogie boards and food.

Expect to pay a $3 entrance fee for parking in addition to $3 per person over age 12. Many island businesses offer specials that include passes and discounts.

At Fort Gaines (51 Bienville Blvd.; 251-861-6992), you will see cannons, a working blacksmith, stables, bunkers and more. The historic Civil War fort was instrumental in the Battle for Mobile Bay – the battle from which Adm. David Farragut coined the phrase "Damn the torpedoes! Full speed ahead!" The view from atop the fort is striking as you can see the Sand Island Lighthouse in the distance. The lighthouse is listed as one of the most endangered in the country due to erosion and damage by hurricanes.

FUN ON THE WATER

Dauphin Island offers plenty of outdoor activities including kayaking and fishing. Kayak rentals are available by calling Dauphin Island Kayak Rentals and Tours (251-422-5285). Operators will deliver and pick up kayaks, and you can schedule a tour.

Dauphin Island is also home to the Alabama Deep Sea Fishing Rodeo, the world's largest saltwater fishing tournament (listed in *Guinness World Records*). The first rodeo took place in 1929, attracting 260 fishermen.

Today, the rodeo attracts more than 75,000 visitors and more than 3,200 anglers. Participants compete with catches of king mackerel, speckled trout, tuna, shark, swordfish and other big game fish. If you can't make it for the annual three-day summer event, you can still plan your own in-shore or deep-sea fishing excursion with more than half a dozen outfitters and charter captains operating out of the Dauphin Island Marina.

WHERE TO EAT

Lighthouse Bakery (919 Chaumont Ave.; 251-861-2253) serves breakfast and lunch items including muffins, sandwiches and subs. Locals love the Sunday special, a crab omelet. The bakery is open Wednesday through Sunday.

Blooming azaleas and bright greenery of spring draw visitors to Bellingrath Gardens and Home.

PLACES TO STAY

Lodging on Dauphin Island includes rental houses, condos, a motel and a campground. Good resources for finding beach lodging include the South Mobile County Tourism Authority (251-861-8747) and the Dauphin Island Chamber of Commerce (251-861-5524).

Gulf Breeze Motel (1512 Cadillac Ave.; 251-861-7344) is the only motel on the island. It sports a retro vibe from its back-in-the-day exterior down to the metal room keys. The modest-looking hotel was featured in the movie *October Baby*.

The Fish Camps at Dauphin Island are at the end of the large bridge leading onto the island. These pastel-colored structures are built on piers and are occasionally available for rent.

The Dauphin Island Campground is located on the island's east end. To get there, take a left at the water tower. The campground offers 150 sites with power and water, a store, bathhouses, showers, barbecue grills and free boat launches.

It also has fun activities for the kids, including walking trails, a playground, bike rentals, horseshoes, volleyball and shuffleboard.

NEARBY TOWNS WORTH THE TRIP

Bayou La Batre, the "Seafood Capital of Alabama," is renowned for its fresh Gulf seafood and is featured in the Academy Award-winning movie *Forrest Gump*. Visitors can watch the shrimp boats return to the dock with the day's catch. Annual events such as the Blessing of the Fleet in May and Taste of the Bayou in September pay tribute to the town's fishing industry. Bayou La Batre was known as a resort town in the late 1800s through the early 1900s and was home to numerous historic waterfront homes and hotels frequented by wealthy vacationers from throughout the region.

Nearby Grand Bay is well known for its watermelons. The Grand Bay Watermelon Festival, which has been a July Fourth tradition here since 1973, allows visitors the juicy opportunity to sample locally-grown watermelons. Farmers in the area also grow pecans, peaches and satsumas. While here, be sure and visit the Grand Bay National Wildlife Refuge (228-475-0765). It encompasses 10,188 acres to help protect one of the largest remaining expanses of wet pine savanna habitats on the Gulf Coast.

The town of Theodore's claim to fame is the ever-popular Bellingrath Gardens and Home, near Mobile. The garden estate of Walter and Bessie Bellingrath features 65 acres of landscaped beauty and includes a conservatory, nature walk, water elements, several themed gardens and the home. Theodore is also the site of the Alabama Pecan Festival each November.

The event features music, arts and crafts and the signature sweet Southern pecan prepared and served in a variety of ways.

An excellent way to see the island is on a bike. Rentals are available from the Dauphin Island Bicycle and Kayak Rentals (251-861-2222). Call for bike pickup and delivery anywhere on the island.

GETTING THERE

Dauphin Island is approximately 30 miles south of Mobile. From Mobile, take Interstate 10 west to exit 17. Head south on Highway 193 (Dauphin Island Parkway) and continue to follow 193 to Dauphin Island. If traveling east, take exit 4 and follow Highway 188 south. Continue on 188 and turn right on Highway 193 (Dauphin Island Parkway).

ALABAMA'S COASTAL CONNECTION:
NATIONAL SCENIC BYWAY
by Colette Boehm

Shrimp boats alongside the Billy's Seafood dock at Bon Secour

Beautiful beaches, authentic downtowns, wildlife preserves, historic sites and the freshest of seafood are all yours to enjoy on Alabama's Coastal Connection, a nationally designated scenic byway. Alabama's southern tip is one of those places where even first-time visitors will find a place to belong. Traveling the byway, you'll experience the link between the traditions of the Deep South and a more laid-back island lifestyle. And, amid the thousands of acres of preserved lands, the beautiful coastal waterways, and the good life of a beachfront vacation, you'll discover a myriad of opportunities to make your own connection to Alabama's Gulf Coast.

CONNECT WITH NATURE

From migratory birds and sea discoveries on Dauphin Island to the 7,000 acres of wildlife habitat at Bon Secour National Wildlife Refuge (12295 AL Highway 180, Gulf Shores; 251-540-7720), the first leg of this nature journey is filled with amazing views. A safe haven for an abundance of threatened and endangered species of wildlife, flora and fauna, the refuge is comprised of five separate units in Mobile and Baldwin counties and has been named one of the 10 natural wonders of Alabama.

From Bon Secour, stop at Orange Beach Marina (27075 Marina Rd., Orange Beach; 251-981-4207), Zeke's Landing (26619 Perdido Beach Boulevard; 251-981-4044) or any one of the nearly two dozen other boat harbors. Make plans to spend the day having fun watching dolphins in their natural habitat, experiencing the deep waters of the Gulf on a guided fishing charter or going parasailing for the afternoon.

If you've got a hunger spot, you'll find two excellent restaurants on the premises of Orange Beach Marina. The restaurants are housed under one roof, that of Fisher's at Orange Beach Marina (27075 Marina

Rd; 251-981-7305). Fisher's Upstairs is fine dining in a relaxed environment; whereas, Fisher's Dockside, downstairs, is more casual. At Zeke's Landing, Wolf Bay Lodge is the downstairs restaurant by the docks at Zeke's Landing. It offers home-style Southern cooking, seafood and more in a casual, family-friendly atmosphere. At the Shrimp Basket at Zeke's, you can enjoy a refreshing cocktail inside the café or under a covered patio while waiting for your perfectly grilled, steamed or fried seafood.

There are lots of recreational opportunities along the Coastal Connection, but if fishing sets the order for your day, then you'll want to be geared up to catch the big one. Lost Bay Tackle and Guide Service (25405 Perdido Beach Blvd.; 850-748-5076) is located about two miles west of Zeke's Marina on Highway

ABOUT ALABAMA'S COASTAL CONNECTION

The Alabama Coastal Connection is one of 150 treasured places in 46 states recognized by the Federal Highway Administration as a National Scenic Byway. It connects the people and places in coastal Mobile and Baldwin counties and showcases the rich culture and flavor of Alabama's Gulf Coast region.

182. Lost Bay is one of several places to find live bait, rod and reel combinations and just about anything else you could possibly want to meet your fishing needs, plus Lost Bay offers guided fishing trips as well.

Another one of the Coastal Connection marinas, SanRoc Cay (27267 Perdido Beach Blvd., Orange Beach; 251-981-5423) offers you the opportunity to enjoy everything from courtyard events, shopping and dining to parasailing, fishing charters, scuba diving or simply spending the day relaxing by the beautiful Gulf. The Dock Store at the marina is great for buying bait, tackle and ice, but is also an excellent source for purchasing snack foods and some everyday items you may have forgotten to bring with you. There are also some exclusive stores at SanRoc, ranging

A regal blue heron fishes in the shallows at Weeks Bay Reserve.

THE BLESSING OF THE FLEET

This leg of the scenic byway winds its way through Bayou La Batre, approximately 30 minutes from Mobile. On the first Sunday in May, Alabama's Gulf Coast fishing and shrimping communities come together to offer prayers for a bountiful harvest, the safety of boating vessels and the people on board during the annual Blessing of the Fleet. Hosted by St. Margaret's Catholic Church (13790 S. Wintzell Ave.; 251-824-2415), the celebration includes land and boat parades, arts and crafts, a gumbo cook-off, seafood dinners, live entertainment and boat tours.

from women's dress shops to a soap and skin-care shop.

From Orange Beach, your connection to nature moves onward to Weeks Bay, which is home to many species of waterfowl and one of few National Estuarine Research Reserves (11300 U.S. Highway 98, Fairhope; 251-928-9792) in the country. This leg of your trip concludes along the eastern shore of Mobile Bay, where calm waters are framed by stately oaks in the quaint coastal communities of Daphne, Fairhope, and Spanish Fort. This portion of the Coastal Connection is abundantly rich in art, antiques and history, and is one of the most charming areas in the state.

CONNECT WITH LAND AND SEA

A salute to the people who make their living from the land and sea, another trip portion of the byway begins in Grand Bay. For more than a century, farmers in this once vibrant community have thrived on crops of pecans, cotton, soybeans and watermelons. The Grand Bay Watermelon Festival (Grand Bay Odd Fellows Festival Park, 10327 Taylor F. Harper Blvd., Grand Bay; 251-865-3456) celebrates the agricultural heritage of the area

annually around the Fourth of July. The event offers lots of arts and crafts, entertainment, a pretty baby contest and all the free watermelon you can eat, so come hungry.

CONNECT WITH THE PAST

From Bayou La Batre, point your car in the direction of Dauphin Island. Along the way, discover the floral beauty of Bellingrath Gardens (12401 Bellingrath Gardens Road; 251-973-2217) in nearby Theodore. This world-renowned property showcases acres of gardens, blooming all year long. Then cross the waters of the Mississippi Sound onto Dauphin Island. You can also retrace the steps of history from Fort Gaines (51 Bienville Blvd., Dauphin Island; 251-861-6992) to Fort Morgan (110 AL Hwy. 180 W., Gulf Shores; 251-540-7202), where the echoes of battles past still ring. Imagine naval gunboats sailing up river and troops planning to occupy the city of Mobile.

All along the route, local museums tell the story of the heritage and traditions of coastal Alabama, as well as the storms that have affected the area.

History buffs will not want to miss the chance to cross the bay and imagine the smoke of the big guns as Farragut cried, "Damn the torpedoes! Full speed ahead!" during the Battle of Mobile Bay. The Mobile Bay Ferry is an auto ferry that makes the trip between Historic Fort Gaines and Fort Morgan part of the adventure.

They also showcase the resilience of the region, its communities and residents, who have rebounded stronger after each event.

CONNECT WITH OTHERS

For added adventure, you can set your own pace and your own path along Alabama's Coastal Connection. Get lost on purpose on a coastal hideaway, head out for a day of charter fishing or dine your way from one great restaurant to the next. You'll find a number of great places to eat on the Gulf in Alabama Tourism's "100 Dishes to Eat Before you Die." Spending time your way with your favorite folks is the best way to enjoy the byway.

WHERE TO EAT

Seafood is king on the Coastal Connection! There are plenty of elegant dining options to choose from, but for a good old, casual seafood feast, try any of the three Tacky Jacks locations, each overlooking the water. Dine at the beautiful Playa at Sportsman Marina (27842 Canal Rd.; 251-981-9891) in Orange Beach, which is run by the team at Fisher's at Orange Beach Marina.

WHERE TO STAY

Lodging options along the byway offer variety for all types of travelers. From quiet out-of-the-way bed and breakfast inns to luxurious beachfront condominiums, local tourism offices can direct you to the accommodations that will make your stay complete. For more information, visit the Alabama Coastal Connection website.

HISTORIC HOUSE MUSEUMS OF MOBILE

Mobile's historic homes offer everything from antebellum mansions with spiraling staircases and moss draped oak trees to Creole cottages and bungalows. Some of the other architectural styles you'll see are Italianate, Greek Revival, Victorian and Revivalism. This Historic House Museums of Mobile Road Trip takes you on a tour where you'll hear stories of the families that built the homes and see personal keepsakes, antiques, furniture and workmanship that make the stories come alive. From the grand Bragg-Mitchell to the Richards DAR House Museum, the historic house museums of Mobile are sure to provide a memorable experience for those who love history, architecture and a good story.

GETTING STARTED

The Fort of Colonial Mobile (150 S. Royal St.; 251-802-3092), known around Mobile simply as Fort Conde is the official visitor's center for Mobile and is a great first stop for brochures, coupons and information on historic homes in the downtown area. Fort Conde is the site of the French fort built in 1723 to protect Mobile; however, it has been reconstructed and represents only about one-third the size of the original fort. Here you can see cannons, guns, old barracks and other artifacts from the era. Admission is free.

THE HISTORC HOUSE MUSEUMS

The Conde-Charlotte Museum House (104 Theatre St.; 251-432-4722) is next to Fort Conde and sits on land that originally housed the city jail. In fact, you can still see the jail cells in the garden out back. A small, square portion of the floor in the downstairs parlor is covered in Plexiglas to show the

remnants of the old jail. You can see shackles, a bucket and utensils.

Outside the Conde-Charlotte Museum House you will see five flags that represent the entities that have ruled over Mobile during its 300-year history: France, Spain, Britain, the Confederate States of America and the U.S.. Also, each room is decorated with period furnishings depicting Mobile's history under each of the five flags. The house was built by Jonathan Kirkbride and his wife, Elizabeth, in 1850. It is owned and operated by the National Society of the Colonial Dames of America in the State of Alabama. Hours are Tuesday through Saturday,. 11 a.m.-3:30 p.m., with the last guided tour starting at 3 p.m.

Oakleigh Historic Mansion (300 Oakleigh Place; 251-432-1281), the official period house of Mobile, is located in the Oakleigh Garden Historic District and sits at the highest elevation in the neighborhood. The two-story house was originally built as a gentlemen's escape and is constructed of

pine and cypress in a raised Greek Revival Villa-style. It has belonged to several families through the years and has been modified. Though not available for touring, the Cook House at the back of the property has been restored. It is one of the city's last-standing detached kitchens and servants' quarters. The Oakleigh Mansion is open for tours Friday through Monday 10 a.m. to 4 p.m. and on Sunday from 1 p.m. to 4 p.m.

A few highlights to point out include the dinner table in the dining room; it's one of the first pedestal tables. Also, according to docents, the wallpaper design in the dining room is replicated from a pattern on one of

Don't Miss This

MOBILE HISTORIC HOMES TOUR

Each year in March, the Mobile Historic Preservation Society holds an annual Mobile Historic Homes Tour. The tour includes the Oakleigh and Bragg-Mitchell mansions in addition to many homes not normally open to the public.

Bragg-Mitchell Mansion

Martha Washington's gowns. The children's room upstairs overlooks the backyard and is equipped with period toys and dolls.

The Bragg-Mitchell Mansion (1906 Springhill Ave.; 251-471-6364) is located just outside downtown Mobile. You can't miss the gorgeous expanse of lawn with a grove of tall oak trees draped in Spanish moss. Built in 1855, the antebellum home is indeed a grand Southern mansion with Greek Revival, Italianate and Georgian features throughout. It was built for Judge John Bragg who also

Call the mansion for information on specifics. **Tip:** *The mansion holds its holiday open house where you can see it decorated in all of its period Christmas finery.*

The Richards DAR House Museum (256 N. Joachim St., 251-208-7320) is an Italianate-style townhome built in 1860 for riverboat captain Charles Richards. It's located in the De Tonti Square neighborhood on a small street just east of Dauphin. This is Mobile's oldest neighborhood.

As you walk up the steps to the home, you

The docent tells the story that the granddaughter sold silver coins with her grandfather's image to make the tea set. The fireplaces in the home are made of Carrara marble and display intricate workmanship.

WORTH THE DRIVE

The Bellingrath Home (12401 Bellingrath Gardens Rd., Theodore; 251-973-2217) at Bellingrath Gardens (about 20 minutes from downtown Mobile) is a 15-room, 10,500-square-foot home built in 1935 and

Ladies in period costume welcome visitors to Oakleigh Mansion.

Mobile is a port city located on Mobile Bay along the Gulf of Mexico that came under the rule of five governments during its 300-year history: France, Spain, Great Britain, the Confederacy and the U.S. Mobile was founded in 1702 by Jean Baptiste Le Moyne de Bienvielle and Pierre Le Moyne d'Iberville as the capital of French Louisiana. It did not become a part of the U.S. until 1813 when it was captured by American forces.

The city is also home to Mardi Gras which had its early beginnings in the city in 1703. Several parks are located in squares in the downtown area, one being Bienville Square. The historic city park is located on Dauphin Street and is named after the city's founder.

owned a home in Lowndes County outside Montgomery, but the Union Army destroyed that home.

When you walk through the front door into the large foyer, you will see a Waterford crystal chandelier and a beautiful staircase leading to the second floor. Although the house sat vacant for 15 years before opening as a museum, there are still a large number of furnishings original to the home.

A typical tour takes about an hour but expect to stay longer if you have questions. Be sure to take time to visit the gift shop on the second floor. The home is open for tours Tuesday through Friday, 10 a.m.-4 p.m. with the last tour starting at 3 p.m. Often in December, the mansion offers a holiday open house or other holiday-related activities.

will notice the ironwork on the porch. Look closely within the wrought iron to see the depiction of each of the four seasons.

Step through the front door and you will see the beautiful handcarved mahogany staircase to the left. Turn around and view the beautiful ruby-red stained Bohemian glass framing the door. The furnishings in the home are not original, but they are period pieces dating from 1870 and earlier, which makes the Richards House the only house museum in Mobile where you can sit on the furniture, according to docents. The only original piece of furniture is the Weber box grand piano in the entryway.

In the dining room, you will see a coin silver tea set and just above it hangs a portrait of George Washington's granddaughter.

designed by prominent Mobile architect George B. Rogers. Wanting the architecture to reflect the Gulf Coast region, Rogers constructed the exterior from handmade brick salvaged from the 1852 birthplace of Alva Smith Vanderbilt Belmont in Mobile. The ironwork also came from Mobile, from the demolished Southern Hotel. The home features flagstone terraces, a central courtyard, balconies and covered galleries and a slate roof with copper downspouts. The stone paths throughout the gardens were taken from the old city sidewalks of Mobile. The architectural result was dubbed "English Renaissance" by Rogers. The Bellingrath Home appears as it did when the family lived in the house. It's open to visitors for daily tours from 9 a.m.-3:30 p.m. During Magic Christmas in Lights, tours end at 8 p.m.

All of the original furnishings are on display to guests and include porcelain figurines from France and England along with Meissen porcelain from Germany. You'll enjoy seeing the "ultra modern" pink bathrooms of 1935, the kitchen with its original appliances and state-of-the-art dishwasher, German silver countertops and sinks, and the butler's pantry overflowing with a collection of silver, crystal and china that belonged to the home's owners, Walter and Bessie Mae Bellingrath.

The adjoining guest house and garage was completed in 1939 and has housed a collection of Boehm porcelain since 1967. This fine American porcelain collection was a gift to the Bellingrath-Morse Foundation by the Delchamps family of Mobile. This building also serves as a visitor's lounge and adjoins the family chapel.

After your visit to the home, stop at the Magnolia Café at the Bellingrath Gardens & Home Visitor's Center and gift shop for a bite to eat. The chicken salad is listed in the "100 Dishes to Eat in Alabama Before You Die" brochure.

Though an hour outside Mobile, the Swift-Coles Historic Home in Bon Secour (17424 Swift-Coles Lane; 251-949-5550) is a site that historical-home-lovers will not want to miss. This house was originally built in

1882 as a four-room cabin. The Swift family bought it in 1898 and expanded it to fit their ten-person household. In 1976, Nik Coles purchased the home, filled it with foreign antiques, and, in 2007, bequeathed it to the Baldwin County Historic Development Commission. Now, the home is now listed on the National Register of Historic Places. Tour the home for $10 on Tuesdays and Fridays from 10 a.m. to 3 p.m., or call to arrange a private tour. If you visit around the holidays, you might have the change to attend an open house at the home.

GETTING THERE

To get to Bellingrath Gardens and Home from Interstate 10, take exit 15A (Hwy. 90 West/Theodore exit). Travel approximately 2 miles and turn left at the Bellingrath billboard onto Bellingrath Road. Travel six miles south on Bellingrath Road and turn left.

To get to the Swift-Coles Historic Home from Mobile, head east on I-10, across Mobile Bay, and head south on scenic Highway 98. Continue east on 98 at Barnwell, and then head south on Highway 49 until you reach Bon Secour. Though stretching 40 miles southeast of mobile, this beautiful drive exposes you to the beautiful coastal towns of Daphne, Fairhope, Point Clear, and more.

WHERE TO EAT IN DOWNTOWN MOBILE

The Spot of Tea (301 Dauphin St., 251-433-9009) is located in beautiful downtown Mobile across from Cathedral Square and the Portier House. It's open for breakfast and lunch. There's a wide variety of menu choices that include Eggs Benedict Cathedral which is listed in the tourism brochure, "100 Dishes to Eat in Alabama Before You Die."

HISTORICAL PLACES TO STAY

The Fort Conde Inn (165 St. Emanuel St., 251-405-5040) is a boutique hotel located in an 1836 house, the second oldest in Mobile.

It is tucked away behind Fort Conde on a quiet street surrounded by Victorian homes.

The inn and other surrounding historic homes were renovated and restored in 2010 to house guest rooms. The inn has 22 guest rooms and suites 3 cottages including the Blakely and Gonzales cottages. It serves a scrumptious breakfast prepared daily by the chef and served from 7:30 – 9 a.m.

The hotel manager, Alan Waugh, is a delight and very welcoming. Plans are underway to renovate several homes on the same street to add to the total number of rooms available.

Kate Shepard House (1552 Monterey Place, 251-479-7048). This Queen Anne home turned B&B was built in 1897 for Mr. C.M. Shepard by architect George F. Barber. Beginning in 1910, this home was used by Mr. Shepard's daughter, Kate, for a private boarding school for prominent Mobile children. Today, the house is a B&B owned by Wendy and Bill James. The three rooms of the B&B will typically cost $160 per night. That includes a gourmet breakfast with offerings of Pecan Praline French Toast, Southern Scotch Eggs, biscuits, bacon and beignets.

The Admiral Hotel (251 Government St., 251-432-8000). This historical property opened its doors in 1940 and was the first building in Mobile with air conditioning. The hotel has 152 guestrooms that channel the sophisticated allure of the 1940's gilded age glamour with flourishes of modernity. The hotel has a pool, courtyard and two restaurants. Corner 251 is a laidback bar and bistro, and Launch Urban Upscale Dining is a fine-dining eatery.

The Battle House Renaissance Hotel (26 N. Royal St., 251-338-2000) is a AAA Four Diamond historic hotel in the heart of downtown Mobile with 207 rooms and 31 suites.

Three restaurants in the hotel, the Joe Cain Café, Trellis Room and the Royal Street Tavern offer breakfast, lunch and dinner. The spa and pool are located across the street, but easy to get to with the hotel skywalk. The hotel is pet friendly.

FORT MORGAN, DAUPHIN ISLAND, THEODORE:
GULF COAST BIRDING

Alabama's Gulf Coast is a stopover point for birds as they return from Central to North America in the spring, so it's the perfect place to see herons, seagulls, pelicans and more.

The Alabama Coastal Birding Trail (877-226-9089) spans Baldwin and Mobile counties and is a bird watcher's paradise. You can watch pelicans fly in formation as they prepare to nose dive into the Gulf of Mexico for the catch of the day. Or see great blue herons sail across Mobile Bay and watch a breathtaking sunset.

The trail winds through more than 270 birding sites and is enhanced by directional and interpretive signage. Loops are close enough that you can easily drive from one to the other. Along the way you'll find plenty of places to eat, sightsee and soak in the local flavor, so grab your binoculars and head out for a walk on the wild side.

EXPLORE A WILDLIFE HABITAT

On your way to Fort Morgan, stop and visit the Bon Secour National Wildlife Refuge located off Fort Morgan Road (12295 AL Hwy. 180, Gulf Shores; 251-540-7720). The refuge is made up of 7,000 acres of wildlife habitat for migratory birds, sea turtles and the endangered Alabama beach mouse. The refuge has been named one of the 10 Natural Wonders of Alabama because of its wild, undeveloped land. More than 370 species of birds have been identified at Bon Secour during migratory seasons. Visitors can explore the area by walking one of the five trails within the refuge. The Jeff Friend Trail meanders along a maritime forest and lagoon, the

Centennial Trail winds around sand dunes and swamps, the Pine Beach Trail takes you along an ecosystem that includes a saltwater and freshwater lake, and the Dynamic Dunes Beach Trail takes you along the waters' edge. The tours are for both beginners and experienced birders.

AN ISLAND BIRD SANCTUARY

After bird watching at Bon Secour, drive to the ferry landing at Fort Morgan (251-861-3000). The ferry takes you across Mobile Bay to Dauphin Island, named one of North America's best places for migratory bird watching.

You can enjoy watching birds in the 160-acre Audubon Bird Sanctuary on Dauphin Island (109 Bienville Blvd., Dauphin Island; 251-861-3607), considered one of the top bird watching sites in the United States. In 1988, the town designated the entire island a bird sanctuary. In fact, *WildBird* magazine named Dauphin Island a top-four location in North America for viewing spring migrations. Also, stroll down the trail system to the freshwater lake, an interactive nature loop, forests and white-sand beaches.

Each October, local birders host the Alabama Coastal BirdFest. The event includes workshops, demonstrations, and guided bird tours. Participants can sign up for guided or unguided trips to explore some of the best birding spots on the coast. You can also shop for bird-related merchandise

Bird perched on Dauphin Island marsh grass silhouetted by setting sun

Don't Miss This

BIRD-BANDING AT FORT MORGAN

Start your birding trip in Fort Morgan (110 AL Hwy. 180W; 251-540-5257) at the historic Civil War site where for two weeks each spring and fall bird watchers can enjoy the banding season. You'll be able to see a variety of birds at this banding station, including hummingbirds.

DAUPHIN ISLAND

While on Dauphin Island, be sure to visit the Estuarium and Sea Lab (101 Bienville Blvd.; 251-861-7500) where you will find marine life native to Alabama's Gulf Coast. Located at the ferry landing, the Sea Lab features a 10,000-square-foot exhibit hall with interactive exhibits and living displays showcasing the area's marine life. The educational facility highlights the four key habitats of coastal Alabama: the Mobile Tensaw River Delta, Mobile Bay, Northern Gulf of Mexico and the Barrier Islands. Outside is a living marsh boardwalk that meanders along portions of the fourth-largest estuary system in

the U.S. It's great for all ages.

Across the street from the Sea Lab is a Civil War fort famous for its role in the Battle of Mobile Bay. You can almost hear Admiral David Farragut shout the famous command, "Damn the torpedoes – full speed ahead." Visitors can tour Fort Gaines (51 Bienville Blvd.; 251-861-6992) for a look at how soldiers lived in the 1860s. A tour of the 19th-century brick seacoast fort includes a working blacksmith shop, bakery, officer's quarters, cannons and more.

THE BEAUTY OF BELLINGRATH GARDENS

As you leave Dauphin Island, your next stop should be in Theodore at Bellingrath Gardens and Home (12401 Bellingrath Gardens Rd., Theodore; 251-973-2217). Located on the west side of Mobile Bay, 30 minutes south of Mobile, this area also offers excellent bird watching opportunities and is home to the largest public gardens in the state.

Originally the fishing camp of Walter Bellingrath, who made his fortune bottling Coca-Cola in Mobile, the gardens opened to the public in 1932. An avid gardener, Mrs. Bellingrath's dream was to create a "Charm

Spot of the Deep South." She succeeded. The couple constructed a 10,500-square-foot mansion around a central courtyard on their 65-acre estate. You'll see a variety of migratory birds as you stroll through the tranquill setting that's filled with seasonal flowers year round. Camellias are in bloom in the winter, azaleas in the spring, roses in the summer, and chrysanthemums in the fall. The 15-room, 10,500-square-foot house, built in 1935, is open year-round for tours. Across from the home is the Delchamps Gallery of Boehm Porcelain that houses a large collection of painted porcelain animals and birds.

Enjoy walking on the 1,500-foot-long Bayou Boardwalk trail at Bellingrath that will take you through the backwaters to see cranes, eagles and more. Interpretative panels identify wildlife and plants along the way. You'll also see flora and other creatures native to the area.

Behind the house is the pavilion where you can enjoy views of the Fowl River. Visitors will also see wildlife and birds in their natural habitat.

Ferry prices for the Mobile Bay Ferry start at $18 for one car and one driver. If you don't have a car, the price is $6 per person. Children younger than six are free. The ferry departs every 1.5 hours during the summer. Hours vary by season, so it's best to check ahead for schedules and prices.

WHERE TO EAT

Enjoy breakfast or lunch at the Lighthouse Bakery (919 Chaumont Ave.; 251-861-2253) on Dauphin Island that offers sandwiches, soups, hot breakfasts and pastries.

For lodging and dining options in the Dauphin Island and the Mobile area, visit the following websites: www.dauphinisland-chamber.com and www.mobilebay.org.

Bird watching is a fun and easy family affair.

FOLEY AND ELBERTA:
ART, ANTIQUES AND MODEL TRAINS

Foley's railroad heritage is featured on the grounds of the city archives and museum.

Eight miles north of the white sand beaches of Alabama's Gulf Coast sit two small towns rich in culture and heritage, Foley and Elberta. You'll find everything from modern art, antiques, a train depot and a medical museum where visitors have claimed to have seen ghostly spirits, to a soda fountain and, in Elberta, a museum with artifacts from pioneer days. Foley is a small town that's big on places to shop, while Elberta is home to the German Sausage Festival and Baldwin County Heritage Museum.

SHOPPING IN FOLEY

Foley is a great place to find antiques and collectibles in shops like the Gift Horse Antique Centre (209 W. Laurel Ave., 251-943-3663), Hollis Ole Crush (204 S. McKenzie St., 251-943-8154), Antiques on Alston (323 S Alston St.) and Old Armory Mall (812 N. McKenzie St., 251-943-7300). The shops are all within walking distance of each other.

The town is also home to the Tanger Outlet Center (2601 S. McKenzie St., 251-943-9303) where you can shop till you drop at more than 150 brand name stores, from Coach and Ralph Lauren to J. Crew and Polo. The outlet is located approximately two miles from downtown Foley on Hwy. 59.

Shops are open Monday through Saturday, 9 a.m.-9 p.m. and Sunday, 10 a.m. to 7 p.m.

GRAB A CUP OF COFFEE FOR A DIME

After shopping, stop by for a treat or a cup of coffee for 10 cents at Stacey's Rexall Drugs & Old Tyme Soda Fountain (121 W. Laurel Ave.; 251-943-7191). Since 1929, Stacey's has been offering ice cream, handmade milkshakes, malts, ice cream sundaes, sandwiches and sodas. The fountain also houses a pharmacy with some unusual over-the-counter remedies.

Enjoy the beauty and fragrance of the roses along the paved public walking trail that winds through the heart of downtown Foley.

MODEL TRAINS, ROSES, ART AND MEDICINE

The Foley Alabama Railroad Museum (125 E. Laurel Ave.; 251-943-1818) is located in the Old L&N Railroad Depot and houses Foley's archives. The first depot was built in 1905 when John B. Foley of Chicago used some of his own money to bring the railroad to the southern part of Baldwin County. This first depot burned and a second station took its place in 1908. The museum contains reminders of the days when Foley was a thriving agricultural center and the railroad played a major role in its prosperity. It's open Monday through Saturday 10 a.m. to 3 p.m.

After touring the train museum stop to smell the roses, literally. Take a leisurely stroll along the Wilbourne Antique Rose Trail and camellia path that begins just outside the train depot. The paved public walking trail winds through the heart of downtown Foley following the path of the old railroad line. You'll enjoy the beauty and fragrance of the roses along the one-mile trail. Enjoy the camellias in Heritage Park and continue north across Violet Avenue where the rose trail begins.

The Holmes Medical Museum (111 W. Laurel Ave.; 251-970-1818) served as

Don't Miss This

THE QUARTER MILE MODEL TRAIN EXHIBIT

Step inside the railroad museum where families will enjoy the "O" gauge model train exhibit with one-fourth mile of track. The layout represents the 1950s era, when the rail lines were in the transition of being run by steam to running on diesel fuel. There is a Main Street USA, complete with a fire station, car wash, church, bus station and a city park with an "N" gauge train that carries children around the park. You will see a farm, a sawmill and a coal company on one end of the layout and an oil refinery on the opposite end. Also, Thunder Road, an old Robert Mitchum movie, is playing at the Hub Drive-In.

Enjoy a different type of trail while riding a horse at Sea Horse Stables (Hwy. 59 at County Road 24; 251-971-RIDE). The stables are open year-round and offer trail rides, birthday parties, hayrides and cookouts.

Balloons glow in the dusk at Foley's annual Hot Air Balloon Festival.

ABOUT FOLEY

Foley is located at the heart of Baldwin County, one of the largest counties east of the Mississippi River. Just minutes from the white-sand beaches of Gulf Shores, Foley has seen many influences, including Native American, Spanish, French and English. Its proximity to Mobile Bay made it home for settlers from France, Germany, Sweden, Russia, Greece and Africa.

For more information on Foley, stop at the Foley Welcome Center (104 E. Laurel Ave.; 251-943-1300) located next to the Holmes Medical Museum (251-970-1818). The center is open Monday through Friday 8 a.m. to 5 p.m.

THE GULF COAST HOT AIR BALLOON FESTIVAL

The Gulf Coast Hot Air Balloon Festival (251-943-3291) takes place every Father's Day weekend in Foley. Nearly 50 hot air balloons float in the Gulf Coast skies, and the evenings provide spectacular balloon glows.

You can even take your own hot air balloon ride with Taking Off Hot Air Balloon Company (251-970-FLYU) where you will soar 1,500 to 2,000 feet over the Gulf Coast.

Baldwin County's first hospital from 1936-1958 and remains mostly unchanged since it was in operation. On display are many original medical artifacts including surgical instruments, operating room machinery and a human skeleton. It's said that some of the former patients are still around keeping watch. Visitors have told stories of seeing ghosts.

Downtown Foley is also home to two art galleries and studios. Jan's Art Studio (115 W. Laurel; 251-971-3836) sells arts and crafts by local artists and also offers art supplies and art classes. The local crafts make great gifts and souvenirs. Across the street from Jan's is the nonprofit art center and gallery, the Foley Art Center (211 N. McKenzie St.; 251-943-4381). As you shop, you just might discover your hidden gem. Displays in the large gallery include paintings, mixed media, pottery, jewelry, clothing and many other crafts. The center also offers art classes.

WHERE TO STAY

The quaint Hotel Magnolia (115 N. McKenzie St.; 251-943-5297) has celebrated more than 100 years of history. Built in 1908 by John B. Foley himself, the Hotel Magnolia closed in 2012 and was reopened in 2014 to serve a new generator of visitors.

With all the elegance and craftsmanship of a bygone era, visitors can enjoy the hotel's luxurious and charming atmosphere, which includes antiques, comfortable, graciously appointed rooms and exquisite mosaic-tiled bathrooms,

for about the same price as a garden-variety motel room.

A nearby option is the Magnolia Springs Bed & Breakfast (14469 Oak St., Magnolia Springs; 251-965-7321). This B&B with five guest rooms sits on a quiet street lined with old oak trees draped with Spanish moss. It has been featured in *Southern Living* and on HGTV.

WHERE TO EAT

The lunch buffet at the Gift Horse Restaurant (209 W. Laurel Ave., 251-943-3663) will satisfy your appetite for Southern food. Their apple cheese casserole is listed in the "100 Dishes To Eat in Alabama Before You Die" brochure. Other dishes on the buffet include fried chicken, seafood bisque, baked chicken, salads, turnip greens, fish and more. If you have room, there are freshly baked cakes like German chocolate, coconut and red velvet. Housed in a 100-year-old building, the restaurant is open for lunch and dinner 4:30 p.m. to 8:30 p.m

VISIT ELBERTA

Just 10 minutes and 5.8 miles from downtown Foley on Hwy. 98 awaits the community of Elberta founded by farmers from Germany in the early 1900s.

The Baldwin County Heritage Museum (25521 US Hwy. 98 E.; 251-986-8375) offers a place for visitors to reconnect with the early history of the area. The museum has created a home for historically significant buildings, tractors, farming materials, documents and artifacts.

GULF SHORES AND ORANGE BEACH:
SPRING BREAK

Volleyball is a popular shoreline activity.

Pack the car and head down I-65, U.S. Hwy. 231 or across I-10 and down to Alabama's beautiful white sand beaches. You can soak up the sun on 32 miles of sugar-white sand beaches, see exotic animals at the world famous "Little Zoo That Could" or hop on an eco-cruise to watch dolphins play.

The beach communities of Gulf Shores and Orange Beach offer visitors a wide variety of fun, and this road trip is sure to be a vacation that will leave you coming back for more. It's the perfect getaway for spring break or a family-friendly vacation.

KICK BACK AT THE HANGOUT

As you drive south on Gulf Shores Parkway (AL Hwy. 59) and arrive at AL Hwy. 182, the scenery of the beaches and the smell of the ocean breeze will leave you wanting to hop out of your car and run to the white sand beaches. There is public beach access here, so

ABOUT ALABAMA'S GULF COAST

Alabama's Gulf Coast boasts 32 miles of turquoise water, sugar-white sands, fresh seafood and activities for the whole family. From Gulf Shores and Orange Beach to the mouth of Mobile Bay and the Florida state line, the coast is the perfect place to kick back and relax.

you can do just that at one of the hottest places on the beach, The Hangout (101 E. Beach Blvd., Gulf Shores; 251-948-3030). Here, you can grab a bite to eat and the kids can play at The Hangout by building sand castles in the play area and getting lost in the suds with a bubble machine. The casual dining area is open so that you can feel the Gulf breeze, and the outdoor bar features live music. The restaurant is open for lunch and dinner and offers seafood, burgers, sandwiches and salads. It's a great place to take the family and a great place to relax, play, have a bite to eat or just hang out.

The Hangout restaurant sponsors the annual Hangout Music Fest each May. Hangout Fest has become one of the most popular events for Alabama residents and visitors alike, featuring acts such as the Dave Matthews Band, Red Hot Chili Peppers, Foo Fighters, Cee-lo Green, Paul Simon, Widespread Panic and more. The three-day event takes place right on the beach in Gulf Shores.

SEE FLIPPER AND HIS FRIENDS

For a special experience you won't soon forgot, you'll want to take a dolphin cruise. A variety of outfitters offer tours of the Intra-coastal Waterway.

Glass Bottom Dolphin Tours by Dolphins Down Under (28101 Perdido Beach Blvd., Orange Beach; 251-968-4386) offer glass-bottom boat dolphin tours. Besides dolphins you will have the chance to see osprey, great blue herons,

Ferris wheel at The Wharf in Orange Beach

stingrays, sea turtles, and many other wetland creatures and birds in the bay area. They also offer snorkeling tours.

Southern Rose Parasailing and Dolphin Cruises (27212 Marina Rd., Orange Beach; 855-524-8837) offers cruises about a spacious double-deck boat with inside and outside seating on both decks and air-conditioned seating on the top deck. The company also offers parasailing, flyboarding, Jet Ski, and other watersport adventures.

Blue Dolphin Cruises (29603 Perdido Beach Blvd., Orange Beach; 251-981-2774) offers dolphin sightseeing tours on a 51-foot, seaworthy, heated/air-conditioned bi-hull boat with inside and outside seating, gift shop and snack bar.

OFF-THE-BEACH FAMILY FUN

A must-visit is the Alabama Gulf Coast Zoo (1204 Gulf Shores Parkway, Gulf

Shores; 251-968-5732). It became known as "The Little Zoo That Could" on the Animal Planet channel. See more than 500 animals, including lions, tigers, bears, primates, leopards, and wolves. It's a day of fun for the entire family.

Visit the Bon Secour National Wildlife Refuge (12295 AL Hwy. 180, Gulf Shores; 251-540-7720), a short drive from the beaches down Fort Morgan Road. The refuge consists of nearly 7,000 acres of coastal lands with plants, flowers and animals native to the area. It's open during the day for hiking, fishing, bird watching and enjoying nature. You can walk along a variety of trails such as Gator Lake Trail, Centennial Trail, Jeff Friend and Pine Beach. The trails range from one to four miles.

For a little speed, fun and adventure head to the Waterville USA Park (906 Gulf Shores Pkwy./AL 59, Gulf Shores; 251-948-2106). Experience daring water slides, enjoy mini golf and race around a small track in go-carts. All ages are welcome at this 20-acre water park.

Take a ride or walk along the Hugh S. Branyon Backcountry Trail (24037 Perdido Beach Blvd.; 251-981-1180) in Orange Beach. Tour guides will take you along the paved trail that winds through moss-lined trees, flora and fauna native to Alabama's Gulf Coast. You might even run into the Cat-Man, a legendary wild man who is purportedly half cat and half man.

Visit the Orange Beach Arts Center Hot Shop (26389 Canal Rd., Orange Beach; 251-981-2787) to take home a great souvenir from the beach. You'll find jewelry, paintings or a variety of other crafts in the shop. You can even make your own piece of glass art in the shop by signing up for an art class or purchase a piece of glass art in the gallery. The Hot Shop is the only public access glass studio in the state of Alabama.

Drive a short distance inland to hop on the Southeast's tallest Ferris Wheel at The Wharf (4985 Wharf Pkwy., Orange Beach; 251-224-1000) for a ride with a view. You'll be 120 feet high above the Intracoastal Waterway in Gulf Shores with views of scenic wetlands and a marina. The Wharf is an entertainment area with a 9,500-capacity amphitheater, boutique shops, restaurants and accommodations.

WHERE TO EAT

You've probably heard the Jimmy Buffet song "Cheeseburger in Paradise," but have you actually tried one? It's on the menu at his sister's restaurant in Gulf Shores, LuLu's at Homeport Marina (200 E. 25th Ave., Gulf Shores; 251-967-5858), located on the Intracoastal Waterway. Also try the wild shrimp and L.A. Caviar on the menu. The main ingredient is black eyed peas. The family atmosphere provides loads of fun activities for kids and there's live music nightly. Small kids will love playing in the sandy beach area while the Mountain of Youth ropes course is geared toward older kids. The ropes course sits high above LuLu's and is a three-story climbing tightrope apparatus.

WHERE TO STAY

With more than 17,000 rooms, Gulf Shores and Orange Beach have a variety of places to stay, from hotels and condos to beach houses. Visit www.gulfshores.com/lodging to help you find a place to park your flip-flops for the night.

Father and son gather shells at the high tide line.

PICTURESQUE GULF STATE PARK

When renovations were made to Gulf State Park, it wasn't just to add a new conference center, but to make it one of the most innovative environmental sites in the country. The 6,150-acre Gulf State Park in Gulf Shores features restored sand dunes, expanded walking and biking trails, new interpretive centers, a learning campus and a new lodge and conference center. The Lodge at Gulf State Park, a Hilton Hotel, opened in November 2018 and has 350 rooms including 20 suites. It offers guests access to 28 miles of educational hiking and biking trails, a nature center, outdoor classrooms, an interpretive center, tennis, kayaking, guided nature walks, a butterfly garden, a forest and beach pavilions.

Perhaps most importantly, it is designed to be one of the country's cutting-edge environmental sites. The Interpretive Center at Gulf State Park is in the process of obtaining a Living Building Challenge environmental designation currently afforded to only 16 buildings in the world. The park's Eagle Cottages are undergoing an evaluation to become the first lodge in the Southeast and one of only seven in the country to be designated a National Geographic Unique Lodge of the World.

If you want to fish during your stay, a state fishing license is required for anyone 16 years and older; Alabama residents over 65 do not need a license.

Down 182 at Lake Shelby you will find a picnic area, golf course, camping store and trails. Other activities to enjoy include tennis, swimming, boating, fresh and saltwater fishing, skiing and other outdoor recreation. If you want to spend the night at the state park, there are 11 remodeled cottages and 20 cabins for rent within walking distance of the golf course and 2.5 miles from the beach. All cottages are three-bedroom, three-bath with screened porches overlooking Lake Shelby. The cabins are equipped with full kitchens and all utensils.

ALABAMA'S GULF COAST:
GOLFING AND FISHING

Sometimes a guy just has to leave the day-to-day grind behind and head out with his buds to a place where possibility blows on the breeze. The 32 miles of Alabama's sugar-white sands are a fine place to land, where the sea is refreshing, the sun rejuvenating and the play just plain fun. You'll find enough to entertain from sunup to sundown and on into the wee hours of the morning if that's your thing. This is the kind of trip where great stories are made that you'll tell for years to come. So head on down to the coast.

HITTIN' 'EM STRAIGHT

You'll find stunning views from the emerald greens of the Gulf Coast golf clubs, where there are courses created for every level of golfer. While you can probably walk in to most facilities without a reserved tee-time – especially in the off-season – you'll uncover the best deals if you reserve a space in advance. Many properties offer discounted rounds in the afternoons. That means you can expect the biggest crowds on the greens in the mornings.

The winds blowing off the Gulf can play havoc with drives at Kiva Dunes (815 Plantation Dr., Gulf Shores; 251-540-7000), a Jerry Pate designed course, but the seaside views

Gulf Shores Peninsula Golf Club

ABOUT ALABAMA'S GULF COAST REGION

With 32 miles of white-sand beaches, the Gulf Coast region is the state's most popular tourist destination. In addition to the bountiful recreational activities that can be found in Gulf Shores and Orange Beach, visitors come here to explore the history and culture of places such as Mobile and Dauphin Island.

more than make up for any trouble. It's located off of Fort Morgan Road, about 15 minutes west of Gulf Shores. The accompanying resort offers condo accommodations and a lovely spa for easing tired muscles after a game.

While you're out in that direction, play the three nine-hole championship layouts at Peninsula Golf and Racquet Club (20 Peninsula Blvd., Gulf Shores; 251-968-8009), an Earl Stone design. Meticulously landscaped, the manicured fairways wind around lakes and streams for narrow landing surfaces that challenge seasoned golfers.

Two lovely courses at Craft Farms, Cotton Creek and Cypress Bend (3840 Cotton Creek Cir., Gulf Shores; 251-968-7500), sit on the north side of the Intracoastal Waterway not too far from the new toll bridge leading to Orange Beach. The only public courses designed by Arnold Palmer in the state of Alabama, they feature mature trees, hillocks and dwarf Bermudagrass. You can find stay-and-play deals that match up accommodations around Gulf Shores and Orange Beach with rounds of Craft Farms golf.

INSHORE OR OFFSHORE, FISHING IS FINE

When a bull redfish grabs your line and runs, you'll feel every muscle tense to reel in the fighter. The passes between the bays and the Gulf host these big sport fish. Yet there's so much more to catch. Plate-sized flounder, slender trout and silvery

Lights of the Gulf State Park pier reflect along the shore at dusk.

Alabama deep-sea fisherman with a prized Amberjack

pompano all clamor for bait here too. And that's just the inshore fishing.

Book a charter that motors miles into the Gulf, where you can crank in snapper, grouper, tuna, wahoo, mackerel, mahi-mahi and amberjack. It's a sportsman's dream.

All the marinas from Orange Beach west past Mobile Bay host charter captains who know where the fish are biting every day.

When you book a trip, know that the captains generally provide your fishing license, gear and bait. All you need to bring is your own food and drinks, plus tips to pay the deckhands when they put you on that trophy catch. All captains accept cash, but only a few will accept credit card payments, so check in advance. Here are a few of our favorite charters:

- Capt. Mike's Deep Sea Fishing (650 Lemoyne Dr., Dauphin Island; 251-861-5302) captained by Mike and Skipper Thierry, runs two boats out of Dauphin Island.

- Action Charter Service (27844 Canal Rd., Orange Beach; 888-558-3889, 251-986-6855) floats a 65-foot Bonner out of Zeke's Landing in Orange Beach

with Capt. George Pfeiffer that's ideal for full day and overnight trips.

- San Roc Cay Marina (27267 Perdido Beach Blvd., Orange Beach; 251-981-5423) and Zeke's Landing (26619 Perdido Beach Blvd., Orange Beach; 800-793-4044, 251-981-4044) hosts a fleet of boats for groups small and large.

WHERE TO EAT

One of the best parts of a guys trip is that you get to eat where you want to.

If you like to settle into a seafood dive for fresh catch, drop by King Neptune's (1137 Gulf Shores Pkwy., Gulf Shores; 251-968-5464).

A LITTLE NIGHT MUSIC

Don't have to get up early in the morning? Then take on the nightlife. The Gulf Coast's late hours are some of the most fun along any shore. Wander through the dozen or so different barrooms – inside and out – at the famed Flora-Bama (17401 Perdido Key Dr., Orange Beach; 850-492-0611) that straddles the Alabama-Florida state line. Another

storied beachfront late-night place, the Pink Pony Pub (137 East Gulf Pl., Gulf Shores; 251-948-6371), brings in live entertainment alongside good grub and cocktails. The best place to dance to the music is at the Hangout (101 East Beach Blvd., Gulf Shores; 251-948-3030), especially during its May festival.

WHERE TO STAY

One of the finest places to lay your head at the beach is in the two blue towers known as Turquoise Place (26302 Perdido Beach Blvd., Orange Beach; 800-210-7914). The three- and four-bedroom units boast comfy furnishings with full luxury amenities – a grill and hot tub on the balcony overlooking the Gulf, separate wine fridge and ice makers, gourmet kitchen, and private baths for each bedroom. There's an excellent gym on the premises, indoor pools, a lazy river and outdoor pools. The place will spoil you – you'll bring your family back to stay next visit.

But sometimes all you want is a place with a view where you can sleep and shower. The Hampton Inn & Suites in Orange Beach (25518 Perdido Beach Blvd., Orange Beach; 251-923-4400) is right on the Gulf, with comfortable rooms.

Don't Miss This

COOKING YOUR CATCH

So you've spent the day out on the water and you're too tired to think about cooking all that fresh fish, but you really want a taste of your day's efforts. Take your catch to Fin and Fork (24131 Perdido Beach Blvd., Orange Beach; 251-981-1213), Cobalt, The Restaurant (28099 Perdido Beach Blvd., Orange Beach; 251-923-5300), Bill's By the Beach (300 West Beach Blvd., Gulf Shores; 251-948-5227) or several other restaurants in Orange Beach, and they'll dish it up.

The Lodge at Gulf State Park